P9-AFE-848

Huntington Library Publications

PORTRAIT OF DAVID C. BRODERICK
BY WILLIAM STEPHEN SHAW
Courtesy of E. B. Crocker Art Gallery, Sacramento

David C. Broderick

☆☆☆☆☆☆ A Political Portrait

☆☆☆☆☆☆☆☆☆☆☆☆☆

DAVID A. WILLIAMS

1969
THE HUNTINGTON LIBRARY
SAN MARINO, CALIFORNIA

The publication of this volume has been assisted by The James Irvine Publication Fund of the Huntington Library.

San Marino, California
Library of Congress Catalog Card Number 79–85342
Printed by Kingsport Press, Inc., Kingsport, Tennessee

TO RUTH

Preface

Few writers of fiction have dealt with incidents and characters more dramatic than those found in the life of David C. Broderick. Born in the shadow of the nation's Capitol, where his father was employed as a stone carver, Broderick climbed the steps leading to political power to sit eventually as a senator beneath the handiwork of his father. The road to eminence was filled with obstacles for this son of Irish Catholic parents. In January 1857 the long years of striving culminated in his election to the United States Senate, and Broderick returned to his birthplace from California as a member of the Thirty-fifth Congress. Overshadowed by such established figures of American politics as Stephen A. Douglas, Jefferson Davis, William H. Seward, Charles Sumner, and Sam Houston, he was expected to follow precedent and play the role of obscurity allotted to a freshman member. Contrary to what was expected of him and what has been written about him, Broderick became a vigorous protagonist in the Senate. In the final analysis, he did as much as any senator to determine the settlement of the most important questions that confronted Congress on the eve of the Civil War. Before death removed him from the scene, he became a leading figure of the antislavery wing of the Democratic party and a man of established national reputation.

Broderick's remarkable rise to national prominence took place in a little more than two years, a period of change in the political arena. As the conflict increased in violence, the friends and allies of slavery utilized their domination of the Democratic party to drive opposing members of the party to cover. Broderick, the ally of Stephen A. Douglas and the man who put iron in the backbone of the Little Giant, became one of their chief targets. Douglas, Broderick, and their supporters represented a locus of power which—given appropriate direction—might have prevented the disruption of the single national political organization that had the capacity to prevent dissolution of the American Union.

Although, in the tradition of Hamilton, Broderick was concerned with the utilization of governmental power in behalf of the expanding economy of the United States, he considered himself a champion of the working class from which he sprang. He advocated the accelerated development of internal improvements such as the steamship, the transcontinental railroad, and the telegraph, but he was also concerned with the rights of the working farmer, the artisan, and the mechanic. He was committed to the realization of Jefferson's ideal of a society of landed yeoman farmers through the distribution of the public domain among America's landless.

In life an enduring enemy of slavery, Broderick did as much as any man of his time to restrain its advance into the Trans-Mississippi West. His death was a portent of the fratricidal war which was imminent. The story of his life, his times, his successes, his failures, and his death sheds light on California, the nation, and the generation whose blood was tapped on the battlefields of the Civil War.

An objective, dispassionate, and balanced attitude toward Broderick is difficult to maintain. An enduring hazard to objectivity is the fact that the principal manuscript sources are those of his enemies. The Mandeville and Terry collections in the Huntington Library represent such lodes. Both contain hundreds of letters which deal with the political milieu of Broderick. The Mandeville Collection is composed of the letters of an adamant foe of Broderick and the antislavery sentiments he championed; the Terry Collection contains the letters and papers of David S. Terry, the California supreme court justice who put aside his judicial robes to meet Broderick on the "field of honor" on a fateful day in September 1859. To measure a politician by what his political enemies said about him is to produce an appraisal which will do violence to the real man. A better bench mark is essential.

The problems of a biographer of Broderick are compounded by the lack of a substantial collection of Broderick papers. This deficiency is offset, to some extent, by other materials that relate to him and his times. He was a dominant figure in California's political scene in the 1850's—so significant that almost all political letters, diaries, newspapers, legislative journals, and the like reflect his presence and influence. In the absence of introspective personal writings by Broderick, one is forced to lean upon the more objective evidences of the past. In some respects this is an advantage, for the portrait that emerges from an examination of what he advocated, supported, and campaigned for is more likely to be objective than one which is based primarily upon what other politicians said about him or what he said about himself.

In the course of this work, which began as a dissertation, I have become indebted to a great many people. Dr. Arthur R. Kooker, Dr. Donald C.

Cutter, Dr. Manuel Servín, Dr. Ray Allen Billington, and a great many others encouraged me to pursue it. Dr. Allan Nevins suggested that the subject was promising, spurred me on in times of discouragement and fatigue, and gave me the benefit of a careful reading and of comments on the deficiencies and strengths of the manuscript. Dr. Billington joined him in an evaluation of it which also guided me in the work of revision. I am most grateful to these scholars and of course absolve them of any responsibility for errors of fact or judgment which may be found herein.

I have everywhere met the customary courtesy and cooperation of librarians and archivists. The staffs of such institutions as the Bancroft Library at the University of California in Berkeley, the Library of Congress, the National Archives, the Pennsylvania Historical Society, the California Historical Society, the California State Library, the New York Public Library, the Archives of the State of California, and the libraries of the University of Chicago, the University of Southern California, the University of California at Los Angeles, and the New York Historical Society put their facilities at my disposal under conditions that made my work fruitful as well as pleasant. The Huntington Library staff was especially helpful, Miss Anne Hyder, Dr. Edwin Carpenter, Miss Haydée Noya, and the then Director, Dr. John E. Pomfret, extending assistance which revealed their commitment to historical scholarship. I am also grateful to the late Father Joseph Thompson, O.F.M., who made the De la Guerra Collection available to me, and to the John Randolph and Dora Haynes Foundation, which extended me a fellowship in 1960–1961. My colleague Dr. Robert Frazier put his skilled editorial pen to work in the course of a careful reading, and Mrs. Anna Marie Hager shared her extensive knowledge of Californiana with me. Mrs. Anne Kimber and Mrs. Nancy Moll of the Huntington Library Publications Department were most helpful in the final stages of the manuscript. My family also contributed in many ways which, although unstated here, are well known to husbands and fathers who are beset with the manifold problems of teaching and writing as well as filling those roles. The special research leave extended to me in the spring of 1967 enabled me to put the finishing touches to the manuscript.

David A. Williams

California State College, Long Beach
May 1967

Contents

CHAPTER ONE

The Formative Years

David C. Broderick was born in a troubled time, a member of the generation that grappled with the problems which eventuated in the Civil War. His life began in the week that saw the birth of the Missouri Compromise—the first major attempt to create a modus vivendi between the antagonistic societies which comprised the American federation. He came to maturity while this system provided for accommodation of differences between the dynamic society of the North and the static southern society based upon slavery. His most productive political years were those which preceded secession, when he served as a bold advocate of the new society which was to emerge from dissolution, Civil War, and reunion.

It was his political fate to rise to eminence and play a leading role as the political structure of the United States was subjected to great stress. A new order impended, and the guardians of the old resisted the eclipse of the old. It was Broderick's personal fate to come to great power in an arena where the representatives of the old order were entrenched. Faced with oblivion, these representatives of an anachronistic society focused their hostility on the archenemy of slavery in the Trans-Mississippi West. A short time after Broderick's death in 1859 a congressional speaker predicted that the senator's last words, "I die because I was opposed to the extension of slavery," might yet be "trumpeted at the mouths of cannon on the field of war." Within months, the cannon were roaring.

There was nothing in Broderick's birth or his antecedents which indicated that he would become one of the great political figures of the Civil War period. His parents, Thomas and Honora Colbert Broderick, were born in Ireland around the turn of the nineteenth century. Both were descended from a long line of stoneworkers. Thomas was the son of Michael Broderick, a stonemason who plied his craft in Limerick for a number of years before moving to Little Island, Cork County, where he died in 1840. Thomas followed his father's trade, as Michael had followed that of his father. Honora Colbert was also the child of a stonemason, who lived in a village near Little Island. Her parents were close friends of Michael and Ellen Broderick. The marriage of Honora and Thomas in 1816 was the natural outgrowth of that friendship.[1] A highly romantic and probably inaccurate version of their marriage pictures Thomas as the son of an upper-class family who married beneath his station and was thereafter alienated from them—a rebel against family authority as well as a radical in political persuasion, who emigrated to the United States when his family refused to welcome his bride. Actually, Thomas and Honora came to America at the invitation of a federal agent who sought artisans in the Old World to work on the public buildings of the District of Columbia. Thomas was doing similar work on the harbor improvements of the Cove of Cork when he was approached. He left Ireland not in flight from parental censure or endemic poverty but as an artisan who was assured of employment upon his arrival. The couple landed, probably in Baltimore, in 1817.[2]

Evidently an artisan of great skill, whose talent in fashioning stone approached that of a sculptor, Thomas was put to work on the Capitol building in the spring of 1817. Several years earlier, during the War of 1812, British troops had captured, burned, and destroyed a large part of the city. Public buildings, including the Capitol, were especially hard hit; a number were left fire-gutted ruins. Thomas was part of the work force gathered to repair and rehabilitate, as well as build. For a short time he was employed in the quarry, but the greater part of his employment was spent in cutting, shaping, polishing, and placing the stone which adorned the columns and walls of the Capitol. Each year he became more skilled. By the summer of 1825, he was working

[1] Affidavits of Richard Forrest and John Kirby, in California Supreme Court Transcript, *People of California* v. *McGlynn,* Calif. State Archives File No. 3494, Sacramento, hereinafter cited as *People* v. *McGlynn.*

[2] William E. Griffis, *Townsend Harris: First American Envoy in Japan* (Boston and New York, 1895), p. 16; Affidavit of John McDonnell, in *People* v. *McGlynn; Wilkes' Spirit of the Times* (New York), Oct. 22, 1859.

on the Capitol Centre, where the most accomplished of the stone carvers were employed.[3]

On February 4, 1820, while Thomas Broderick labored on the symbol of the nation and the lawmakers within the edifice worked on the legislative arrangements to be known as the Missouri Compromise, a son was born to Honora Broderick. A month later the boy was christened David Colbert Broderick in St. Patrick's Church with a small group of friends as witnesses. Afterwards the group returned to the Broderick home on East Capitol Street for a modest celebration.[4]

Honora Broderick was a self-effacing woman who was devoted to her husband and her firstborn. The boy responded in kind. For the next twenty-three years, until her death in 1843, David was her favorite, although she bore two other children, Hannah, who died in infancy, and Richard. For the rest of his life Broderick was marked by that attachment to his mother. He sometimes referred to the influence she had had on his life. He never married, and there is little evidence that he ever succeeded in establishing warm personal relationships with women.

The family lived in Washington, D.C., for a number of years while the father worked on the Capitol. The city was then a small town, scattered across the landscape, possessing little of its present grandeur. Evidently the family prospered, for Honora was soon sending home substantial sums to a sister in Ireland. In 1825, Thomas Broderick's employment came to an end. Soon after, the family left for New York City, where they settled in what is now known as Greenwich Village. This was a semirural district of farms, gardens, pastures, and scattered residences; but it was not to remain long in its state of pastoral simplicity. The city was on the verge of a period of rapid development; the village lay in the path of immediate growth. By 1850, the once rural area was part of a sprawling metropolitan complex. The construction boom in those years of rapid development furnished Broder-

[3] Records of the United States General Accounting Office, Record Group 217, Miscellaneous Treasury Account Series, 1815–25, National Archives.

[4] Baptismal Register, St. Patrick's Church, Washington, D.C., May 1819 to December 1836; Judah Delano, comp., *Washington Directory, Showing the Name, Occupation, and Residence of Each Head of a Family* (Washington, D.C., 1822), p. 20. Broderick's birthplace and birth date are reported incorrectly in a number of places, including Hugh Quigley, *The Irish Race in California, and on the Pacific Coast* (San Francisco, 1878), p. 298, which states: "We had it from the best authority, namely, his own lips, that he was a native of Kilkenny, Ireland."

ick with steady employment. Homes, warehouses, stores, streets—all required the services of building craftsmen, and stonemasons found ready employment. The two boys, David and Richard, grew up in this city of rapid change. They survived in spite of widespread hygienic poverty characterized by impure water, periodic outbreaks of disease, and inadequate diet. They attended the ninth ward public school for a time, David for little more than a year. At fourteen he was apprenticed in the trade of his father; hands turned from books to the mastery of a trowel.[5]

Under the direction of his father, David began the mastery of stonework; but the tutelage was cut short when Thomas died. At fourteen, the boy was faced with the burden of providing for himself, his mother, and his younger brother. The father had evidently given his son a solid training in stone carving, for within a few years David obtained a release from his indentures as an apprentice and assumed the status of an artisan. Meanwhile the young man was not to carry the total burden of providing for the family. Shortly after the death of her husband, Honora Broderick opened a small chinaware shop. Its limited profits, supplemented by David's income, enabled the family to survive.[6]

Out of his mother's venture came an association with a self-made man, a china importer named Townsend Harris, which had a profound effect on the life of Broderick. Harris lived near the family and doubtless came to know them as a result of Honora's shop. Reared in a rural area of limited educational opportunities, Harris immersed himself in reading and study in mature life and in time became a well-educated as well as successful businessman. Harris was a complex individual. Like Broderick, he was attached to his mother and never married. In his youth he was associated with the publication of a number of ephemeral newspapers and magazines in New York City. He was also involved in politics and became a member of the Tammany Society. Apparently he was not the typical politician of his time, eager for "place and pelf," although his activities led in 1846 to the presidency

[5] Affidavit of William E. Dennis, in *People* v. *McGlynn; Wilkes' Spirit of the Times*, Oct. 22, 1859.

[6] Wilkes stated that Thomas Broderick died in 1837, but this is probably incorrect. Honora Broderick was listed as a widow in *Longworth's Directory of New York City, 1836–37* (New York, 1836), p. 116. An exhaustive search of Gertrude A. Barber's "Death Notices Taken from the New York *Evening Post* in the Nineteenth Century," typescript in New York Public Library, failed to uncover an obituary notice for Thomas Broderick.

of the Board of Education. Here he began to implement his egalitarian educational ideas. He initiated a campaign to establish a free, publicly supported college, open to students of ability regardless of means. Despite considerable opposition, he succeeded. The City University of New York stands today as a monument of sorts to this nineteenth-century chinaware importer.[7]

Evidently discerning unique qualities in Broderick, Harris became his tutor soon after the boy lost his father. David's mind and thirst for knowledge doubtless delighted the older man and gave him additional evidence of the validity of his egalitarian ideas. Harris opened his personal library to Broderick, guided him in his reading, and provided him with the opportunity to test his thinking in lengthy discussions. The boy read in the systematic manner outlined by his tutor—in history, literature, philosophy, and political economy. Gradually his educational achievements became impressive. These hours of reading, study, and discussion had a lasting influence on Broderick. Of equal importance to the knowledge were the habits and attitudes that he developed. Reading and study became second nature to the young man, something to be preferred to idle pastimes, something to turn to for guidance, sustenance, and pleasure. In later years he could lose himself in a book in the midst of a turbulent political gathering. He read extensively and built an impressive personal library. He learned that books contained ideas, solutions, and answers, and he used them accordingly. Quick intelligence, sharply honed ambition, and the knowledge of man and society derived from study with Townsend Harris transformed Broderick. His contemporaries, especially those who were familiar with his background, were frequently amazed by the breadth and depth of his mind.[8]

[7] *Longworth's Directory of New York City, 1836–37,* p. 116; J. Frank Kernan, *Reminiscences of the Old Fire Laddies and Volunteer Fire Departments of New York and Brooklyn* (New York, 1885), p. 119; Carl Crow, *Harris of Japan* (New York, 1935), pp. 26 ff. Harris' membership in the Tammany Society is indicated in Tammany Soc. Minutes, 1845–46, MS in New York Public Lib., under date of Oct. 21, 1846; his election to the Board of Education is reported in the New York *Post,* June 2, 1846; his role in the establishment of the college is in Emilio Cosenza, *The Establishment of the College of the City of New York as the Free Academy in 1847* (New York, 1925), pp. 16 ff.

[8] James O'Meara, *Broderick and Gwin: The Most Extraordinary Contest for a Seat in the Senate of the United States Ever Known* (San Francisco, 1881), pp. 8–11; George W. Sheldon, *The Story of the Volunteer Fire Department of the City of New York* (New York, 1882), pp. 374–378; *Colonel Alexander K. McClure's Recollections of Half a Century* (Salem, Mass., 1902), pp. 32–34; *Wilkes' Spirit of the Times,* Oct. 22, 1859; John B. Haskin in *Cong. Globe,* 36th Cong., 1st Sess., p. 752.

Broderick was shaped in a number of ways by his apprenticeship. Stonemasonry required strength, skill, and foresight. The mason as he works with stone, mortar, level, and plumb line must plan for the end result as well as check and double-check his work as he proceeds. A style of thinking and operating emerges from such experience. In later life, Broderick exhibited that style. He planned for the ultimate as well as the immediate objective; he envisioned the steps which led toward the major goal and subjected his work to frequent checks as he proceeded. A member of a political family of much experience, Charles Washburn, editor of the San Francisco *Times,* was often critical of Broderick but declared flatly that he was a gifted organizer and administrator. His apprenticeship in stonework was partially responsible.[9]

The years of arduous stonework marked Broderick in other ways. Naturally robust, he developed a strong muscular frame. His shoulders, arms, and hands never lost the strength that lifting, placing, cutting, and polishing stone gave them. His health, however, was affected by his work. Chronic respiratory ailments became a serious problem, and he began to cast about for other employment. In 1840 he opened a tavern which catered to the working-class residents of the Washington Square area. It was called The Subterranean, named perhaps for the radical newspaper which was then edited by his friend Michael Walsh.[10] Townsend Harris was a silent partner in the venture and probably furnished the bulk of the capital. From the first day it opened its doors, it was a successful enterprise which furnished its proprietor with an adequate income. It produced a number of additional benefits. Relieved of the toil of stonemasonry, Broderick was provided with a chance to pursue his interest in books and ideas. He set aside a place in his tavern for a study and began the systematic building of a library, a practice which he continued for the rest of his life.[11]

[9] San Francisco *Times,* Sept. 14, 1859.

[10] *Wilkes' Spirit of the Times,* Oct. 22, 1859; Jeremiah Lynch, *Life of David C. Broderick* (San Francisco, 1911), p. 13. Broderick is listed as a tavern keeper, "143 Barrow," in John Doggett, comp., *New York City Directory for 1842 and 1843* (New York, 1842) and in the same publication for the years 1843–44 and 1844–45; *The Directory for the Cities of New York and Brooklyn for 1845–1846* (New York, 1845) also lists him as the operator of a "tavern, 366 Hudson Street."

[11] Crow, *Harris of Japan,* pp. 34 ff., reports Harris' involvement with Broderick's tavern. See also *Wilkes' Spirit of the Times,* Oct. 22, 1859, and Haskin in *Cong. Globe,* 36th Cong., 1st Sess., p. 752.

A fusion of the man of action and the student, Broderick must have puzzled some of his patrons. The incongruous sight of a tavern keeper parsing sentences amidst the paraphernalia of a bar was not easily forgotten. The quarrelsome among his patrons came to know him as a quiet man who was slow to anger but who, when the occasion demanded, came forth with the work-worn hand of a master stonemason. After settling a dispute, he returned to his books; he was always reluctant to leave and eager to return to his study.

About the same time that he opened a tavern, Broderick joined a volunteer fire company. The volunteers were the only organized fire fighters in New York at the time. Unpaid and often unsung, they enrolled the active young men in the city who found in the battle with the flames an opportunity to display their strength, courage, and manliness. The companies had many of the characteristics of fraternal organizations. A social room was usually maintained at each headquarters building, where the men often gathered in the evenings to while away the time. Dances, picnics, parades, and similar social occasions cemented bonds between the members. Ostensibly nonpolitical, the companies played a political role, as evidenced by the fact that six mayors of the city during the first half of the nineteenth century came out of their ranks. There were dozens of companies in the 1840's scattered throughout the city. The membership of such companies ranged upward to sixty; together the volunteer firemen represented a sizable bloc of voters and a formidable organization. A quick descent into political oblivion awaited the politician who ignored or antagonized the firemen. Conversely, the aspiring politician who was able to harness the volunteer firemen for political work thereby secured a major advantage.[12]

Broderick became a member of one of the oldest companies in the city, the Howard Company. Shortly after he joined, he was elected foreman, a distinct honor, for he was less than twenty-one years of age. The selection of a man so different from the other members of the Howard Company was an unusual tribute to this self-educated tavern keeper. The Subterranean, located near the headquarters of his company, became a favorite gathering place for the volunteers and active Democrats of the ward.[13]

[12] Sheldon, pp. 40–42, 82–83; A. E. Costello, *A History of the New York Fire Departments, Volunteer and Paid* (New York, 1888), p. 613.

[13] O'Meara, *Broderick and Gwin*, pp. 4–5; Costello, pp. 176 ff.; Matthew P. Breen, *Thirty Years of New York Politics Up-to-Date* (New York, 1899), pp. 71–73.

It was also about this time that Broderick formed another friendship which was to have a lasting influence on him and his career. George Wilkes and Broderick were strikingly different in temperament and outlook; but they were to have a lifelong relationship, and Wilkes inherited Broderick's estate. Wilkes, a man of obscure antecedents, was quick and alert, almost dandified in dress. His pen, which sustained him most of his life, was wielded with great skill, producing a quantity of prose which ranged from a book of Shakespearean criticism to a history of Oregon. He founded one of the great magazines of general circulation of the nineteenth century, publicized bold proposals for the construction of a transcontinental railroad, and during the Civil War was (in the judgment of James Parton) the best of the war correspondents.[14]

Wilkes was a man of violent likes and dislikes who evinced a lifelong interest in social questions. Usually calm, he had a volcanic personality which could produce violent eruptions. His journalistic career, spanning the middle years of the nineteenth century, encompassed the founding of the *National Police Gazette* and one of the major sporting journals of that time, *Wilkes' Spirit of the Times.* The *Gazette* which is published today is similar in format, style, and content to the publication which he launched. One of his last books, entitled *In Defense of the Paris Commune,* is evidence of his enduring interest in social and political questions. In the course of his career he wrote, edited, published, organized railroads in Russia, promoted prize fighting, introduced pari-mutuel betting to America, and worked in the political arena.[15]

In the early 1840's, Wilkes became a friend, confidant, and tutor to Broderick. To supplement the work that Harris had done, Wilkes encouraged his pupil to broaden his reading. Once limited to history and political economy, Broderick now began to dip into the great

[14] *Dictionary of American Biography;* New York *Times,* Sept. 25, 1885, p. 2, col. 5; O'Meara, *Broderick and Gwin,* p. 8; *Wilkes' Spirit of the Times,* Oct. 22, 1859.

[15] See Clarence B. Bagley, "George Wilkes," *Washington Hist. Soc. Quart.,* V (1914), 3–11, for a highly laudatory account of Wilkes's career as well as a list of his publications. Robert S. Holzman, *Stormy Ben Butler* (New York, 1954), pp. 184–185, cites a number of letters from U. S. Grant to Wilkes which reveal Wilkes's role in attempting to reconcile Benjamin F. Butler and Grant. The San Francisco *Daily Town Talk,* Mar. 17, 1855, on the eve of the departure of Wilkes from California and the dissolution of the Broderick-Wilkes political partnership, printed this characterization of Wilkes: "Excitement is a necessity of his nature, and, under the smooth surface of his exterior deportment, induced by habitual caution, lurks a perfect volcano of passion and feeling."

works of English literature. Before long, the onetime stonemason was quoting Byron and Shelley, his favorite poets. His interest in literature, once awakened, never waned. When he was a senator, sorely beset with a hundred pressing political problems, he immersed himself in reading the works of Daniel Defoe.[16]

Both men were strongly interested in political theory as well as practical politics, and both became active in the Democratic party. Wilkes preferred the role of writer and manager, while Broderick plunged into the mainstream as a candidate. Wilkes never held a political office, although he once ran for Congress; however, his competence and understanding of American politics were recognized by major figures of both parties. In the course of Broderick's career the two men worked as a team on several occasions.[17]

In 1843 Broderick was shaken by the first of two personal tragedies. Honora Colbert Broderick's death, some nine years after that of her husband, left David and his younger brother as sole survivors. Two years later Richard was killed in an unusual accident, when he and a friend were watching a salvage operator attempting to remove caked powder from a shell which had been dredged from the ocean floor off Sandy Hook. Suddenly the shell exploded. Both boys, who had crossed the street a moment before to observe, were killed instantly.[18]

After this final tragedy, David was subject to deep depressions, brooding in solitude and speculating on the meaning of life and death. At such times he withdrew into himself. As melancholia seized him, friends who were aware of the series of tragedies which had stalked him were inclined to be understanding and considerate. Broderick himself was convinced that he was fated to lead a tragic and unhappy life.[19] He sometimes referred to the fact that there was "not another human being in whom a single drop of my blood courses." After the death of his brother and for the remainder of his life he was unencumbered by close personal ties. However, he generated warm and affectionate feelings in his associates. He never married and apparently never seriously considered marriage. A perceptive observer declared that the lack of family explained Broderick's readiness to champion

[16] San Francisco *Times,* Sept. 20, 1859; John S. Hittell, *A History of the City of San Francisco* (San Francisco, 1878), p. 282.

[17] New York *Times,* Sept. 25, 1885.

[18] New York *Post,* June 21, 1843; New York *Tribune,* Mar. 26, 1845.

[19] *Wilkes' Spirit of the Times,* Oct. 22, 1859; John W. Forney, "On David C. Broderick," San Francisco *Post,* Mar. 8, 1879.

the interests of groups which had no claims on him: that he was the "son of the people and his heart beat in response to theirs" was a part of this explanation.[20]

That he was abundantly endowed with the attributes of leadership was apparent. Personal ambition led him to devote himself to reading and study. Intelligence was a great lever which lifted and transformed him. Pride and aspiration kept him from indulgence in the soft pleasures of the flesh, which were so prominent in his milieu. In the midst of a battle for his political life he declared that no man could truthfully say he had ever seen Broderick in a gambling hall or a brothel.[21]

[20] Haskin in *Cong. Globe,* 36th Cong., 1st Sess., p. 752; F. F. Low, "Political Notes," p. 54, MS in Bancroft Lib.; Theodore Hittell, *History of California* (San Francisco, 1898), IV, 277.

[21] *McClure's Recollections,* p. 32.

CHAPTER TWO

Genesis of a Politician

Had Broderick compiled a balance sheet of political assets and liabilities in 1840, it would have included a number of personal items. Membership in a large immigrant group—the Irish Catholic—was both an asset and a liability. While people of like derivation might support his aspirations, a substantial part of the population despised the Irish. The winds of nativism were beginning to stir in America in the 1840's. Not yet the hurricane that swept the land in the form of the Know-Nothings of the mid-fifties, these hostile forces would make Broderick's climb to political power more difficult.

His enduring ambition was a significant asset—almost indispensable in American public life of that time and this. The sources of that drive to excel are concealed, but the ambition of Broderick was repeatedly displayed. It enabled him to endure and rise above defeat; it made it possible for him to persist in the face of adversity; it made him sensitive to opportunity. Political setbacks tempered him; ambition brought him back to the fray. Early in his career he set his sights high, scorning minor offices that he might have secured.[1]

He was a proud man whose self-image matched aspiration and ability. In the beginning he had little money and few men of influence to encourage him. As a result he had to make his way alone. He was forced to depend on his personal resources and to develop attributes of leadership. He became knowledgeable about human motivation, able to work with people of diverse background, and capable of earning

[1] *Wilkes' Spirit of the Times,* Oct. 22, 1859.

the loyalty and respect of associates. His friends were tied to him with "hooks of steel," complained a political enemy.[2]

Broderick's political training ground was one of instability and change. In it new parties appeared and disappeared, new factions rose and fell from power, new organizations and methods were tested and either adopted or discarded. It was a time when political clubs of strong-armed men who were ready, willing, and able to use muscle in convention, campaigning, and balloting were coming to the fore. It was a time when volunteer fire companies played a political role. Federal patronage appointees in the customhouse and in the post office were increasing and becoming a locus of power which could determine the outcome of events. Groups of city and state employees had similar functions.[3]

In upstate New York the legendary Albany Regency, its days of greatest glory in the past, still clung to power. Where others used the heavy hand, the Regency used finesse and taught friends and foes some of the subtleties of effective political manipulation. Among those who learned something about the art and science of politics was Broderick. In the city itself, which was growing and expanding rapidly, politics was becoming the great diversion which professional sports were to be at a later date. The speeches, the conventions, the torchlight parades, the balloting, the shoulder-strikers—all made politics exciting, dramatic, interesting, and diverting.[4] In many respects this milieu was similar to that of the 1850's in San Francisco, where Broderick rose to such eminence that he was called a "field marshal" who towered above his rivals. In part, that rise to power in San Francisco could be traced to his training in the world of politics of New York in the late thirties and early forties.[5]

[2] A. A. Selover Statement, MS in Bancroft Lib.; John W. Forney, "David C. Broderick," San Francisco *Post,* Mar. 8, 1879; San Francisco *Times,* Sept. 20, 1859; Milton S. Latham to James W. Mandeville, Nov. 18, 1856, Mandeville Coll., Huntington Lib.

[3] Alexander C. Flick, ed. *History of the State of New York* (New York, 1935), VII, 140 ff., discusses the changed conditions that led to the appearance of the political gangs. I. N. Phelps Stokes, *The Iconography of Manhattan Island* (New York, 1915–28), III, 634, describes the changes that accompanied the growth of the city and the broadening of the franchise.

[4] Lewis Mumford, *The Culture of Cities* (New York, 1938), p. 182.

[5] The comment appeared in the Sacramento *Weekly Times,* Jan. 10, 1857, in a review of the California career of Broderick. John S. Hittell, *History of the City of San Francisco* (San Francisco, 1878), p. 319, describes the manner in which Broderick's political power in California was based on his organization in San Francisco.

Among the short-lived parties in New York in the 1830's was the Workingmen's Party, which gave rise to the term "Locofoco." Once used to denote a member of the Workingmen's Party, in time the term was used to label Democrats, especially Democrats of radical persuasion. Broderick was often so labeled. In some respects it was an accurate designation, for Broderick shared some of the radical political sentiments of the Locofocos.[6]

The political arena of New York City in the early forties was filled with crosscurrents. A short-lived but vigorous movement among Democrats to push the presidential ambitions of John C. Calhoun was one such eddy that muddied political waters. It enlisted the services of proletarian editor Michael Walsh, who publicly proclaimed in the columns of *The Subterranean* that Calhoun was the greatest statesman of the age. Fitzwilliam Byrdsall, a fixture of the Locofoco movement, also shared Walsh's admiration of Calhoun, but David C. Broderick remained aloof. However, while Broderick avoided a Calhoun commitment, he identified with another southern aristocrat, John Tyler.[7]

Destined to complete a single term as president, Tyler was active in 1842 in putting together an organization which might produce reelection. Among the small cogs in the machine which he and his lieutenants assembled in New York was Broderick, who was appointed a customhouse inspector in 1843. From that vantage point, provided for past and prospective political services, Broderick saw another aspect of American politics—the manner in which patronage appointees were marshaled in behalf of political objectives. He held the position for a short time. When James K. Polk frustrated the aspirations of Tyler, Van Buren, and other presidential contenders and succeeded to the White House, there was a general removal of lesser appointees. Among these was Broderick. It was his first and last

[6] The most authoritative account of the Locofoco movement is Fitzwilliam Byrdsall, *The History of the Loco Foco or Equal Rights Party* (New York, 1842). A recent scholarly account which concentrates on the movement in the 1830's is Walter Hugins, *Jacksonian Democracy and the Working Class: A Study of the New York Workingmen's Movement 1829–1837* (Stanford, 1960). James O'Meara, *Broderick and Gwin* (San Francisco, 1881), p. 6, labels Broderick a Locofoco.

[7] Margaret L. Coit, *John C. Calhoun, American Portrait* (Boston, 1950), pp. 303–304, describes the admiration of Walsh for Calhoun. The correspondence of the New York City politicians involved in the "Calhoun boom" is in Charles H. Ambler, ed. "Correspondence of Robert M. T. Hunter, 1826–1876," American Hist. Assn., *Annual Report, 1916* (Washington, D.C., 1918), pp. 39–62. See also Joseph A. Schoville to John C. Calhoun, Oct. 25, 1842, in J. Franklin Jameson, ed. "Correspondence of John C. Calhoun," American Hist. Assn., *Annual Report, 1889* (Washington, D.C., 1889), pp. 855–856.

appointment to such a position. On another occasion he made a serious effort to obtain a similar appointment, but failed. However, the lessons which he had learned stayed with him. For the balance of his career he was concerned with patronage and its uses.[8]

It is difficult to pinpoint the exact date when Broderick's interest in political matters was transformed into aspiration. In part those forces which molded and shaped him were personal, and there can be little doubt that Townsend Harris and George Wilkes were influential. Perhaps Michael Walsh ignited the spark of ambition. In any case, in the early 1840's Broderick turned to the political arena. From that time on, his name frequently cropped up, a representative of the new breed of politician which was spawned by a new milieu. Before he left for California in 1849, he was a comer in New York City politics, a prominent figure of the Democratic party, and a major figure in the fifth congressional district of the city.[9]

The political arena was permeated by a spirit of change and development during the late thirties and early forties as New York was transformed. In rapid succession the city became the commercial head of the country, its principal manufacturing city, and its chief financial center. It grew rapidly in population, expanding and absorbing surrounding villages until it emerged in mid-century as a great urbanized complex. The body politic changed more slowly. The municipal government, appropriate for a small city, continued to function along traditional lines, although each passing year brought evidence of the need for change.

As New York grew in size and complexity, there was an increased need for municipal services. The water supply was insufficient, fire-fighting facilities were inefficient and inadequate, street sanitation was irregular, and educational services were limited and poorly administered. The crime rate, recurrent epidemics, fires which caused exten-

[8] Edward Curtis to Walter Forward, Jan. 16, 1843, in Customhouse Nominations, New York, March 4, 1841, to March 4, 1845, Treasury Dept. Records, Fiscal Division, National Archives; a record of Broderick's employment in the New York Customhouse as one of seventy-six inspectors in 1842–43 is in *Register of All Officers and Agents, Civil, Military and Naval, in the Service of the United States* (Washington, D.C., 1843), p. 71. His position is scarcely the "lucrative patronage position" reported by O'Meara, *Broderick and Gwin,* p. 6; his effort to secure a similar position in 1844 is revealed in Broderick to Alexander Gardiner, Jr., Nov. 12, 1844, ALS in Yale Univ. Lib.

[9] Broderick is mentioned in political stories in the New York *Herald,* Sept. 3, Oct. 7 and 10, 1846; the new political milieu which reflected the accelerated growth and development of the city is described in *United States Magazine and Democratic Review,* N.S., XVIII (1846), 400 ff.; see also Stokes, III, xxix.

sive damage—all pointed to the need for an expanded city government. As the number of public employees increased, almost all serving at the pleasure of the appointing power, they came to represent a formidable political bloc when properly organized.

The rising demand for changes in the municipal government was accompanied by a need for changes in the political system of the city. The broadening of the franchise and the assembling of a great population which included a large number of immigrants created new problems and presented new opportunities to enterprising politicians. Once political matters had been arranged by the insiders, the aristocrats of land and market place, and then endorsed by a limited number of voters; now in the forties, with the decline of the aristocracy, came opportunity to the strong and able leaders of the masses. Dan Sickles was of this new breed; Michael Walsh profited from the changes; Fernando Wood was to find advantage in the new political environment; and Broderick was to find opportunity in this new arena.[10]

The Tammany Society was one of the more important political organizations in New York City in the 1840's. Born in the closing years of the eighteenth century, it had survived through the decades. Sensitive and responsive to political conditions, it was a tightly controlled group generally allied with the Democratic party. In later life Broderick was often labeled a Tammany politician who had mastered the arts of chicanery as a member of the society. However, the surprisingly complete records of the society indicate that he was never a member, although many of his friends and associates were affiliated with it. Not only was he not attached, but he incurred the open hostility of the society from time to time.[11]

Broderick's following in New York was not derived from an alli-

[10] W. A. Swanberg, *Sickles the Incredible* (New York, 1956), pp. 77–87; O'Meara, *Broderick and Gwin,* pp. 6–8; Arthur M. Schlesinger, Jr., *The Age of Jackson* (Boston, 1946), p. 408; Samuel A. Pleasants, *Fernando Wood of New York* (New York, 1948).

[11] Gustavus Myers, *The History of Tammany Hall,* 2nd ed. (New York, 1917), p. 63; Allan Franklin, *The Trail of the Tiger, Being an Account of Tammany from 1789* ([New York?], 1928); M. R. Werner, *Tammany Hall* (New York, 1928), pp. 53 ff. The Kilroe Collection of Tammaniana in Columbia Univ. Lib., the Minutes of the Tammany Society in the New York Hist. Soc. Collections, and the Tammany Society Minutes in the New York Public Lib. have been examined to establish the relationship of Broderick to the society. No evidence of either his membership or his candidacy as a member was found. A number of his associates were members; Moses E. Flannagan, later a political aide to Senator Broderick, was accepted for membership on Mar. 9, 1846 (Tammany Minutes, 1845–49, New York Hist. Soc. Lib.). Flannagan also served as secretary (Tammany Society: Constitution and Roll of Members, 1789–1916, New York Pub. Lib.).

ance with the Tammany Society but was largely of his own making. It was chiefly confined to the ninth ward of the fifth congressional district, where political sentiment was divided between Whig and Democrat. In addition to the major parties, there was a substantial number of members of the National Reform Association in the district. Sectarian reformers who pushed a radical program involving the public domain, banking and currency, the court system, elections and apportionment, they vigorously and insistently pointed the way to a better life. As a practical matter, they were of limited importance in elections although they had a newspaper, *Young America,* and a city-wide organization. Broderick was never formally affiliated with the National Reform Association, but he often advocated similar policies. Michael Walsh and George Evans, the editor of *The Workingman's Advocate,* could work together, but Broderick apparently preferred his affiliation with the Democracy of New York City to identification with the association.[12] Though some members of the association objected to Broderick's occupation, his personal life was above reproach. His contemporaries considered this a matter of some importance and frequently commented on it. While he associated with rough and rowdy characters (as tavern keeper he was host to many), a friend pointed out, "It is worthy of observation that his most unscrupulous enemies . . . were obliged to stop inside of the quotation of one single act of questionable integrity." [13]

There were any number of people who were critical of Broderick, and at times they were sharp and caustic. Philip Hone, of aristocratic social inclinations and Whiggish political sentiments, expressed his objections to Broderick in his diary as "a precious nominee of Tammany Hall." His opinion was shared by others, who attacked Broderick's undistinguished ancestry, occupation, and background. To some it was enough that he was the son of an Irish Catholic stonecutter and a man who kept a "three-penny groggery." As infuriating as anything else was his insensitivity to the role that was assigned him by his

[12] The National Reform Association newspaper printed on its masthead the pledge it expected its candidates for political office to accept; see *Young America,* Mar. 21, 1846. The program of the association was printed as an extra in the form of a pamphlet entitled *Principles and Objects of the National Reform Association or Agrarian League* (n.p., n.d.), 16 pp.; a copy is in New York Pub. Lib. Michael Walsh and George Evans combined the newspapers *The Subterranean* and *The Workingman's Advocate* for a time in 1844. See the tribute to Walsh paid by his co-editor in the issue of Oct. 12, 1844.

[13] *Wilkes' Spirit of the Times,* Oct. 22, 1859.

betters. Thus, when President Tyler visited the city in 1843, it was Broderick who took over the welcoming ceremony in complete disregard of the minor role he was assigned. Before his first campaign for a major office began, there were a number of people in New York who looked forward eagerly to the time when he would receive his "comeuppance." [14]

Before that first race took place, Broderick participated in the convention to revise the city charter, which met in the summer of 1846. The need to revise the state constitution as well as the charter of the city had become more apparent with each passing year of the 1840's. Pressure to revise, first aired by the Locofocos, finally became irresistible, and a revision was authorized by the legislature of 1845. Two conventions were to be held, one to rewrite the constitution, the other the charter. Broderick was elected a member of the latter group in June 1846, his first successful try for an elective office.[15]

The convention which assembled was overwhelmingly Democratic —only three Whigs were in the group of thirty-five—but it was not a monolithic political group. On the contrary, political sentiments ranged from conservative to radical. Broderick was identified with the latter. Since the gathering was to deal with almost every aspect of the system, from who should be allowed to vote to how frequently elections would be held, it was possible for an observer to learn much about the political philosophy of the delegates who participated.[16]

The gathering displayed a businesslike approach to the tasks at hand, and from the beginning Broderick participated freely in the deliberations, airing his opinions and taking positions. When the convention was over, many people knew a great deal about the political sentiments of the onetime stonemason. For example, one of the first steps of the convention was the adoption of the usual rules of order with the modification that its president would have the right to appoint

[14] Philip Hone, Diary, Oct. 26, 1846, MS in New York Hist. Soc.; Jeremiah Lynch, *The Life of David C. Broderick* (New York, 1911), pp. 7–9; O'Meara, *Broderick and Gwin,* pp. 18–20.

[15] New York *Tribune,* June 2, 1846. Byrdsall, pp. 163–165, prints a proposed constitution to replace the existing plan of government. The National Reform Assn. vehemently demanded constitutional reform in *Young America,* Feb. 7, 1846. Stokes, III, 651, describes the problems arising out of rapid development of the city, which demanded revision of the charter.

[16] *Journal of the Convention in Relation to the Charter of the City of New York* (New York, 1846), pp. 1–4, lists the members. Stephen Hasbrouck, a delegate, was a fixture of the Locofoco movement. See Byrdsall, p. 55, and Hugins, p. 67.

all committees. Broderick led the fight to restrict the power of the president and have the membership of committees determined by the convention. He failed. It was the first of a number of rebuffs.[17] Contrary to the reports of enthusiastic biographers, Broderick was never the president of this convention. However, he attended almost every meeting, took an active role in the proceedings, aired his opinions, and voted his convictions. He was appointed to the committees on assessments and taxes, elections and appointments, police, and education. In each he was active.[18]

Like many Jacksonian Democrats, Broderick championed the principles of popular democracy. He advocated the election of a wide range of city officials, restriction of the appointing power of the mayor and the common council, annual elections, and special elections within thirty days in the event of a vacancy between elections. Not only the mayor but such minor functionaries as the receivers of taxes as well would be elected. A city governed by such arrangements could rightly claim to be operating in accordance with the Jacksonian principle of rule by the people through officials selected by them at frequent and regular elections.[19]

Broderick proposed a number of changes in the way law was to be enforced and justice administered. Justices and clerks of the courts as well as police officials, including the policemen in each ward, would be elected. An autonomous police department would be established for each ward, to be supervised by an elected official. In this way, said Broderick, "the result will be, that efficiency will be a man's only claim to retention in office and his constituents placed in a situation to observe impartially his conduct, will take a pride in returning only the most faithful and capable men."[20] In the assessing and taxation of property, Broderick thought assessors should be elected and paid salaries rather than receiving fees for their work. They should be elected by the voters of the ward in which they functioned; thereby

[17] Broderick was absent from the sessions only on Sept. 24, Oct. 8, 13, and 26, 1846; see *Journal of the Convention* for those dates. The adoption of the rules and Broderick's rebuff appear on pp. 9–18.

[18] *Journal of the Convention,* pp. 52, 92, 167, 517; New York *Tribune,* July 15, 1846.

[19] *Journal of the Convention,* pp. 661–662, 305–315.

[20] The report of the committee on police is in *Documents of the City Convention, 1846, for Forming a New or Revising and Amending the Present Charter of the City of New York* (New York, 1846), pp. 347 ff.

their work would be scrutinized by the voters and those who assessed unfairly or dishonestly could be retired by the electorate.[21]

Broderick was especially critical of the existing apportionment under which city councilmen were chosen to represent wards which ranged in population from six thousand to forty thousand. With a limited number of allies he pressed for changes that would make representation directly reflect population. A New York *Tribune* reporter commented on the "warm discussion" of the debate and the role which Broderick played. Only three delegates stayed with him to the end of the contest, where he suffered another setback. The convention preserved the existing apportionment and its inequities.[22]

The convention dragged on through the summer of 1846. As the days passed into weeks and then months without progress from the meeting to revise the charter, the city's press lost interest in the proceedings. War news from Mexico helped to drive the convention from prominent columns. Broderick stayed throughout, although his first campaign for a major office was in the offing. Day by day he compiled a record. Time after time he was recorded in the minority, a dissident in an overwhelmingly Democratic gathering. Ostensibly of the Democratic persuasion, he made it obvious that his concept of the party's credo differed sharply from that of his fellow Democrats.

On October 20, two weeks before its work was to be submitted to the electorate for ratification, the convention adjourned. In a crucial meeting preceding final adjournment, the conservative Democratic majority placed in a select committee the power to write a complete draft of the charter. Broderick fought the step vigorously, but was defeated. Carte blanche authority was given the select committee; subsequently, its work was ratified by the full convention.[23]

The charter that was approved by the convention did not incorporate many of Broderick's ideas. The conservative cast of the gathering insured the rejection of most of the concepts of this primitive democrat, who sought the establishment of a municipality in which real political power would be in the hands of the general population. The city he defined in his proposals was far different from the one that

[21] *Journal of the Convention,* pp. 255, 664–665; New York *Tribune,* Sept. 12, 1846.

[22] *Journal of the Convention,* pp. 217, 222, 304, 365, 390–395; New York *Tribune,* Oct. 2, 1846.

[23] New York *Tribune,* Oct. 20, 1846.

existed or the one which was to come into being. It remained an amorphous dream, a vision valuable chiefly for the insight it gives into the mind, attitudes, and values of the politician from Washington Square.

In the city which Broderick designed, voting would be a universal right of the citizenry. Public officials, from the mayor to the policeman on the corner, as well as the presiding judge of the local municipal court, would be elected. The power of the mayor and the council to appoint would be sharply curtailed. The municipality would be divided into rational units based on wards of congressional districts. In effect, a collection of small cities would be created which would comprise the metropolitan complex of New York. Power and authority would be wielded by officials of the various wards, who would be chosen at frequent elections. Clearly such a government would derive its authority from the consent of the governed and would be more responsive as well as responsible to the people.

Broderick's participation in the convention affected his political career in several ways. It had an immediate effect in bringing him to the attention of a number of Democrats. The views he had announced, the policies which he had pushed, and the uncompromising manner in which he played his role as a delegate stamped him as a man of independent and advanced political views who deviated from the party line. To conservative Democrats he was a radical who should be eliminated. The first opportunity to send him into political oblivion was the forthcoming election in which he was a candidate for a congressional seat in the fifth district. In effect, Broderick through his convention activities waved a provocative banner in the faces of conservative Democrats. They responded to that provocation.

A more beneficial result of his participation was the polish and experience he got from it. This was the first time in which he had appeared before a group of knowledgeable, experienced, and educated men. For the first time he had been called upon to express his opinions, defend his point of view, direct himself to devising immediate responses to questions and suggestions. In the course of the convention he was exposed directly and at length to a parliamentary body. The intricacy of procedure, of motion and countermotion, of the formalized patterns of debate, became familiar. A few years later he was to preside over the California Senate, chosen for the role because of his mastery of parliamentary procedure, and showing a competence that reflected his experience in the convention of 1846.[24]

Shortly after the final session of the convention, Broderick began his pursuit of a congressional seat in the fifth district with more energy and direction. Political aspirations were to be transformed to the world of reality. The road was filled with uncertainty, but there were a number of reasons for him to look with optimism upon his first important campaign. A man of standing and reputation in the district, he had a large personal following in the ninth ward, which was a sizable part of the area. Political assets included his membership in the volunteer firemen, his experience as a delegate to the convention, his short-lived tenure as a customhouse appointee, and his membership in the Irish Catholic community which comprised a considerable part of the population of the district.[25]

His identification with the Irish Catholic community made him a natural target for the animosity of nativists. It was to be generations before the Irish were to meet with real acceptance in the political arena, and a part of the population was never to accept Catholic participation in American politics. Nativist hostility was a serious problem, and as one of the first Irish Catholic candidates for major office, Broderick was certain to incur such hostility and opposition.

Moreover, Broderick was a Jacksonian Democrat of the Locofoco variety. The Jacksonians were a conglomeration of diverse groups which coalesced under the Democratic banner. They were united chiefly because of their common antipathy to the financial monopolies of the big cities of the Atlantic Coast. Lawyers, mechanics, teachers, journalists, and enterprising capitalists, they found sufficient appeal in an amorphous program of antimonopoly, antibank, and antiaristocracy to unite on the field of political strife. The Locofoco segment of the coalition was comprised of the highly vocal opponents of privilege, the spokesmen for egalitarianism whose opposition to monopoly was exceeded only by their distaste for "rag-money" bankers. In the latter part of 1837, after a period in which they were independent, the

[24] San Francisco *Alta California,* Jan. 10, 1851.

[25] New York *Herald,* Oct. 10, 1846; *Wilkes' Spirit of the Times,* Oct. 22, 1859; *Journal of the Convention,* pp. 82–83. Hugins, pp. 203–218, presents a series of charts that facilitate an analysis of the wards of the city in terms of voting preferences, population, assessed valuation, etc.

Locofocos merged with the Democratic party. They never recovered from the "embrace"; that is, they found their radical program muted and their influence sharply curtailed. The powers that reigned in the Democratic party were not about to allow these vociferous radicals a major voice in party affairs.[26]

A dedicated group of the Locofocos insisted on the preservation of an independent organization which they dubbed the "National Reform Association" or "Equal Rights Party." A sectarian group with a far-reaching program of reform that included an end to the traffic in public lands and the reservation of the public domain to actual settlers, the National Reformers must have been delighted with a number of Broderick's convention stands. However, while Broderick was identified as an ideological sympathizer of the National Reformers by his activity in the convention, apparently securing their support, he was alienating the more conservative segments of the Democracy of New York. Their antipathy led to an effort to sabotage his first race for Congress. The fact that he was the regular nominee of the party measured the depth of their antagonism to Broderick and his principles.[27]

The elections of 1846 produced a number of memorable results in New York, some of which had national implications. Governor Silas Wright, luminary of the Albany Regency, ran for a second term in 1846. His friends saw this as a necessary step toward the White House, and his reelection was considered so certain that a leading Democratic journal announced it as a fact before the returns were counted. To the chagrin and amazement of its editors, Wright was defeated. The upset was the result of a number of factors, including the defection of thousands of normally Democratic voters and the active intervention of the representatives of the Polk administration. The same powers that had put Polk over as the first dark-horse presidential candidate, in the Baltimore convention of the Democracy

[26] Joseph L. Blau, ed. *Social Theories of Jacksonian Democracy* (New York, 1947), p. xxvii, emphasizes the diversity of Jacksonian Democracy; Hugins tends to agree but stresses the role of the Locofocos within the conglomeration. Byrdsall, pp. 67–70, describes the merger as a cardinal error for the Locofocos; for a contrary view see William Trimble, "Diverging Tendencies in the New York Democracy in the Period of the Locofocos," *American Historical Review,* XXIV (1919), 396–421.

[27] *Young America,* Jan. 24 and 28 and Feb. 6, 1846; O'Meara, *Broderick and Gwin,* pp. 20–21. The program of the National Reformers is analytically described in Hugins, pp. 131–147.

in 1844, used patronage to frustrate the ambitions of Wright and the Regency in New York in 1846.[28]

Like Wright, Broderick encountered the antagonism of Democratic leaders. In the primary meetings in the fifth district, he had bested more prominent Democrats for the congressional nomination, including the preferred candidate of the Empire Club, led by the notorious Isaiah Rynders. The *Herald* declared Broderick's election to be "beyond a doubt, as he carries with him the active, energetic and progressive forces of the district." The New York *Post,* a few days before the election, printed an assault on Broderick which was a portent of what was to come. Attacking him because he had "neither the education or kind of talent" to make him useful or influential and because he was lacking in the "moral fitness necessary to command the whole vote of the party," this prominent Democratic newspaper expressed the hostility of powerful elements in the party toward Broderick and the Locofocos.[29]

The opposition did not confine itself to writing letters. A short time before the election, Conservative Democrats prevailed on John Bloodgood to run in the fifth district. The objective was to prevent the election of Broderick, for Bloodgood could do little more than secure a small part of the vote and thereby insure the election of a Whig. In 1844 a Whig had carried the district by two hundred votes, less than two percent of the total. In a contest confined to Broderick and his Whig opponent, Frederick Tallmadge, the former would have had a good chance, but the entry of a ticket-splitting Democratic candidate apparently doomed him to defeat.[30]

Meanwhile another political faction in the district presented a problem. The National Reformers debated their course for some time

[28] *United States Magazine and Democratic Review,* XIX (1846), 349–356 and 419 ff. James C. N. Paul, *Rift in the Democracy* (New York, 1951), pp. 177–178, describes the episode from the national point of view. See also John A. Garraty, *Silas Wright* (New York, 1949), pp. 364 ff.; Herbert A. Donovan, *The Barnburners: A Study of the Internal Movements in the Political History of New York State* (New York, 1925); and John Bigelow, ed. *The Letters and Literary Memorials of Samuel J. Tilden* (New York, 1908), I, 47–48.

[29] New York *Herald,* Oct. 10 and 20, 1846; New York *Post,* Oct. 20, 1846.

[30] Lynch, p. 6, describes Bloodgood as an "aristocratic Democrat"; O'Meara, *Broderick and Gwin,* p. 21, describes him as a "man of ancient Knickerbocker stock." John B. Haskin (*Cong. Globe,* 36th Cong., 1st Sess., p. 752) reported: "The aristocracy of the party turned their backs" on Broderick. For election results of 1844 see New York *Tribune,* Oct. 24, 1846.

before they decided to run a complete slate of candidates. In the fifth district Louis Ryckman, longtime member of the association, shoemaker by trade, and chief state organizer of the party, was to carry the banner. Under fire from the conservative Democrats in his own party, Broderick now came under fire from the radical left. The National Reformers were determined to preserve their political identity, and the fact that Broderick was in sympathy with much of their program could not forestall this threat from the left.[31]

The roll call of candidates was completed with the announcement that David E. Wheeler was to run as the candidate of the Native American party. Forerunners of the Know-Nothings of the 1850's, the "natives" in 1846, capitalizing on the mindless animosity which was directed at the immigrant, entered Wheeler, a former member of the Democracy of New York. In the fifth district, where relations between the Irish and the rest of the population were frequently strained, a nativist candidate was assured a sizable vote.[32] The candidacy of Wheeler was the device whereby Broderick was denied a congressional seat. When the votes were counted, he was short of the magic number. Tallmadge had a small plurality; Bloodgood, the stalking horse of the conservative Democrats, had a handful; Ryckman, of the Reformers, polled an insignificant number. The real margin of difference between Broderick and Tallmadge was represented by the "nativist" vote polled by Wheeler.[33]

A chastened Broderick analyzed the defeat, its consequences, and the groups which were responsible. He had neglected his personal affairs and thrown himself into the campaign, but it had ended in galling frustration. The perfidy of men of his party hit home, and in a

[31] *Young America,* Feb. 14 and 21, 1846; New York *Tribune,* Oct. 23, 1846.

[32] New York *Herald,* Sept. 29, 1846. The district was not the Democratic stronghold described by O'Meara, *Broderick and Gwin,* pp. 21–22. *United States Magazine and Democratic Review,* XIX (1846), 414–415, describes Wheeler and analyzes the election in terms of the respective strength and weaknesses of the two major parties.

[33] New York *Herald,* Nov. 4 and 5, 1846; New York *Post,* Nov. 6, 1846. *Niles' National Register,* Nov. 21 and 28, 1846, contrasts the elections of 1844 and 1846 in New York state. An analysis of the city and state election results appears in the *United States Magazine and Democratic Review,* XIX (1846), 419; it emphasizes the influence of local issues and factionalism within the New York Democracy. Philip Hone, Diary, Nov. 7, 1846, MS in New York Hist. Soc., has a trenchant comment on the defeat of the city charter: "The new charter of the city which has occupied the valuable time of a set of idle fellows all summer at the expense of the city has shared the same fate [defeat]." Cf. Walsh's characterization of the convention delegates in *The Subterranean,* June 6, 1846: "the deliberations of such despicable and imbecile loafers as compose the great majority of those elected."

long letter to the Secretary of the Treasury, Robert J. Walker, he complained bitterly of the role played by patronage appointees of the Treasury Department. "The Customhouse was responsible," he declared, "It was a portion of this influence that defeated me." [34]

Broderick's analysis of the election was incomplete. While he emphasized the perfidy of the "customhouse," he failed to mention a number of other factors. The dimensions of this "Waterloo defeat of the Democracy" became apparent as soon as the polls closed. Silas Wright left the city with an insignificant majority, a portent of the massive defeat which was inflicted on the Democrats. The election represented not simply a victory of Whig over Democrat but also a backlash of major proportions. The revised constitution as well as the revised charter were rejected; the constitutional provision establishing Negro suffrage was rejected by a margin of five to one; antirent animosities focused on Wright and the Democracy—all were involved in this "confused melee in which whigs, democrats, natives, abolitionists, anti-renters and the various sections into which these several parties are divided, took part." [35]

His enemies rejoiced, but they were mistaken if they thought this was to be the end of Broderick's career. It was a beginning rather than an end—and a most significant beginning, for it represented an initial effort by a figure from the Irish Catholic community to break into the American world of politics. The fact that Broderick lost was not nearly as significant as his candidacy. The entry of the first of a long line of Irish Catholic politicians into the American political arena was a signal event.

The practical lessons to be learned from campaigning are many and varied, and most of them cannot be learned in any other school. The completeness with which Broderick mastered them in 1846 was demonstrated repeatedly in his career. The matrix that produced a congressional nomination was not duplicated in the years that followed his defeat in 1846, but he continued to play an active role in Democratic politics. In 1848 his associates pressed on him a nomination to the state Assembly, but he abruptly declined. His party regularity was evidenced in his support of Lewis Cass, the Democratic presidential

[34] Broderick to Mary and Bridget Colbert, Apr. 19, 1847, in *People* v. *McGlynn*, p. 167; Broderick to Walker, Nov. 14, 1846, Miscellaneous MSS, New York Hist. Soc.

[35] For additional analysis of the election, see New York *Herald*, Nov. 4, 5, and 10, 1846.

nominee that year. For a time he toyed with the idea of running for Congress, but rejected the notion before he had made a firm commitment.[36]

In the spring of 1849 Broderick joined the gold rush. Jonathan Drake Stevenson, commander of the New York Volunteers, a regiment which had been raised in New York and sent to California during the Mexican War, urged him to come. But Broderick's decision to head west was a personal one, for he later explained, "I left the scenes of my youth and manhood for the 'far West,' because I was tired of the struggles and jealousies of men of my class, who could not understand why one of their fellows should seek to elevate his condition above the common level." [37]

One of a group of eleven New Yorkers who pooled their resources and traveled together, Broderick left the city on April 17, 1849. The group, which included Frederick Kohler, George W. Green, William McKibbin, Jacob Howe, and Michael Phelan, was dubbed the "Republic Company" when they embarked on the steamer *Crescent City* for Panama. Ahead lay an arduous trip which led across the isthmus and up the west coast to San Francisco.[38] In mid-June the steamer *Stella* made its way through the Golden Gate, ending the two-month trip of Broderick and his associates of the Republic Company. The land of the new beginning lay before them. The trip had taken its toll. Broderick narrowly missed finding obscurity in one of the dozens of graves that marked the route across the isthmus. His robust constitution pulled him through the crisis of a tropical fever, and ten days at sea as the ship steamed northward brought him a measure of recovery, but he was not completely well when the anchor plunged into the light green waters of the bay. Soon after their arrival, most of his associates left for the gold fields and the strike that would transform them into

[36] *Wilkes' Spirit of the Times,* Oct. 22, 1859; Fitzwilliam Byrdsall to Calhoun, July 19, 1847, in Jameson, ed. "Correspondence of John C. Calhoun."

[37] Stevenson had once been prominent in the Tammany Society and the New York Democracy. He was a former assemblyman of New York elected at the same time that Alexander Wells, later a California supreme court justice, and Samuel J. Tilden were elected; their certificates of election are in Bigelow, I, 394. Stevenson was aware of the rewards of public life in California as evidenced by a letter which Col. Richard B. Mason wrote him; see Mason to Stevenson, Jan. 23, 1849, Stevenson Papers, Univ. of Calif., Los Angeles, Lib. Lynch, p. 9, states Stevenson urged Broderick to make the trip. Wilkes, in *Affidavit of George Wilkes* (n.p., n.d.), Bancroft Lib., declared he financed Broderick's trip to California. Broderick's explanation is in *Cong. Globe,* 35th Cong., 1st Sess., App., p. 193.

[38] Lynch, pp. 11–13.

men of wealth.[39] Broderick remained behind, his poor health making him a prisoner of the city.

The Broderick who arrived in California was a far different person from the apprentice stonemason who had begun his political career in New York. The previous five years had been rich in political experience. Extensive reading in law, literature, and history had given him intellectual polish. Before long he was applying the lessons he had learned in the New York political arena to California.

[39] Edgar H. Adams, "Private Gold Coinage in California," *American Journal of Numismatics,* XLV (1911), 174–178, reports the organization, membership, route, and activities of the members of the group.

CHAPTER THREE

The Land of the New Beginning

San Francisco had a turbulent, restless, and cosmopolitan population. A way station for many who were en route to the gold country and impatient of delay, it was to become one of the great cities of the western hemisphere. In 1849, however, it was a sprawling collection of improvised shelters which fronted on a bay crowded with ships. Most of its inhabitants looked upon their stay as a temporary one, but Broderick did not share that view. Soon after his arrival he became a San Franciscan, obviously bent on making the city his permanent home.[1]

The problem of making a living was pressing, for costs were high and his purse was sadly depleted by the expenses of the trip. Frederick D. Kohler, a longtime friend and political associate from New York, stepped into the breach and offered him a partnership in a minting and assaying business. Doing business under the name of Kohler and Company, the two men soon had a thriving establishment in operation. Kohler, onetime jeweler, contributed his know-how and the bulk of the capital. Broderick brought to the enterprise a limited amount of money and a willingness to work and learn. Kohler and Company became one of the more successful of the fifteen or so establishments of this nature that operated in the city in the early 1850's. In addition to assaying, the company cast gold slugs to the order of its customers. The private coins it issued contained a slightly smaller amount of gold than the value stamped on them. The difference was the margin of profit for Kohler and Broderick, whose coins circulated readily in the

[1] Frank Soulé, John Gihon, and James Nisbet, *The Annals of San Francisco* (San Francisco, 1855), p. 823.

city's commercial and business world. Broderick returned to the arduous labor of former years—swinging a sledge and doing much of the heavy work involved.

A short time after the partnership was formed, the two men branched out and began to invest their profits in real estate. In the latter part of 1849 they made a number of purchases in the name of the firm, and in the opening months of 1850 Broderick bought land in his own name. The purchases were astute investments. Land in and near the city was limited, and the demand increased as San Francisco grew; those who purchased in the early years realized enormous profits. Broderick added to his real property holdings from time to time; within a short period he was a man of considerable means. At his death his estate included hundreds of lots and parcels in the city—many prime pieces of real estate.[2]

The acquisition of property under these circumstances was to have a marked and lasting influence on the career of Broderick. Then, as now, money played an important role in political affairs. Thanks to the income derived from his investments, Broderick was provided with the means to further his political career. When money was needed to rent a hall or pay for signs, banners, or a band, Broderick's political funds were available. Of modest tastes and inclinations in matters of food, dress, and lodging, Broderick found his income adequate to provide for his personal as well as his political needs. In time he came to spend a substantial portion on the latter; but thanks to his extensive holdings of real property "he experienced no real want of money for his political campaigns." [3]

Although he was a man dominated by his political interests, Broderick was also a whole man who became deeply involved in the life of San Francisco. During the primitive early years he participated in fighting fire, an ever-present hazard to the sprawling, wind-blown city of frame buildings and tents. On one occasion he and his partner

[2] Edgar M. Adams, "Private Gold Coinage in California," *American Journal of Numismatics,* XLV (1911), 174–178; newsclipping, ca. 1850, in Benjamin Hayes Scrapbooks, XVII, 94, Bancroft Lib.; San Francisco *Pacific News,* May 1, 1850. Among specific purchases made by Broderick and Kohler were those made at the sale of city water lots in January 1850, when they purchased lots 543 and 75, the former for $225; see Reports of the Alcalde, Vault 23, Calif. Hist. Soc., San Francisco. For the size of Broderick's estate and nature of his land holdings, see David A. Williams, "The Forgery of the Broderick Will," *Calif. Hist. Soc. Quart.,* XXXX (1961), 203–214.

[3] Jeremiah Lynch, *The Life of David C. Broderick* (New York, 1911), p. 68; *Wilkes' Spirit of the Times,* Oct. 22, 1859.

shoveled mud against fire-threatened buildings, and he played a leading role in organizing the first group of volunteer firemen in the city. He obviously prospered. When a collection was made in San Francisco for the benefit of destitute overlanders in 1850, his personal contribution was exceeded only by several corporate gifts. His fortune in 1851 was estimated at $30,000, a sizable sum for that time.[4]

He made his home with Tom and Emma Maguire, transplanted New Yorkers, in the early years of his stay in San Francisco. Maguire was a pioneer theatrical producer who built and operated the Jenny Lind Theater and made substantial profits by providing his patrons with crude roughhewn amusements which ranged from jugglers to grand opera. His persistent attempts to popularize Rossini and Mozart, despite repeated losses, cost him dearly. The man who worked with such figures as David Belasco and William O'Neill, father of Eugene O'Neill, died penniless in New York City in the 1890's.[5] Life with the Maguires brought Broderick into contact with other members of the world of theater. That the arrangement was not completely satisfactory was indicated by his departure in 1854. Thereafter he lived in one of the better hotels and took his meals at any one of a dozen restaurants. His quarters were ample and provided the privacy that his political situation required. He was, above all things, a *homo politicus*.

Broderick's California political career began with his election to the state Senate in January 1850. His predecessor, Nathaniel Bennett, resigned to accept an appointment to the supreme court. In the special election called to fill this vacancy as well as a number of posts in city government, all sorts of tickets appeared. The profusion of slates reflected the absence of well-organized political groups. Some candidates campaigned vigorously. Bands paraded through the streets on wagons plastered with slogans and names, beseeching the attention of voters. The electorate performed in a creditable fashion, and editors complimented the voters and the city for the orderly fashion in which the election was conducted. Among the victorious candidates was Broderick, whose victory was so apparent and overwhelming that it was among the first to be reported. Apparently he campaigned effec-

[4] Julia C. Altrocchi, *The Spectacular San Franciscans* (New York, 1949), p. 76; *Alta California*, Jan. 9, 1850.

[5] Lois Foster Rodecape, "Tom Maguire, Napoleon of the Stage," *Calif. Hist. Soc. Quart.*, XX (1941), 299.

tively and doubtless secured the support of thousands of former New Yorkers in San Francisco. The magnitude of the triumph was reflected in the totals of the candidates: Broderick, 2,508; Frank Moore, 28; Elcan Heydenfeldt, 20; and 53 for a number of others. In late January Broderick entered the state Senate. From this time until his death he was to be a major figure in the political world of California.[6]

As a member of the state's first legislature, Broderick shared the tremendous tasks involved in writing a body of laws that would implement the constitution and provide a legal foundation for society. The quality of the work is to be seen in the printed volume of laws which was published shortly after adjournment. Its pages of clear and precise language indicate the unjustness of the oft-repeated characterization of this body as the "legislature of a thousand drinks." [7]

This was Broderick's first parliamentary experience in California, and he lost no time in making an impression on his fellow lawmakers. Contrary to what has been published by careless or enthusiastic biographers, Broderick was not a member of the California Constitutional Convention. However, as a member of the first legislature, he played a leading role. Appointed to some of the more important committees of the upper house, Broderick participated in a direct and active manner.[8]

In New York, Broderick had been a member of the Locofoco faction of the Democracy—committed to a program of broad social and political reform. On the left of the political spectrum of that day,

[6] Calif. *Senate Journal,* 1st Sess., 1850, pp. 108–109.

[7] *Statutes of California Passed at the First Session of the Legislature* (San Jose, 1850); F. F. Low, Memoirs, p. 51, MS in Bancroft Lib.; Theodore Hittell, *History of California* (San Francisco, 1898), II, 807.

[8] Broderick has been described by several authors as a member of the California Constitutional Convention of 1849: *Wilkes' Spirit of the Times,* Oct. 22, 1859; Lynch, p. 41; *Biographical Directory of the American Congress, 1774–1949,* p. 892. There is much evidence, however, that Broderick did not participate in the convention. His name is not included in the list of delegates and alternates printed in the *Alta California,* Aug. 2, 1849, nor is he mentioned in the most authoritative account of the convention, J. Ross Browne, *Record of the Debates in the Convention of California on the Formation of the State Constitution* (Washington, D.C., 1850). Broderick is not mentioned in the William M. Gwin Memoirs, MS in Bancroft Lib., in relation to the convention. In none of his public speeches did Broderick mention participating in the writing of the constitution. An autobiographical sketch which Broderick authored was reprinted in the Sacramento *Bee,* June 5, 1886, with explanatory comment by Winfield J. Davis; it fails to mention Broderick's participation. It seems safe to conclude that Broderick did not take part in the convention. His official entrance into the Senate is noted in Calif. *Senate Journal,* 1st Sess., 1850, p. 114; his committee assignments, Public Schools and Judiciary, are noted on p. 175.

Broderick advocated such measures as the distribution of the public domain to the landless and urban poor as well as the election of all public officials through universal suffrage. In the course of his legislative career it became readily apparent that he had lost little enthusiasm for these principles of his political youth.

A violently antiforeigner "Act for the Better Regulation of the Mines and Government of Foreign Miners" presented him with an opportunity to demonstrate his commitment to democratic principles. Ostensibly aimed at the replenishment of the state treasury through the taxation of foreign miners, the bill represented a vigorous assault on all miners who could not establish their citizenship. The act specified that alien miners must secure a license every thirty days at a cost of twenty dollars. Those who failed to secure licenses were to be barred from mining, and continued violation could lead to imprisonment and heavy fines. Collectors, armed with the necessary papers, were to issue licenses in the field, and they were to receive a commission of three dollars for each license sold.[9] Enforcement of the act was to be left to the county sheriffs, whose authority was to be bolstered, when necessary, by a delegation of citizens. It was apparent from the text of the law that all sorts of abuses might result from its enforcement. Collectors were presented with the means whereby they could "mine the miners"—a golden opportunity that could be as rewarding as a promising placer deposit. Claim jumping sanctioned by law was possible, and the provisions for enforcement seemed designed to bring about widespread collisions between citizens and noncitizens in the gold fields.[10]

Broderick vigorously attacked this assault on the rights of the foreign-born, but in spite of his opposition the bill was passed. It was subsequently repealed, after it had produced little revenue and a great deal of violence in the mining counties. Broderick's opposition to the law reflected his own Irish-immigrant background and his conviction that all groups in California's population were entitled to full participation and equal rights. He expressed his concern for the rights of the foreign-born repeatedly; and Californios, Mexicans, French, Negro, German, and Irish residents of California came to look upon him as a

[9] *Statutes of California,* 1850, p. 221.

[10] Introduction of the act is noted in the *Senate Journal,* 1st Sess., 1850, p. 232; the Finance Committee's favorable report, couched in nativist phrases and concepts, is on pp. 494–497.

friend and ally. But while such convictions brought him friends, they also steeled and multiplied his enemies. In the political upheaval that spawned the Know-Nothings during the middle years of the 1850's, Broderick was a principal target. On this occasion the apostles of prejudice joined hands with the advocates of slavery to work against him.[11]

The Chivalry, as defenders of slavery were called in California, represented one of the more powerful groups in the political arena during the 1850's. For the most part they were of Democratic affiliation, although the Whigs included a number of representatives of the South. On two occasions during the 1850's the Chivalry deserted the Democratic party en masse, for the Whig party in 1853 and the Know-Nothing or Native American party in 1855. In both instances the mass defection followed a victory that Broderick and his associates had won in the Democratic party which enabled them to dominate the selection of a slate and the writing of a platform.[12]

The slavery issue was one of the principal questions dividing parties in the turbulent political world of California during the decade that preceded the Civil War. In California, as in many other states, it did more to dominate political campaigns than any other issue. In conventions, with their traditional smoke-filled rooms, in legislative chambers, and in mass meetings the passionate rhetoric of proslavery and antislavery groups revealed the ascendancy of this paramount question. It created friendships, alliances, and allegiances—sometimes uniting men of diverse background—but it also destroyed such ties.

Broderick took his first public stand against slavery soon after his election to the state Senate. The introduction of a resolution labeling the slavery question an abstraction brought into legislative chambers for "unholy, unpatriotic, and partisan purposes" provided him with a chance to display his antislavery convictions and his mastery of parliamentary tactics. The resolution asserted that Congress had no right to interfere with slavery in the territories and advocated popular sovereignty as the best means of settling the status of slavery in the West.[13]

[11] Leonard Pitt, "The Beginnings of Nativism in California," *Pacific Historical Review,* XXX (1961), 23–28, is one of the more scholarly accounts of the impact of the law and its implementation in the mining camps; cf. Charles H. Shinn, *Mining Camps* (New York, 1965), p. 212.

[12] Etta Olive Powell, "Southern Influences in California Politics before 1864" (unpubl. M.A. thesis, Univ. of Calif., 1929).

[13] *Senate Journal,* 1st Sess., 1850, pp. 372–374.

Clearly determined to prevent the passage of a resolution which would label antislavery political activities as "unholy, unpatriotic, and partisan," Broderick began his campaign with a motion to refer the resolution to a select committee. This was rejected by the Senate. A motion for indefinite postponement met with a similar fate. When Broderick then moved to amend the resolution with an antislavery assertion, it met with the support of a majority of his colleagues. However, once antislavery and proslavery sentiments were merged in a single resolution, it became difficult for anyone who felt strongly about the issue on either side to vote for the resolution. Further debate revealed the dilemma that faced a number of senators. When Broderick again moved to postpone the matter indefinitely, the Senate voted for this in spite of the fact that such a step had been rejected a short time before. The Senate had seen a skilled parliamentarian convert a handful of votes into a majority. It also became plain to a number of observers that the senator from San Francisco was an effective spokesman for the antislavery position.[14]

Broderick must have been pleased with this victory. It was not to be duplicated often, for he was in the minority on many questions. However, he was frequently able to take advantage of the rules or of the divisions within the opposition to make his position known and muster maximum support for it. This was to be his approach on a number of occasions. One such battle involved Broderick in a direct clash with the governor as well as a majority of both branches of the legislature. Governor Peter H. Burnett initiated the contest when he urged the passage of legislation to prevent the entry of "Free Negroes and Persons of Color" into California. He found support in the legislature, for the law was passed by the Assembly, and a majority of the upper house favored it. Opposition to such a proposal was obviously based on principle, for there was much political hazard in such a stand and little advantage to be realized by championing "Free Negroes and Persons of Color."

Broderick took full advantage of the rules, the crowded legislative calendar, and the imminent adjournment of the legislature in his battle against the bill. When it came up for a second reading, he moved indefinite postponement and indicated that he would use whatever dilatory tactics were necessary to block its passage. His adamant

[14] *Senate Journal,* 1st Sess., pp. 379–380.

opposition threatened to postpone consideration of other measures and upset all sorts of legislative plans. As adjournment loomed and the pressure mounted on lawmakers, it became quite clear that passage of the governor's immigration bill would doom other legislation —at least for this session. Eventually enough votes were mustered, some coming from frankly hostile members, to kill the measure. The result once more demonstrated Broderick's parliamentary skill and the depth of his commitment to equal treatment of all Americans.[15]

The Chivalry pursued two legislative goals with vigor during this first decade of California's statehood. One objective was the enactment of a fugitive slave law to supplement the national fugitive slave act of 1850. The other was the passage of legislation to convene a state convention—first step toward the division of California into two states. One of the new political entities would be open to slavery, and its entry into the Union would redress the balance which the South had lost when California's admission gave the free states a majority in the United States Senate. Broderick played a major role in the battle against each proposal.

A number of members of the legislature were aware of the real objective of proposals to "amend and change" the state constitution. Antonio María de la Guerra, representative from Santa Barbara, described the activity of the constitution amenders to his brother and concluded: "There is a suspicion here that all these questions are only a pretext to put in time awaiting division." Another knowledgeable observer made a similar charge in an entry in his diary: "The proposition now before the legislature, to submit the question of a constitutional convention to the people, has for its secret purpose the introduction of slavery." [16]

In spite of the fact that considerable sentiment might develop in favor of the scheme in the southern half of the state, where complaints about under-representation in the legislature and a heavy tax burden were heard, the delicate matter required discretion and finesse on the part of the Chivalry, for the bulk of the state's population opposed the

[15] *Senate Journal,* 1st Sess., 1850, p. 347. The action of the Assembly is recorded in *Journal of the California Legislature,* 1st Sess., 1850, pp. 1232–1233, hereinafter cited as *Assembly Journal.*

[16] Antonio María de la Guerra to Pablo de la Guerra, Feb. 4, 1852, De la Guerra Collection, Santa Barbara Mission Archives. C. E. Montgomery, "Lost Journals of a Pioneer," *Overland Monthly,* 2nd Ser., VII (1886), 179; the entry in question is dated Feb. 12, 1852. See also Samuel H. Willey to B. D. Wilson, Dec. 30, 1854, Wilson Coll., Huntington Lib.

introduction of slavery although a substantial portion might accept division into two states. Opposition to slavery was often based upon naked self-interest rather than humanitarian considerations, but in any case the majority would not support division which was accompanied by the introduction of slavery.

The Chivalry pushed the scheme vigorously. Their determination measured their desire to restore the balance of power lost by the South when California was admitted. As was pointed out, however, the proposal contained a number of hazards. Assuming that the convention was a success, an observer declared that when the new state created applied for admission to the Union, a firebrand would be thrown into the confederacy which would "light a conflagration disastrous to our country and to the cause of liberty in the world." [17] The debates of 1850 would be renewed and perhaps the dissolution of the Union, so narrowly averted in 1850, might follow.

The first steps toward the division of the state were taken in the legislature of 1852. The Chivalry, led by astute and bold men like Henry A. Crabb and Richard P. Hammond, successfully guided through the Assembly an act calling for a constitutional convention. Broderick, from his vantage point in the Senate, bided his time until he mustered sufficient support. Once his majority was assured, he acted with dispatch. His motion to postpone the measure indefinitely was passed. As soon as the result was known, Broderick moved to reconsider. This time the vote was apparently adverse to the senator from San Francisco, for the motion to reconsider was rejected by a substantial margin. Under the rules, however, the second vote barred any further consideration of the proposal during that legislative meeting. In effect, Broderick had put the measure in a legislative coffin and then screwed the lid down tight with his motion to reconsider.[18]

The struggle was not ended, for in the following legislature the measure was passed. This time Broderick was not present, and the Chivalry succeeded. It was a most difficult problem for Broderick to deal with, for it seemed hardly proper for a Democratic leader to assail a measure passed by a Democratic legislature and apparently in accord with the American tradition of democratic government and constitution writing. However, at the Democratic state convention in

[17] *Alta California,* Feb. 29, 1852.

[18] Hubert H. Bancroft, *History of California,* VI (San Francisco, 1888), 668–669.

1863, Broderick once again displayed his mastery of the art of political maneuver.

The proposal to call a convention and revise the constitution did not provide for the subsequent ratification of a new constitution by the electorate. This made it vulnerable, and Broderick moved decisively. After pointing out to the convention that the people were not to be given an opportunity to ratify any changes, Broderick proposed a resolution to correct this "oversight." In effect, he sought to have the convention declare its opposition to any proposed change without a vote of the people of California. The applause of the delegates indicated their approval, and a majority vote in favor of Broderick's proposal was soon recorded.[19]

The convention's action was a bitter pill to the Chivalry, for they had labored long to pass the act and were apparently headed for a successful culmination when Broderick placed this insurmountable roadblock in their path. The possibility of the electorate's endorsing changes in the constitution which would divide the state and establish slavery in the southern half was nonexistent. The whole thing might have been done quietly and unobtrusively; but when the resolution threw a searchlight on the scheme, most of its supporters were ready to admit defeat. Once again the Chivalry had reason to look with antagonism on this plebeian Democrat.

In the contest with the Chivalry over the fugitive slave law, Broderick further demonstrated his understanding of parliamentary processes and his willingness to go to great lengths in behalf of a principled position. Henry A. Crabb, stalwart champion of the Chivalry, led the battle to enact such a law in the legislature of 1852. It was not a fierce contest until it reached the Senate, for the majority of the lower house supported it. For that matter, a majority of the Senate favored it as well. Described as "no better and no worse than any other fugitive slave laws," it was, in fact, an arbitrary law that menaced the personal liberty of every Negro in California.[20] Couched in legal phrases, it discarded many aspects of "due process" and gave legal sanction to almost any effort by almost any white man to claim almost any Negro as a fugitive.[21] It authorized any judge, justice, or magistrate to issue a

[19] Winfield J. Davis, *History of Political Conventions in California, 1849–1892* (Sacramento, 1893), p. 25.

[20] Hittell, *History of California,* IV, 97–98.

[21] The full text of the law is in *Statutes of California,* 1852, pp. 67–69. Powell, "Southern Influences," pp. 110 ff., describes the interest of the Chivalry in the act.

warrant authorizing the removal of a fugitive upon oral or written statement. The statement of the alleged fugitive was inadmissible; and the law "forbade any molestation of anyone acting in pursuance of the certificate by any court, judge, justice, or magistrate or any other person whomsoever." To strip the fugitive of all defenses, the act provided that any person who "knowingly hindered or obstructed the claimant of a fugitive" was liable to fine, imprisonment, and civil damages. Fines as well as civil damages could be levied against any persons, including sheriffs and other peace officers, who failed to "carry out, obey, and execute all warrants and precepts" issued under the act. In effect, the fugitive was stripped of defenses and those who came to his aid endangered themselves.

As objectionable as any feature of the law was the section which defined fugitives. Section Four was freighted with the language of the barrister: "Any person held to labor or service who was brought or introduced within the limits of this state previous to admission who shall refuse to return to such labor shall be held and deemed a fugitive within the meaning of this act." Thus, in spite of California's constitution, which prohibited slavery, the status of slaves was extended until the admission of the state. The act also endangered slaves who had come to the Golden State under an agreement to work for a time in exchange for their freedom. In the final analysis, no Negro in California could consider himself beyond the operation of the act.

Broderick towered in the battle against this law.[22] He began by moving its reference to the judiciary committee, where his presence insured a proper hearing of the antislavery viewpoint. There it lay, unattended by the committee but not forgotten by the Chivalry. Demands that it be reported upon finally brought it out of the committee, but without a recommendation—an indication of the balanced composition of the committee and the presence of Broderick.

The battle then shifted to the floor of the Senate, where Broderick again led the opposition. Centering his fire on Section Four, Broderick advocated an amendment which would limit the act to "such slaves as were brought hither prior to the adoption of the constitution." Since but a handful of slaves were in that category, this amendment would have gutted the law. The amendment was rejected. Broderick then

[22] *Senate Journal,* 3rd Sess., 1852, Feb. 7 and 17, Mar. 12 and 16, Apr. 8, 1852. The involved parliamentary maneuvering and the debate that preceded the passage of the act are reported in the *Alta California,* Apr. 8, 9, and 10, 1852.

attempted to amend the bill so as to exempt anyone who had come to California under a contract to labor for a time in exchange for his freedom. This too was rejected by a substantial margin.

The next day Broderick returned to the battle with an ingenious parliamentary move that enabled him to reopen the questions settled on the previous day. Rejection of the amendments, by the rules, barred any further debate on the disputed section. Having been repulsed in his attempt to amend, Broderick now moved to strike the pertinent section. Thereby, general debate was reopened. While his opponents thumbed parliamentary guides to ascertain if this could be done, Broderick demanded that the section be deleted. He declared that the antislavery prohibition of the constitution clearly applied; and, therefore, the attempt to write a law which would apply to persons brought to California after the constitution had been adopted was unconstitutional.

As the debate continued, voices were raised, and soon heated and emotional terms like "doughface" and "abolitionist" were heard. When a vote was finally taken following protracted debate, Broderick's motion to strike was rejected. Still the battle continued, for each section of the law could be attacked in this manner. Broderick freely utilized the tricks of the parliamentary procrastinator to frustrate the will of the majority. Points of order, motions to adjourn, and a call of the Senate were used to delay; but his opponents successfully surmounted each obstacle. With darkness approaching and the usual hour of adjournment long past, the patience of the Senate wore thin. Candles were lighted to offset the gathering darkness, food was brought in to sustain the senators, and the battle continued into the night. The Chivalry, scenting victory, were determined to force a vote. A call for the previous question finally produced the division that Broderick had sought to avoid. The battle was over and the Chivalry rejoiced—a bit grimly.

Within two months, the dangers to free Negroes inherent in the act were to be seen in a Sacramento courtroom where two alleged fugitives were examined. Although both had been brought to California under contracts to labor in exchange for their freedom, they were held to be subject to the law, which was declared constitutional by the California supreme court.[23]

[23] The case cited is described by a member of the Sacramento bar in C. E. Montgomery, "Lost Journals of a Pioneer," p. 180, entry of June 11, 1852.

The eventual passage of the act was to be expected in view of the proslavery character of the legislature of 1852. Only Broderick's utilization of parliamentary procedures had blocked the lawmaking machinery for a time. An informed observer, who watched the battle in its various stages, commented admiringly on Broderick's role. Among other comments was a phrase which described his discussion of the fugitive slave law as "the strongest constitutional argument yet delivered in the Senate." In the battle, Broderick had traveled the lonely road where one man and the right made a majority.[24]

Broderick took a number of positions in the legislature which revealed his political philosophy. Someone familiar with his Locofoco background in New York would have found most of them consistent with the ideas he had expressed as an aspiring politician of the ninth ward. He vigorously supported a law which exempted a personal holding of real estate from forced sale—a typical Locofoco position. On another occasion, he objected vigorously to a provision in a proposed law granting special privileges to state bondholders. Despite his opposition, the measure passed; however, it required a suspension of the rules to overcome his resistance. His Jacksonian animus to "rag-money" doctrines was never more clearly expressed. He pushed legislation that doubled the rate of taxation on the property of banks. Clearly he was willing to treat these organizations of the "money power" differently than other more acceptable lines of enterprise. His position in such matters was not based upon primitive animosity, for he was informed in financial affairs. For example, he vigorously supported a funding bill designed to liquidate the municipal debt of San Francisco. A modern student of fiscal legislation would find much in it to admire.[25] This act provided for the issuance of interest-bearing stock, in hundred-dollar denominations, which was to be retired by a sinking fund. Interest-bearing scrip was to be exchanged for the stock, which was to be retired at the rate of $50,000 annually. The sinking fund was to be raised by setting the assessment rate high enough to cover current expenses of the city plus $50,000. Five prominent men, named in the law, were to supervise its operation. Their compensa-

[24] San Francisco *Daily Evening Picayune,* Apr. 10, 1852.

[25] *Senate Journal,* 1st Sess., 1850, p. 347, reports Broderick's support of "homestead legislation," as the measure to prevent forced sale of a personal holding of real estate was termed; his opposition to the law establishing special privileges for bondholders is in the same volume, pp. 116–117.

tion, authority, and activity were carefully spelled out. The law demonstrated a knowledge and understanding of fiscal affairs and taxation that was surprisingly complete and creative.[26]

One of the more difficult problems which troubled politicians of California in the 1850's was the land question. The complicated issues of land title and general land policy revealed much about the philosophy of a political leader. From the beginning of his career in California, Broderick took the position of the Free Soiler and the National Reformer and advocated the distribution of the national domain among landless settlers. The objective was the creation of a society of free and independent landowners—a sturdy yeomanry—the democratic order which Thomas Jefferson envisioned. Broderick shared the vision and took steps to make the dream a reality in California.[27]

Numerous obstacles stood in the path that led to the agrarian and democratic order. The basis for the opposition varied from one group to another, ranging from the simple belief that advancing such a program was contrary to the interests of those already in possession of land to the desire of those who simply wanted to acquire as much land as possible. Land speculators eyed the permanent wealth of California —the acres of rich and fertile soil—and took appropriate steps to insure that they would get a full share of the treasure.

Speculators were active in the city as well as the countryside, searching for opportunities. Their efforts frequently involved attempts to utilize the state legislature. In 1850, for example, an effort was made to pass "An Act in Relation to the Real Estate and Other Property Belonging to the Pueblo or City of San Francisco." The aim was the legislative validation of some rather dubious titles to waterfront property that had come into the possession of the schemers. Broderick led the effort to kill the measure through indefinite postponement in the legislature of 1850. For the moment, the speculators were frustrated.[28]

They were only temporarily balked, however, for in the following year they succeeded in passing two acts which validated some of the titles and established a "permanent line" for the waterfront of San

[26] *Statutes of California,* 1851, p. 387.
[27] Henry Nash Smith, *Virgin Land: The American West as Symbol and Myth* (New York, 1961), pp. 190–195.
[28] *Senate Journal,* 1st Sess., 1850, p. 345.

Francisco and a procedure whereby some of the state's property would be turned over to the city. A prolonged battle took place in the Senate before the acts were passed. Broderick was prominent as a leader of the opposition. The speculators exulted in their triumph; but their elation was short-lived, for in the following session of the legislature Broderick reopened the question of the "water-lot" legislation.[29]

When the lawmakers gathered for the 1852 session, Broderick was a leading figure of the Democracy, acting lieutenant-governor, and a prominent candidate for the Senate seat formerly filled by John C. Frémont. His chief rival was John B. Weller, for it was obvious that Frémont could not be reelected. Weller was the stronger of the two candidates, but the difference between them was small. The situation demanded that Broderick avoid issues that might alienate men or groups in the legislature; it soon was apparent that he would not travel the path of expediency.[30]

A measure of his personal integrity was found in his announcement, prior to the balloting for the Senate seat, that he intended to push the repeal of the "water-lot" legislation. Charging that corruption and fraud had marked every step of their route through the legislature, Broderick demanded that the acts be repealed. The completeness of the corruption was illustrated in his charge that the very text of the bills had been changed by the clerks of the legislature after they had been passed. It was a startling accusation which elicited a heated response.[31]

Joining forces with a self-confessed Free Soiler of 1848, Thomas B. Van Buren, Broderick plunged into the battle. The two men made an effective team, for both were superior speakers and masters of parliamentary tactics, and they refused to bow to the weight of superior numbers. On one occasion the two men "held the Senate at bay from 6 o'clock at night until half-past 1 at night. On most of the

[29] *Statutes of California,* 1851, p. 307; *Alta California,* Dec. 21, 1884.

[30] Frémont's Senate seat remained vacant following the abortive attempt of the legislature in 1851 to elect a successor. See *Senate Journal,* 2nd Sess., Feb. 3–27, 1851, for a detailed account; cf. *Alta California,* Feb. 9 and 17, 1851, and an account which appeared in the San Francisco *Call,* Apr. 3, 1887. An analysis of the respective chances of Broderick and Weller is reported in the *Alta California,* Jan. 26, 1852. See also Henry W. Halleck to Pablo de la Guerra, Jan. 18, 1852, and Antonio María de la Guerra to Pablo de la Guerra, Jan. 19, 1852, in the De la Guerra Coll.; Philip Roach Statement, p. 11, MS in Bancroft Lib.

[31] *Alta California,* Jan. 11, 1852; San Francisco *Daily Evening Picayune,* Mar. 24, 1852.

questions, the Senate stood 20 to 2 and finally the body became almost furious." [32]

The debate was proceeding in a relatively subdued fashion until Broderick began to level accusations of bribery at specific individuals. Declaring the investigating committee was frustrated by witnesses who pleaded privilege or self-incrimination to avoid testifying, Broderick demanded that they be forced to appear before the Senate. "Jonathan D. Stevenson has told me that he bought four members himself to vote for the bill," he declared. "There was fraud about many of the grants, and I want the millionaires who are wallowing in wealth to be made to disgorge," he continued. Then he listed the witnesses he wished to have subpoenaed in addition to Stevenson. Some of the most prominent figures in the city were on the list. These were the men, Broderick charged, who had spent some eighty thousand dollars to corrupt the legislature of 1851. Broderick denied that he had any intention of injuring the innocent: "I am not in favor of taking the property away from innocent holders . . . but most of the property is held by a few men who have only a piece of paper from some rascally Alcalde. Let's take it away from them." Innocent parties, he said, who might be injured by the repeal of the acts could look to the courts for relief.[33]

Senator Philip Roach, of Monterey, confirmed Broderick's charge that the committee on commerce and navigation had been frustrated by witnesses pleading attorney's privilege or self-incrimination. Broderick leveled an accusing finger at two members of the Assembly, Archibald C. Peachy and A. J. Ellis, and demanded that the Senate compel them to appear and testify. In the language of a public prosecutor he declared that "the first act is dripping with corruption . . . here is J. D. Stevenson running about the streets of San Francisco and telling people that he bought four members to vote for the bill himself. Now force him here and make him say so." In spite of Broderick's impassioned oratory, the men he named were not subpoenaed. As if to soften this rebuff, Broderick, Jacob R. Snyder, and Frank Soulé of the San Francisco delegation were added to the investigating committee.[34]

[32] Van Buren's deviation from Democratic orthodoxy was revealed in a Democratic convention. See *Alta California,* July 22, 1852. For a graphic description of the manner in which the two men operated, see the same newspaper, Feb. 29 and Apr. 18, 1852.

[33] *Alta California,* Mar. 21, 1852; *Senate Journal,* 3rd Sess., 1852, Mar. 19, 1852.

[34] Thomas B. Van Buren to Gregory Yale, Mar. 24, 1852, Gregory Yale Coll., Univ. of Calif., Los Angeles; *Alta California,* Mar. 21, 1852; *Senate Journal,* 3rd Sess., 1852, Mar. 19, 1852.

The question of repeal dominated the following day's proceedings. Once again charge and countercharge were made. The session began with a report of the commerce and navigation committee, which recommended repeal of one of the acts. Broderick and Van Buren were livid with anger when it was announced that the committee would report. They demanded to know when it had arrived at this decision. The chairman, Paul Hubbs, replied that the group had met a short time before the session began. When Broderick complained that he and Van Buren had not been notified of the meeting, Hubbs explained that an unsuccessful effort had been made to contact them. Almost as an afterthought, he added that their presence would have made no difference, since they were the only members of the committee who opposed the decision. Broderick and Van Buren protested heatedly that they had understood that the committee was to take no action "until witnesses were examined, until we knew something of the matter." Both men attacked the committee's recommendation to give separate treatment to the two water-lot acts by repealing one and not the other. In Van Buren's words: "The first act was to benefit the holders of Hyde and Leavenworth grants and the second was to benefit holders of Colton grants. Why repeal one without the other? They are both on the same footing." [35]

That Broderick and Van Buren were on the right track became more apparent as the investigation continued. In an extraordinary session of the Senate, Jesse D. Carr, a leading witness, confirmed many of the charges made by Broderick. Much of his testimony would have been inadmissible in a court; but while ironclad proof was not produced, it became apparent that undue influence had played a role in getting the acts through the 1851 legislature. Assemblyman Peachy, accused by Broderick and subpoenaed by the Senate, refused to respect the summons on constitutional grounds.[36]

In general, the effort to uncover the manner in which the acts were passed so that both could be repealed met with failure. As Broderick pointed out, "the examination before the committee amounted to nothing. Whenever we were about reaching the heart of the matter, the witnesses refused to testify." Corrupt means had been used to influence the legislature; but no concrete evidence to prove that spe-

[35] *Alta California,* Mar. 21, 1852.

[36] *Daily Evening Picayune,* Mar. 24, 1852; *Senate Journal,* 3rd Sess., Mar. 24, 1852.

cific members of the legislature received a single dollar in exchange for their votes in favor of the water-lot acts was revealed.[37]

In the final analysis, the investigation and the furor it aroused went for naught, for not a single member of the legislature was ever called to answer for his involvement in the passage of the water-lot acts. However, as both Broderick and Van Buren pointed out, the principal objective was to bring about repeal and not to punish errant lawmakers who had violated their oath of office or the individuals who had seduced them from the paths of parliamentary purity. The two men continued to push repeal of both acts until adjournment in spite of sharp and periodic rebuffs. In the end, they were defeated.[38]

In the course of the controversy, one of San Francisco's leading newspapers, the *Alta California,* applied the lash of criticism to Broderick. Previously it had been neutral, occasionally friendly, but now it examined the manner in which he was attacking the water-lot legislation in a most critical fashion. Pleading that new interests in the property had developed and therefore Broderick should allow "sleeping dogs to lie," the editorial closed with a judgment and a warning: "We have no hesitation in assuring him [Broderick] that his intemperate zeal to prove himself a very paragon of legislative virtue will seal his fate as a politician, without convincing either his friends or his enemies that he is the model of honesty and independence that he evidently desires the public should believe him to be." [39]

When the battle was over, a number of observers turned a searching eye on Broderick and Van Buren and the roles they had played. The journal which had pleaded with him in print to let sleeping dogs lie was quite critical, although it conceded that he was a man of integrity "whose eyes are always open to spy out anything that may savor of special legislation" and that there was "little question that he has been of great value during the present session." Another observer, who obviously wrote from the vantage of a close relationship, paid him a public tribute:

> For his own personal interests and political success, he has been too rigid, too inflexible, too implacable in maintaining what he has thought

[37] Van Buren to Gregory Yale, Mar. 24, 1852, Gregory Yale Coll.; *Alta California,* Mar. 24 and 25, 1852.

[38] The final debate in the 1852 legislature is reported in the *Alta California,* May 2, 1852; an extended discussion of the water-lot legislation appears in the *Assembly Journal,* 3rd Sess., 1852, pp. 284–307.

[39] *Alta California,* Mar. 22, 1852.

right. . . . That he has defects of character and marked ones, none will deny—asperity of temper, stubborn tenacity of purpose, and a lack of consideration and tolerance for the views of others when differing from his own. But these same qualities . . . are precisely those which render him valuable as a public servant, immovable in sustaining right, powerful in opposing wrong. How many times during his public career has he not defeated some premeditated plunder of the people—exposed some deep-laid rascality against the State? Who can justly charge him with participation in any swindling scheme of legislation—any of the thieving operations of the lobby? [40]

There were other occasions on which Broderick displayed a concern for the responsibilities of his office. He and Van Buren championed the selection of a public printer through competitive bidding, but were overruled. They were in the minority again when the "Salary Grab" act was passed, authorizing every member of the legislature to draw a portion of his salary in cash from the hard-pressed state treasury. Toward the close of the session they made an effort to eliminate one of the basic weaknesses of county government in California. County officials retained fees which they collected in the course of their duties. In some instances such fees amounted to as much as sixty thousand dollars a year. County offices became prizes—bonanzas for which candidates would do almost anything.[41] Broderick struck at the heart of the problem with a proposal that all county officials—sheriffs, treasurers, recorders—be limited to an income of ten thousand dollars from fees; money in excess was to be turned into the general treasury of the county. A prolonged debate followed this rational proposal, but it was finally put to rest by an adverse vote. County officials went on to enjoy their lucrative offices for years to come. Perhaps the most important result of the proposal was the host of new enemies that it created for Broderick among incumbent county officials.[42]

One of the more significant bills introduced in this session of the legislature was the work of Archibald C. Peachy, reluctant witness in the water-lot investigation and partner in the legal firm of Halleck, Peachy, and Billings, which specialized in land litigation. The pro-

[40] *Alta California,* Mar. 26, 1852, from letter written in response to an editorial attacking Broderick.

[41] *Alta California,* Feb. 14, 1852, reports Broderick's position on the selection of the public printer; his stand on the "Salary Grab" is reported Mar. 5, 1852.

[42] *Senate Journal,* 3rd Sess., 1852, pp. 164, 380; *Alta California,* May 1, 1852. Among the officials named by Broderick were clerks of the superior courts, sheriffs, and coroners; see *Alta California,* Mar. 6, 1852.

spective law bore an imposing title: "A Bill to Enforce the Observance of Contracts Made Without this State for the Performance of Labor Within the Limits Thereof." In effect, the bill was an attempt to legalize a system of peonage or serfdom in California. Peachy, a well-known figure of the Chivalry, was evidently interested in an approximation of the slave system if the peculiar institution itself couldn't be established in California. His bill was promptly dubbed "Peachy's Coolie Bill" by its opponents.[43]

"Coolie Bill" was an accurate designation, since the measure was concerned with contracts made with Orientals for labor in California. Such contracts were to be assignable and their fulfillment was to be assured by the police authority of the state. Laborers who failed to comply with their contracts or who fled from the contract holder were to be apprehended, imprisoned, and fined by the sheriffs and the courts. Continued imprisonment was to be the punishment of those who refused to work out their contracts. Court costs of such cases were to be deducted from the wages of a laborer, which were to be at least fifty dollars per year. Contracts were limited to a ten-year period. There were obvious similarities between this system of labor and the slightly more odious and oppressive system that prevailed in the South.[44]

Broderick, Van Buren, and Roach announced their vehement opposition to the measure. Their position was reinforced by messages that reached the legislature from mining towns, where the reaction was strong in spite of the provision that such laborers were barred from mining. Columbia, Tuolumne County, held the largest mass meeting in its history and passed resolutions which condemned "the various measures now before the legislature to establish land monopoly, peonage, and degrade labor." Backed by this and similar expressions of public sentiment, Broderick made the bill a special order of business and then succeeded in sending it into legislative limbo through a motion to postpone indefinitely. In the process he demonstrated anew his concern for free labor.[45]

In the waning days of the session, as lawmakers began to contem-

[43] *Assembly Journal,* 3rd Sess., 1852, p. 273.

[44] The complete text of the law is in *Alta California,* Mar. 21, 1852; its more objectionable features were described in the same newspaper, Mar. 7, 1852.

[45] A select committee reported the bill to the floor with a do-pass recommendation. Roach filed a detailed, critical, minority report. See *Senate Journal,* 3rd Sess., 1852, pp. 168, 669 ff., 305. *Alta California,* Apr. 12, 1852, reported the resolutions of the Columbia meeting.

plate the forthcoming adjournment and Broderick the end of his legislative career, the slavery question made its presence felt again. A communication from the New Jersey legislature asked concurrence in its endorsement of the Compromise of 1850. The Assembly promptly concurred, but Broderick and Van Buren objected to the language of the resolution and suggested modification. Eventually a resolution of concurrence was passed, but the committee of conference which authored it produced one far more neutral in tone than the original.[46]

Just before adjournment, Broderick was involved in still another clash with the legislators who tried to serve the land speculators. This time the speculators were concerned with the public land bestowed on California upon admission. Two days before adjournment, a bill which would have authorized sale of a half million acres of school land was defeated. Despite the strenuous objections of Broderick, it was redrafted and adopted. This action required an unusual interpretation of the rules, but despite that problem and the opposition of Broderick, the bill was passed. Again in defeat the San Francisco senator demonstrated a continued concern for the public interest.[47]

The defeat he suffered on this occasion came on the eve of his departure from the California legislature. In late spring the session came to an end and Broderick never again sat in that body. In some ways the final controversy over the disposition of the public lands was symbolic of the man and his philosophy. He fought vigorously in behalf of the public interest and openly opposed all those who would manipulate the government to enrich themselves. On one issue after another he revealed that he was a man of responsibility and integrity. Legislation which sought special advantages for individuals or groups met his vehement opposition. Those who advocated the interests of the slaveholding South found him a formidable opponent. It was largely because of his stubborn determination and his mastery of the parliamentary process that the bill prohibiting the immigration of free Negroes had died a-borning. His identification with free labor was manifested in his battle against the Coolie Bill. The "Salary Grab" act,

[46] *Senate Journal,* 3rd Sess., 1852, pp. 197, 356, 400, 463.

[47] *Alta California,* May 2, 1852. Broderick fought vigorously for the preservation of the public domain to actual settlers but failed in this instance. California's land policies were an amalgam of error, fraud, and incompetency which facilitated the schemes of land speculators and "frustrated to a large extent the avowed objective of government policy: the development of a nation of farm owners." See Paul W. Gates, "California's Agricultural College Lands," *Pacific Historical Review,* XXX (1961), 103–104.

the bill to reduce the swollen incomes of county officials, and the act to fund the debt of the city of San Francisco—all evidenced his integrity.

An observer of the body politic made an appraisal of the San Francisco senator in a few succinct lines. California, predicted this writer, would never find "occasion to regret his unrelenting hostility to the sharpers of politics, . . . his devotion to the public interest and his instinctive stubborn sense of duty that never yet sacrificed the people or prostituted his place as a Senator to a private or unworthy end." [48]

[48] *Alta California,* Mar. 26, 1852.

☆☆☆☆☆☆☆☆☆☆☆☆☆☆

CHAPTER FOUR

Political Foundations

From the first year of his arrival in California until his death a decade later, Broderick was an active and untiring figure in the world of politics. A man of intelligence, purpose, and enduring ambition, he became increasingly skilled in the manifold arts of the politician. An authority once described him bluntly as "by far the ablest and most conspicuous figure" in the political world of his time.[1] It is significant that his friends as well as his enemies utilized extravagant language to describe his mastery of political craft.

His political world was divided into Democratic, Whig, Know-Nothing, and Republican spheres; however, the lines that determined political persuasions were often breached, and individuals as well as groups shifted ground and affiliation during the fifties. Throughout that decade the California Democracy dominated the political arena although, like other political parties, it suffered setbacks from time to time. In the early years of the fifties, the Whig party was a formidable opposition, but the grand old party of Webster, Clay, and Calhoun drifted into political oblivion as the decade passed. By 1854 it was a lifeless organization, beyond recall.[2]

[1] Theodore Hittell, *History of California* (San Francisco, 1898), IV, 142. There are a number of appraisals of Broderick. The most recent, L. E. Fredman, "Broderick: A Reassessment," *Pacific Historical Review,* XXX (1961), 39–46, draws heavily upon an account by John S. Hittell, *Overland Monthly,* 2nd Ser., XIII (1889), 103–106, an extremely hostile evaluation which was apparently intended to answer a favorable review of Broderick's political career published by Hubert H. Bancroft in *History of California,* VI (1888), 659–692, 708–710, 719–735. John Hittell's opinion is largely personal and subjective; Bancroft, in contrast, marshals evidence to sustain his judgment.

[2] There is no satisfactory political history of California for the 1850's. Bancroft, *History of California,* Vol. VI, Chs. xxiii and xxiv, and Vol. VII, Ch. xxi, is the most complete.

Whig decline renewed conflict between two major divisions of the Democracy—the Chivalry or proslavery branch and the antislavery Free Soil wing. Free Soil Democrats were numerous and active in the party. They exhibited varying degrees of hostility to slavery; a commonly shared attitude was their opposition to bringing slave labor and free labor into direct competition. They sometimes were emotional, but for the most part Free Soil Democrats were cold, dispassionate, and objective in their opposition to the peculiar institution. The Chivalry found it difficult to muster popular support for a proslavery political program, but the skill of its leaders and the assistance it obtained from the "federal power" kept the Chivalry in the battle. The conflict between the two wings of the party continued uninterrupted through 1860, occasionally subsiding but always a lurking threat to the peace and unity of the Democracy.

The decline of the Whigs coincided with the appearance of the American party. Better known as the Know-Nothings, they absorbed large numbers of homeless Whigs as well as numerous defectors from the Chivalry wing of the Democratic party and in 1855 swept to an impressive victory at the polls. The remarkable rise of the "party of the dark lantern" was followed by an equally rapid decline. Its demise was accompanied by the growth of a vigorous Republican party, which marshaled behind the banner of John C. Frémont in the presidential race of 1856. The Republican ticket ran second to a unified California Democracy, and its enemies rejoiced. Before the decade came to a close, however, Republicans were organized into a vibrant party which had good reason to look forward confidently to the 1860 elections. Republican optimism was based in part on Democratic division, for once again the California Democracy was divided into hostile wings.[3]

The antebellum Democratic party, then, was not a homogeneous group united by an enduring philosophy and program. On the contrary, it was a broad organization which gave political shelter to people from all walks of life and every section of the Union. The Chivalry drew heavily upon the South for its rhetoric and membership. Many of its leaders were young, intelligent, and vigorous men

[3] Bancroft, *History of California,* VI, 691–692, 697–702. Peyton Hurt, *The Rise and Fall of the "Know Nothings" in California* (San Francisco, 1930), is the best study on the subject. Winfield J. Davis, *A History of Political Conventions in California, 1849–1892,* presents factual information on the growth of the Republican party. Roy F. Nichols, *The Democratic Machine, 1850–1854* (New York, 1923), pp. 17–18, casts light on divisions within the Democratic party and their origins.

who had come to the Pacific Coast to search for gold and remained to found a new society cast in the image of their beloved South. During the fifties the Chivalry in California was an extension of southern influence, devoted to the spread of slavery into the Trans-Mississippi West and the enhancement of southern political power.

The counterweight to the Chivalry was the Free Soil wing of the party. In 1848 and 1852, this fledgling independent party campaigned under a banner inscribed, "Free Soil, Free Speech, Free Labor and Free Men!" Its first national ticket was headed by a former Democratic president, Martin Van Buren, who fled his ancestral political home when proslavery interests came to dominate party councils. The effort to found a national independent organization died a-borning, but the party was a power to reckon with in 1848 when the defection of Democrats to the new banner led to the Whig triumph of Zachary Taylor. Thenceforth "Free Soil" was an odious term which good Democrats eschewed. The Free Soil party disappeared after 1852, but Free Soil sentiments endured. There was a Free Soil faction within the national Democratic party throughout the fifties, and in California it represented a considerable portion of the party faithful. Free Soilers were antislavery, their attitudes ranging from the moralistic abolitionist to the individual who objected to slavery on grounds of naked self-interest. In terms of political program the latter advocated the exclusion of slavery from the territories, the disposition of public land to actual settlers, and the confinement of slavery to its existing domain. Broderick was the principal leader of the Free Soil division of the California Democracy.[4]

A third major grouping within the party included a large part of its membership and the bulk of its professional leaders. This faction took the broad middle ground between the Chivalry and Free Soil factions, reluctant to commit themselves to either unless some concrete advantage was forthcoming. In New York, the term "Hunkers" had been coined to describe these men of flexible views who "hunkered" or "thirsted" for the rewards of politics in the form of place or material advantage. The more accurate and descriptive terms "Conservative Democrat" and "National Democrat" were commonly used to denote

[4] Nichols, *The Democratic Machine,* p. 22; Paul W. Gates, "California's Agricultural College Lands," *Pacific Historical Review,* XXX (1961), 103; Etta Olive Powell, "Southern Influences in California Politics before 1864" (unpubl. M.A. thesis, Univ. of Calif., 1929).

members of this branch of the Democracy. During the fifties both national Democratic administrations were dominated by proslavery figures. Consequently California Democrats of conservative views were subjected to considerable influence as the national Chivalry funneled federal patronage to their political kindred in the California Democracy.[5]

Almost from the day of his arrival in San Francisco in mid-1849, Broderick was involved in politics. Since he arrived before the appearance of an organized system, he was accorded the unique opportunity of molding his political environment. He shaped and influenced his political world, although of course its structure was determined in part by forces which were independent of him. Shortly after he entered the legislature in San Jose, he presided over a Democratic gathering which took steps to set up a statewide organization, supplementing the work which a similar Democratic meeting had done in San Francisco. A number of Broderick's associates were prominent in the city's initial Democratic meeting.[6]

The procedures adopted in the city beside the Golden Gate eventuated in a citadel of political power for Broderick. A general committee was selected to make party policy between conventions. John McGlynn and Frederick D. Kohler, two of Broderick's friends, were chosen members. A party primary supervised by the general committee was to be the means whereby nominees were chosen. These procedures were similar to those which prevailed in Broderick's political training ground, New York City. Party primaries to select nominees entailed a number of factors: among others, that the general membership of the party would play a role in the selection of candidates. Nominees were to emerge from democratic elections—not smoke-filled rooms. It was roughhewn democracy—acceptable to those who could participate and influence, anathema to those who were disadvantaged.[7]

There were many similarities between New York, the metropolis of Broderick's youth, and San Francisco, the city of his mature years. Although the bay city was generations younger, both went through similar stages of evolution. Both were great ports which stood at the

[5] *Alta California,* Feb. 7, 1850.

[6] Preliminary efforts to organize the Democratic party in San Francisco are described in *Alta California,* Nov. 1, 1849; Winfield J. Davis, "Notes on the History of California," p. 3, MS in Huntington Lib.; Davis, *Political Conventions,* pp. 1–3.

[7] *Alta California,* Jan. 26, 1850.

ocean termini of river systems that drained vast hinterlands. Maritime commerce played a major role in the economy of each city. Both were major centers of political power in their respective states; both grew rapidly in the years which immediately preceded the Civil War; both faced urban problems which demanded attention. San Francisco was especially hard-pressed as it struggled with the burdens of providing municipal services and facilities for a cosmopolitan population which grew rapidly. Financing and building streets, public buildings, and port facilities, establishing and staffing a court and police system and the like comprised a complex of problems which would have vexed a modern planner. When Broderick and his associates moved to shape the political world of San Francisco in 1850, they were anticipating the future and envisioning the city which would rise on the hills overlooking the bay.

Democrats capitalized on their early efforts by electing a complete set of municipal officers in the spring elections. As the fall elections approached, the harmony which had characterized Democratic party meetings disappeared. The party primary was by-passed in favor of a nominating committee which produced a ticket described as "an absurd jumble of the little odds and ends of all parties and factions—whiggery, democracy and nativism." This harsh comment was softened by a phrase which declared, "a good, able, talented man was put in here and there for effect." Perhaps Broderick thought those words described him. In any case, the senator from San Francisco, described in election stories as an "independent Democrat," won reelection. His margin of victory in this fall election of 1850 was much more modest than that of the previous spring.[8]

Broderick and his associates made other efforts to structure their political world along familiar lines. In the early summer of 1850, they organized the first volunteer fire-fighting company after a series of disastrous blazes had leveled blocks of the city. It was much like the volunteer companies in New York, and the Empire Fire Engine Company, Number 1, elected Broderick as its first foreman. Under his direction the company fought fire, but it also had a political function. Like the New York companies, Empire Number 1 attended primaries, mustered the vote at election time, assembled delegates at convention time, and staffed the machinery of the party between such

[8] San Francisco *Herald,* Sept. 25, 1850; *Alta California,* Oct. 9, 1850.

important events. In such activities the firemen looked to the political interests of their foreman.[9]

Broderick and his associates took other steps to shape the political world of San Francisco. In the first legislative session he and his supporters guided a charter through the legislature. It blueprinted a municipal government much like that of New York. A common council, composed of aldermen and assistant aldermen, was to be the legislative body of the city, which was divided into wards of approximately equal population, each to be represented on the council. Annual election of a large number of city officials was specified. In effect, it was a thoroughly democratic city government which was established—similar in a number of respects to the municipal government Broderick envisioned in the convention to revise the city charter of New York in 1846. It was also a political system in which men like Broderick could function effectively.[10]

Broderick's political career was given an unexpected boost when Governor Peter H. Burnett resigned shortly after the legislature assembled in 1851. The vacancy was filled by Lieutenant-Governor John McDougal, whose post as presiding officer of the Senate was then filled by Broderick, elected by his colleagues. Thus, within two years of his arrival in California, Broderick had risen to a position comparable to lieutenant-governor. His rise to eminence did not pass unnoticed by his enemies.[11]

The new president of the state Senate set his sights on a still higher office. John C. Frémont's term was coming to an end, and the legislature would soon be faced with the task of choosing a successor. A year earlier it would have been ludicrous for Broderick to picture himself in a senatorial toga, but his California experience widened his political vistas. At the moment there was little chance that he could be elected

[9] San Francisco *Herald,* July 1, 1850. John Henry Brown, *Early Days in San Francisco, California* (Oakland, 1949), pp. 124–125, describes Broderick's involvement in one of the numerous fires that plagued the city in its early years.

[10] The text of the charter is in *Alta California,* May 4, 1850, and in *Statutes of California Passed at the First Session of the Legislature* (San Jose, 1850), pp. 223–229. Broderick's role in pushing it through the legislature is to be seen in the *Senate Journal,* 1st Sess., 1950, pp. 143, 168, 237, 305, 310, and in the *Alta California,* Apr. 15, 1850. The charter was subsequently adopted in a special election in the city described in the *Alta California,* May 1, 1850. Broderick also supported changes in the charter in the direction of consolidation of city and county government; see *Alta California,* Mar. 8, 1851, and *Statutes of California,* 1851, pp. 357–366.

[11] *Senate Journal,* 2nd Sess., 1851, pp. 43–48, 48–49; *Alta California,* Jan. 10, 1851.

to succeed Frémont; under the circumstances his objective was to postpone the election until the following legislative meeting. This he set about to accomplish—exploiting the usual devices of a parliamentary procrastinator. When these were exhausted, he turned to novel procedures which were "without a parallel in the history of the British Parliament or the American Senate." On one occasion he abruptly adjourned, on apparently specious grounds, the joint meeting of the two houses of the legislature. Although without precedent, his tactics were effective; the seat was not filled, and election was postponed to the next meeting of the legislature. Hopefully in the interim the situation would change and Broderick's chances would improve. Thomas Butler King and Solomon Heydenfeldt, scions of the South and the leading candidates for Frémont's seat in 1851, had good reason to look with animosity on the man who had blocked the election.[12]

His work as presiding officer in the state Senate sharpened and deepened his knowledge of parliamentary procedure. He usually operated in an impartial manner when he sat in the chair, but he frequently stepped down into the chamber, where his stance and language were anything but impartial. His vehement style of expressing his views was becoming a trademark. Many of his colleagues appreciated his separation of the roles of presiding officer and senator from San Francisco. At the end of the session the Senate formally thanked him, an appreciation which confirmed an earlier judgment: "He has an abundance of knowledge of parliamentary usages, is prompt and decisive in character and must make a very efficient presiding officer." [13]

While his colleagues appreciated him as a presiding officer, they were not enchanted by his legislative stands. The chief spokesman of the Free Soil Democrats, he frequently collided with members of the Chivalry. Their differences were not confined to the legislature, but frequently spilled over into other gatherings. For example, at a convention called to plan the first state gathering of the Democratic party, the Chivalry elected Thomas Jefferson Green presiding officer. Green was a sometime Texan who had brought slaves to California to work

[12] John Currey to W. Nelson, Jan. 14, 1851, California File, Huntington Lib.; *Alta California,* Feb. 9, 1851. The official albeit abbreviated account of the prolonged effort to elect a U.S. senator is in the *Senate Journal,* 2nd Sess., 1851, Feb. 3–27, 1851; cf. *Alta California,* Feb. 9 and 17, 1851. The account in the San Francisco *Call,* Apr. 3, 1887, is detailed and factual.

[13] *Alta California,* Jan. 10, 19, 21, and Feb. 9, 1851; *Senate Journal,* 2nd Sess., 1851, p. 502.

in the mines, and there were few more militant defenders of slavery. He attempted to keep Broderick from playing a role in spite of the fact that Broderick was a major figure in the party. Green not only kept him off the platform committee but also barred him from the first state central committee.[14]

In spite of the attempt to isolate him, Broderick created a role for himself. After the adoption of the platform, he moved the appointment of a committee to seek its endorsement by other Democrats. The convention adopted this proposal, and Broderick became chairman of the committee. He used this opportunity to broaden his circle of political acquaintances. In the discussion of philosophy and program in a face-to-face setting he was at his best. A number of people learned something about him in the process, and Broderick learned something about them. The exchange in each case worked to his advantage.[15]

The convention, pressed by Broderick, took another step which had a lasting influence on the party and on Broderick's career. The issue was determining representation in the forthcoming convention. Broderick insisted on basing representation on the population of a county; a vociferous minority insisted that each county have the same number of delegates. Since counties varied in population from a few hundred residents to more than twenty-one thousand, it was difficult to square the minority position with democratic practice. Broderick's view prevailed, and representation based upon population became the basic pattern of organization. The decision assured San Francisco County of substantial representation in party gatherings. In fact, during the antebellum period Broderick's bastion, San Francisco, had the largest delegation in Democratic conventions.[16]

Before the 1851 state convention met, Broderick was involved in a controversy which also had an immediate as well as a long-range impact on his career. The matter came to public attention when

[14] Throughout the session most issues were colored by the slavery question. Even a bill on divorce, on which Broderick took a liberal position, brought him into conflict with a colleague of proslavery views, and their discussion on the floor of the Senate revealed the deep antagonism between the friends and foes of the peculiar institution. See *Alta California,* Feb. 12, 1851. See also Leonard Pitt, "The Beginnings of Nativism in California," *Pacific Historical Review,* XXX (1961), 26–28. A detailed account of the convention appeared in the *Alta California,* May 14, 1851.

[15] *Proceedings and the Address and Resolutions of the Democratic Meeting Held at the Capital at the City of San Jose, March, 1851* (n.p., n.d.) in Benjamin Hayes Scrapbooks, XVII, 7–9, Bancroft Lib.

[16] The population figures are from *Alta California,* Dec. 21, 1884. See also *Proceedings and the Address . . . San Jose, March, 1851,* p. 3.

Senator Thomas B. Van Buren, his close associate, introduced a resolution which criticized a number of trials pending in the Seventh District Court. The defendants, James McClatchy, Charles Robinson, and a number of lesser figures of a "settlers' organization," were being held on murder charges as a result of their involvement in a Sacramento riot which resulted in a number of deaths. The deaths occurred when a number of settlers clashed with the local authorities in the course of a demonstration. The settlers were displaying their displeasure with an adverse decision of a local court. They were enraged by the decision as well as by obiter dicta of the bench which declared that there could be no appeal. The matter at issue was title to land in Sacramento, the settlers in conflict with men whose claim was derived from John Sutter. The settlers were skeptical of the validity of Sutter's claims and insisted on viewing the land in and about Sacramento as public domain, subject to preemption. Van Buren suggested that the interest of justice would be served by quashing the charges with a nolle prosequi, and Broderick endorsed this proposal to drop the case.[17]

It was a unique situation in a number of respects. California, although functioning as a state, was not admitted to the Union until September 1850. In the interim, the validity of the decisions of its courts was seriously questioned. Military governors, who exercised authority until admission, declined to intervene in land title disputes, and it was not until 1851 that the federal government established a land commission to look into such matters. Still another four years passed before the commission ruled on Sutter's claim. It required almost a generation of lawyers and jurists to sort out the equities which arose from this situation. Violence was engendered by the lack of accepted legal machinery which could validate and adjudicate land claims. Where possession is nine tenths of the law and there is no established court system, men will determine property rights by a naked contest of will.[18]

[17] *Alta California,* Mar. 15, 20, and 22, 1851, contains detailed accounts of the debates sparked by Van Buren's motion.

[18] The contemporary newspapers detail the confused clash that resulted in the charges. See *Alta California,* Aug. 15, 1851. The San Francisco *Herald,* Aug. 14, 1850, pointed out, "So far as titles are concerned . . . much of the ownership of land here is the result of possession alone. . . ." Such a situation engendered violence. Paul Gates, "California's Agricultural College Lands," pp. 104 ff., succinctly describes the manner in which violence was spawned by the uncertainty of title and the absence of legal machinery to deal with land titles; his views are developed further in

James McClatchy, one of the settlers' association leaders, subsequently carved out an enduring place in California's world of journalism. Born in Belfast, Ireland, he mastered his trade in New York City, where he worked on the *Tribune* with Horace Greeley. Both men were sympathetic to the program of the National Reform Association, and McClatchy, who imbibed deeply of the liberal beliefs of Greeley, was committed to them the rest of his life. Arrested and imprisoned before the riot took place, he was nevertheless indicted for murder. His codefendant, Charles Robinson, who also played a major role in the settlers' movement, was a far cry from the usual type found in the prisoner's dock. Subsequently elected an assemblyman from Sacramento, which he viewed as a popular vindication, he left California in 1851. He was one of the prime movers of the Massachusetts Emigrant Aid Society, which mobilized antislavery forces for the contest for Kansas. He became that state's first Republican governor and was involved in the establishment of the University of Kansas, serving on its board of regents for many years. On this occasion, however, both Robinson and McClatchy were being accorded the treatment reserved to common felons.[19]

Broderick and Van Buren urged the passage of the resolution, "as if their own lives instead of the lives of Robinson and others depended on it." They denied that murder had been committed, for there had been no "premeditation or malice aforethought." Only a strained construction of the law would permit this prosecution, declared Broderick. He pointed out that a private purse of fifteen thousand dollars had been raised to secure conviction, and then in scathing language he denounced the judge who had permitted men to sit on the grand jury

---

"Adjudication of Spanish-Mexican Land Claims in California," *Huntington Library Quart.*, XXI (1958), 213–236; see also his essays, "California's Embattled Settlers," *Calif. Hist. Soc. Quart.*, XLI (1962), 99–130, and "Pre-Henry George Land Warfare in California," *Calif. Hist. Soc. Quart.*, XLVI (1967), 121–148. Josiah Royce, "The Squatter Riot of '50 in Sacramento," *Overland Monthly*, 2nd Ser., VI (1885), 225–246, is quite critical of the "squatters." A balanced treatment of the incident appears in Bancroft, *History of California*, VI, 328 ff. W. W. Robinson, *Land in California* (Berkeley, 1948), pp. 114–116, is a recent but limited account of the Sacramento incident.

[19] A different version and interpretation of the riot and its causes appeared in a biography of one of the principal figures among the settlers, Charles Robinson; see Frank W. Blackman, *The Life of Charles Robinson, the First State Governor of Kansas* (Topeka, 1902), pp. 43–47; a biographical sketch of Robinson appears in the *Dictionary of American Biography*. James McClatchy, pioneer figure in the world of journalism in California, had a long and interesting career, which is described in a biographical sketch in the Sacramento *Bee*, Oct. 26, 1883.

although they had freely expressed their opinions as to the guilt of the accused. As debate continued it became heated. The first day ended with Broderick and Van Buren apparently defeated and subdued, but on the following day they returned to the fight. Van Buren warned that the prosecution and the failure of the legislature to intervene would lead to the formation of a settlers' political party. Broderick conceded that the proceedings were legal, but he vehemently declared that they were not just. He ended on a grim note—an ominous warning that he would organize a force of five thousand men to free the defendants if the legislature did not act. His colleagues listened in amazement and disbelief at this advocate of rebellion.[20]

The opposition countered the logic and vehemence of Van Buren and Broderick with arguments that stressed the separation-of-powers principle. The courts, not the legislature, should handle these matters. Such reasoning did not prevent the passage of the resolution; however, when it reached the governor, he vetoed it. The matter did not end with Governor McDougal's veto, for eventually the Sacramento court utilized the nolle prosequi which Broderick and Van Buren advocated to dispose of the case. Robinson soon afterward took his place as an elected member of the Assembly from Sacramento—a measure of the prosettler influence in the county.[21]

In the course of this controversy Broderick became identified with the settlers. His stand was in accord with his Free Soil convictions: the public domain should be utilized to bring about the Jeffersonian ideal, not monopolized by speculators. Like McClatchy, he continued to support the program of the National Reform Association. It was an unequivocal commitment in 1850 when Broderick employed his voice, parliamentary procedure, and the threat of force to defend the settlers. Robinson, McClatchy, and their followers had good reason to be grateful.

There were other occasions for Broderick to display his readiness to face physical danger in behalf of his principles. Such an opportunity came in the spring of 1851 when a Committee of Vigilance seized authority in the city of San Francisco and set about cleaning the town of the "lawless and disorderly." One of the first incidents in this colorful page of the city's history involved the apprehension of a

[20] *Alta California,* Mar. 15, 20, and 22, 1851. See also *Senate Journal,* 2nd Sess., 1851, pp. 313–337.

[21] Davis, *Political Conventions,* p. 650.

burglar as he fled the scene of his crime. Given a summary trial and sentenced to death, the man's last moments were prolonged when he was provided with the services of a minister to ease his passage from this world to the next. Broderick meanwhile was working feverishly to counter the mob spirit. His efforts met with little success, for when the prisoner was brought to a public square for hanging, he had few allies in the turbulent crowd which assembled to witness the execution.[22]

As the prisoner was brought forth and the noose affixed, Broderick plunged bodily into the crowd, pleading with bystanders to help him prevent the lynching. Restraining hands impeded his progress and the prisoner was hoisted above the mob. In a few moments it was over, and the crowd dispersed. Some of its leaders adjourned to a nearby bar, where they discussed the exciting events of the evening and made plans for the future.

The inquest which followed featured reluctant witnesses who could not or would not furnish the coroner's jury with the names of the participants in the lynching. But when Broderick took the stand, he reeled off the names of the leaders of the mob and described in detail the roles that many of them had taken. Among those he named were some of the city's most prominent citizens. When Sam Brannan subsequently objected to the accusations, Broderick responded with a newspaper card which described in detail the role Brannan had played.[23]

The committee was not harmed by Broderick's disclosures; on the contrary, it grew in numbers, vigor, and prestige. To counter Broderick's testimony, the committee printed a full list of its members with the statement that all were equally responsible for what the committee had done. Broderick continued the battle in spite of the fact that a great part of the city's leaders either were on the committee or sympathetic to it. He organized meetings where he used the vehement language which was his hallmark to persuade others to take a stand. Resolutions were sometimes passed by these gatherings—resolutions which condemned the committee and demanded that "no man should hereafter be hung, whipped, or punished in any manner without due process of law." Broderick had limited impact, for few people attended such gatherings and fewer still were willing to take an open

[22] Gerritt W. Ryckman Statement, p. 2, MS in Bancroft Lib.

[23] *Alta California,* June 12, 1851, published the full text of Broderick's testimony; cf. Porter Garnett, ed. *Papers of the San Francisco Committee of Vigilance of 1851* (Berkeley, 1910), I, 285–353. Broderick's response to Brannan appeared in the *Alta California,* June 14, 1851.

stand. The city's officials meanwhile found a discreet silence their most appropriate response to the committee. Nevertheless, Broderick spoke out loudly, clearly, and repeatedly.[24]

When the committee organized a mass meeting to muster public support, Broderick attended—an uninvited and unwelcome participant. As Hiram Webb, the chairman, called the gathering to order, Broderick pushed his way through the crowd, mounted the speaker's platform, and in the face of a wave of hissing and booing demanded a chance to speak. Unable to make himself heard above the torrent of abuse, he tried to initiate a general dispersal by declaring the meeting adjourned and leaving with a group of supporters. A large part of the crowd remained, so Broderick returned and resumed his denunciation of the committee. The meeting was transformed into a disorganized mob of cheering, hissing, and booing spectators who watched a heated Webb and a determined Broderick battle for supremacy. Eventually Webb produced a set of resolutions, ignored Broderick, and read them at breakneck speed. When finished, he called for a vote of approval, declared them passed, and adjourned the meeting. The crowd thereupon disbanded. The Vigilance Committee objective of the gathering was not realized, for the resolutions provided and read by Webb were neither heard nor ratified.[25]

Having accomplished some of their objectives and finding that the "country had been purged of a goodly number of the worst people," the Vigilance Committee went on a stand-by basis. Since that time the drama of the committee has intrigued writers and historians. It has generally been viewed in a kindly and uncritical fashion. In most accounts the committee is described in laudatory terms, its membership pictured as brave and honorable men of property, its opponents described as lawless and violent men. The committee was a necessity, say some writers, which came into being when the criminal elements of the city became too powerful for the courts to handle. Such interpretations do violence to the reality which spawned the committee. There is in America a long and honored tradition of opposition to summary arrest and trial and private justice administered in a star chamber proceeding. There may have been criminals in the ranks of

[24] *Alta California,* July 11, 1851.

[25] *Alta California,* June 13, 1851; this account is unusually detailed. Cf. A. J. Moulder, "Broderick's Moral Courage: How Single-handed He Stayed a Revolution," *The Argonaut,* III (1878), No. 24, pp. 9–12.

the opposition to the committee; there undoubtedly were men of principle and integrity.[26]

Broderick's opposition to the committee was in accord with his deepest personal values: American freedoms and liberties were the inalienable rights of all individuals; no man should be subjected to trial and punishment by an *ad hoc* group, and every man, regardless of accusation, had the right to due process. In his opposition to the committee of 1851 Broderick once again demonstrated his willingness to assume risks in defense of principle. In this instance he not only risked his life but also endangered his political future when he plunged into the work of organizing the citizenry against the committee, for it was led by powerful and influential people whose antagonism was steeled by Broderick's opposition.

From time to time the enemies whom Broderick acquired in his battle with the Vigilance Committee joined hands with opponents from the ranks of the Chivalry. One such occasion was the 1851 state convention of the Democratic party, which the Chivalry dominated. Despite Broderick's objections the Chivalry elected a former governor of Virginia, William Smith, as chairman. Broderick clashed with the Chivalry again when he questioned the propriety of an appointed delegate representing a county which had not sent a delegation to the convention. He was overruled.[27]

Broderick was more successful in getting the delegates to adopt a proposal that representation in future conventions be based upon one delegate for each two thousand county residents. One consequence was an enhancement of the role which the San Francisco delegation would play in future meetings. Unsuccessful in obtaining a congressional nomination for his Free Soil associate Thomas B. Van Buren, he won other victories. Not only did he succeed in the matter of representation, but he also got the convention to adopt a party structure to function between conventions. The most important phase of

[26] William T. Coleman Statement, pp. 24–28, MS in Bancroft Lib. Almost all treatments of the vigilantes of 1851 and 1856 put them in the best possible light. See H. H. Bancroft, *Popular Tribunals,* 2 vols. (San Francisco, 1887); its dedication to "William T. Coleman, Chief of the Greatest Tribunal the World Has Ever Witnessed . . ." indicates a lack of objectivity which is demonstrated repeatedly in the two volumes. James O'Meara, *The Vigilance Committee of 1856* (San Francisco, 1887), is a critical account. George R. Stewart, *Committee of Vigilance: Revolution in San Francisco, 1851* (Boston, 1964), is the most recent account. William Henry Ellison, *A Self-governing Dominion: California, 1849–1860* (Berkeley, 1950), pp. 192–231, is objective and critical.

[27] *Alta California,* May 20 and 21, 1851.

this plan was the establishment of a state committee of eleven members: four from San Francisco, three from Sacramento, two from Stockton, one from Marysville, and one from Benicia. Broderick was elected by the San Francisco delegation to this committee, which drew seven of its eleven members from the two major centers of population, Sacramento and San Francisco, where his influence was strong. Within a short time the state committee elected him chairman.[28]

The 1851 convention was a time of momentary frustration for Broderick, but when it was over he had good reason to look upon it in satisfaction. The Democratic party had taken a number of steps—some of which were to have a lasting influence. Broderick was partially responsible. Once again he demonstrated the manner in which he could weigh and balance immediate and long-range objectives. His vision undistracted by the baubles of minor nominations, he picked the route that led to great political power. Chairmanship of the state committee, the locus of power in the party between conventions, was an early way station along the road.

The election of 1851 was the first in California which pitted the great parties in a head-to-head contest. John Bigler and William Waldo headed the Democratic and Whig tickets respectively. Bigler was a former Pennsylvanian who had come to California early in the gold-rush years. Although he failed to find a bonanza in the foothills of the Sierras, he became an important political figure in his adopted state. His opponent, William Waldo, was born and raised in Missouri. A man of substance and property who still owned slaves in Missouri, he found considerable acceptance among the Chivalry. Both parties campaigned in lackluster fashion. Some observers expressed dissatisfaction with the campaign, complaining that the issues and rhetoric of yesteryear dominated the stump speeches of Whigs and Democrats. Both parties avoided the question of the status of slavery in the West and its related issue of the uses of the power of the federal government in western development.[29]

Broderick's participation was limited. He made few public appearances and seemed to be generally apathetic. When the totals came in, indicating a Democratic victory, the Whigs cried, "Fraud." They charged that they had been "counted out" after the polls had closed;

[28] *Alta California,* May 22, 1851; *Daily Evening Bulletin,* Jan. 4, 1878.
[29] Davis, *Political Conventions,* p. 13; *Alta California,* July 18 and Sept. 18, 1851.

no evidence was brought forth to sustain these allegations. When it appeared that the Democrats had a majority even after the disputed returns were thrown out, Whigs accepted the result, which put John Bigler in the governor's office.[30]

Shortly after the 1851 election, politicos turned to the approaching senatorial election. John C. Frémont's seat would be filled by a newcomer, declared most analysts, for the West's "greatest pathfinder" could muster little support in the legislature. John B. Weller and Solomon Heydenfeldt were the most prominent candidates for the seat. Broderick was not mentioned as a serious contender.[31]

Overlooking Broderick was a serious error, as his enemies soon discovered. His bitter opposition to the nativist miner's bill and Whig proposals to lease the mineral lands of California rallied considerable support to him among miners and the foreign-born. Championing the homestead bill and the cause of McClatchy, Robinson, and the settlers mustered support in the inland valleys. Opposition to the Vigilance Committee alienated some men of affairs in San Francisco but earned him the support of those who opposed vigilante justice. Championing Free Soil and antislavery sentiments alienated the Chivalry but brought to his side those who shared his antipathy to slavery. It might be difficult to transform this popular support into legislative support, but the situation looked promising.

Democratic strength in the legislature guaranteed the election of a Democrat, although Heydenfeldt, of southern antecedents and Whiggish background, was a serious contender. Sensing defeat, Heydenfeldt withdrew from the race. His withdrawal brought unity to the Chivalry, which had been torn by affection for this transplanted Georgian and fondness for John B. Weller, sometime resident of Ohio who was to make a mark as a distinguished "doughface." The Chivalry of both parties united behind Weller. To the surprise of some observers,

[30] The official election results are entered in a MS ledger in the Archives of the Secretary of State of California at Sacramento, Vol. 1759, labeled "Election Returns." Each set of election results is listed under the appropriate year and tabulated by counties. Davis, *Political Conventions*, p. 15, gives the statewide results. Whig charges of fraud are given some credence by the unusual nature of some of the county returns, but they failed to contest on the basis that disallowance of the disputed returns would make no difference. See *Alta California*, Jan. 9 and 10, 1852.

[31] Frémont withdrew, probably realizing he had little chance to be reelected; see New York *Times*, Oct. 6, 1851; Frémont to Pablo de la Guerra, Aug. 16, 1851, De la Guerra Collection, Santa Barbara Mission Archives.

Broderick, the chief representative of the Free Soil wing of the party, was his major opponent.[32]

Before the actual balloting began in the legislature, a pro-Broderick newspaper sent each candidate a questionnaire designed to elicit his views on important public questions. Weller's responses were almost laconic, but Broderick spelled out his opinions on the Compromise of 1850, public land policy, and Indian affairs. From their replies one could learn a great deal about the views of the two men. Broderick's Free Soil convictions were clearly expressed.[33]

The process of selection began with a caucus where Democratic legislators met to select a candidate. Several ballots ended in failure before the first meeting adjourned. A similar outcome resulted when the two branches of the legislature met and balloted. Stalemate sparked rumors that the election would be left to the following legislature. Broderick trailed Weller in these early ballots by a handful of votes, but "his friends clung to him with a tenacity that was amazing." Among his staunchest supporters were representatives of the Californios—the De la Guerra, Covarrubias, Pacheco, and Pico clans, who stayed with him to the end despite such criticism as "Your friends are utterly astonished to see Covarrubias and your brother voting for Broderick. He is the squatters' candidate." [34]

Eventually the stalemate was ended when a majority of the Democratic caucus voted for Weller. Victory came on the fifth ballot, with Broderick still mustering a total of nineteen votes—including all of the Californios. Broderick accepted the inevitable and the next day withdrew in the convention. Weller was chosen to fill the seat vacated by Frémont for a term ending in 1857.[35]

[32] Henry W. Halleck to Pablo de la Guerra, Sept. 10, 1851, De la Guerra Coll., discusses the composition of the legislature and its implications for the senatorial election; Heydenfeldt was eliminated as a senatorial candidate as a result of his election to the supreme court in the September 1851 election; see Davis, *Political Conventions,* p. 15.

[33] Sacramento *Times and Transcript,* Jan. 27, 1852, contains the questionnaire and responses of Broderick and Weller. The *Alta California,* Feb. 3, 1852, criticized the *Times and Transcript* as the organ of the "Squatter Democracy" for endorsing Broderick.

[34] *Alta California,* Jan. 30, 1852, reports the voting in caucus; *Senate Journal,* 3rd Sess., 1852, pp. 62–66, reports the convention proceedings through the first five ballots. Henry W. Halleck to Pablo de la Guerra, Jan. 29, 1852, De la Guerra Coll., reveals the enduring support of the Californios and the astonishment of the friends of Covarrubias and Antonio María de la Guerra at their support of Broderick, the "squatters' candidate"; cf. *Senate Journal,* 3rd Sess., 1852, pp. 67–70.

[35] *Alta California,* Jan. 31, 1852; *Senate Journal,* 3rd Sess., 1852, pp. 81–82.

However much Broderick might console himself with the thought that he had reached for a major prize before his time, the fact that he had come so close to victory must have made the defeat galling. As difficult to accept as the defeat itself were the tactics of his enemies. In his bitter words, "it would take a ream of paper to contain the account of the prohibited treachery that was used against me during the canvass." He left the details of "prohibited treachery" to another occasion, but that character assassination was used by his enemies was noted by one of San Francisco's leading journals.[36]

Broderick suffered a major setback in the senatorial election of 1852, but he remained a major factor in California politics, as his enemies shortly discovered. Soon the Chivalry was rallying its forces again in an attempt to curb the growing influence of the principal spokesman of the Free Soil Democracy.

[36] Broderick to George Wilkes, Apr. 18, 1852, in *People* v. *McGlynn,* pp. 303–304; San Francisco *Daily Evening Picayune,* Jan. 26, 1852.

☆☆☆☆☆☆☆☆☆☆☆☆☆☆

CHAPTER FIVE

Senatorial Aspirations

The contest between the Free Soil and Chivalry factions continued beyond the 1852 senatorial election. The Chivalry triumphed again when they admitted a "rump" delegation in place of Broderick's contingent at a state gathering to select delegates to the national Democratic convention. Prolonged debate preceded the decision, but the Chivalry won. Its domination of the gathering was graphically demonstrated when a prospective delegate to the national meeting, queried whether he intended to return, declared that he didn't expect to bring his family here "until we made a nigger state of California." His audience reacted with mirth and applause.[1]

The antagonism of the Chivalry displayed itself repeatedly. A few days after the convention, Broderick was involved in a brawl with James L. Freaner, pro-Chivalry wagon-road promoter who made a number of disparaging remarks about Broderick's friend Van Buren. Broderick retorted in kind, one word led to another, and soon they were exchanging blows. Freaner struck Broderick with an inkstand, inflicting a facial wound. Bystanders intervened before any more serious harm was done. Broderick carried the scar and the memory for the rest of his life.[2]

Less than a month later, Broderick was involved in a much more

[1] *Proceedings of the Democratic State Convention Held in Sacramento City the 23 of February, 1852* (Sacramento, 1852), p. 7, declares the vote to reject the Broderick-led delegation was 191 to 65, but the *Alta California,* Feb. 23, 1852, asserts the vote was 100 to 64. The convention's response to the delegate's remarks is described in the *Alta California,* Feb. 27, 1852.

[2] Antonio María de la Guerra to Pablo de la Guerra, Feb. 24, 1852, De la Guerra Coll., Santa Barbara Mission Archives; *Alta California,* Feb. 25, 1852; James O'Meara, *Broderick and Gwin* (San Francisco, 1881), p. 31.

serious form of personal combat. Once again his opponent was a member of the Chivalry. Caleb C. Smith, the son of a former governor of Virginia, took offense at a comment Broderick made about his father. The two men exchanged insults in the press before Smith challenged Broderick to a duel. To the surprise of a number of people, Broderick agreed to meet the militant son of the South on the field of honor. The weapons were revolvers. When the word was given, each man was to fire and continue firing, walking toward his opponent, until his weapon was empty. It was a fearsome business. Broderick's gun jammed, and as he huddled over it desperately trying to free it, Smith's bullets whistled about him. A slug struck Broderick's pocket watch, shattering it and inflicting minor flesh wounds. Broderick eventually freed his weapon and completed his firing. His marksmanship was evidently as poor as Smith's. When the firing stopped, the seconds stepped forward and following a consultation with Smith and Broderick, it was announced that Smith was "satisfied." [3]

The crowd which witnessed the duel was pleased with the drama and spectacle. A newspaper reported that it was conducted "with the strictest decorum." Broderick regarded it as evidence of the hostility of his enemies. "I have been hunted by the Chivalry," were his defiant words, "but I have taught them on all occasions that I was not to be trifled with." The bold sentence revealed a characteristic which was at once a strength and a weakness. His truculence made opponents wary of a personal challenge, but it also provided them with the foreknowledge of the sort of heated response that might be elicited from the senator. A calculating enemy might find a way to provoke him into conflict on the challenger's ground and with the challenger's weapons.[4]

Before the scars of the encounter had been completely healed, Broderick welcomed to San Francisco his friend and mentor from New York, George Wilkes. Wilkes came in response to repeated invitations. He left a promising career in publishing, a sacrifice which was offset by the warmth of Broderick's welcome. The two men became again the team which had given Broderick intellectual polish and launched him on a political career. Wilkes brought a great deal to

[3] San Francisco *Daily Evening Picayune,* Mar. 18, 1852; New York *Times,* Apr. 17, 1852.

[4] Ben C. Truman, *The Field of Honor* (New York, 1884), pp. 486–489, describes the duel in detail. Broderick subsequently "withdrew" remarks reflecting on Smith on the basis of a similar retraction by him. See *Alta California,* Apr. 17, 1852; Broderick to George Wilkes, Apr. 18, 1852, in *People* v. *McGlynn,* p. 305.

the new firm, for he was experienced in urban politics; the shift to San Francisco entailed little more than a change in scene and cast, for the political settings of the two cities were quite similar. Broderick predicted that there was no object beyond their reach; now they were to test that judgment.The two men set off on a journey to the political heights, determined to make Broderick's vision of a seat in the United States Senate a reality.[5]

A number of problems demanded immediate attention. The Chivalry had made serious inroads in what had once been Broderick's San Francisco bastion. The admission of "rump" delegates to the state convention in the place of the legitimate delegation had brought about a state of near civil war in the Democracy. A compromise between the factions had been worked out under which a new election in the city was to be held to determine who should represent the city's Democrats. It was held in the spring of 1852. Broderick's faction won, but by a small margin. That election of reconciliation and the following contest were marked with considerable violence. Democratic head met Democratic knuckle, but Broderick's group carried the day. Unity of a sort had been realized.[6]

The result was more an armistice than a peace. "The old feud between the Broderick and anti-Broderick sections in this city bids fair to be renewed under very favorable auspices," commented an observer. So long as the Chivalry controlled the state organization of the party and the Free Soil faction controlled the city of San Francisco, there would be conflict. The major factions of the party were divided

[5] *Affidavit of George Wilkes* (n.p., n.d.), p. 1, in Bancroft Lib.; the date of Wilkes's arrival in California is not known, although it is recorded that he was in Panama en route to San Francisco about May 6, 1852 (Affidavit of John A. McGlynn, in *People* v. *McGlynn,* p. 303). Broderick and Wilkes worked as a team until the spring of 1854, when they had a serious disagreement over a legislative bill. They continued to collaborate in political matters until Wilkes left for New York in 1855 to resume his career in journalism. See San Francisco *Daily Town Talk,* Mar. 17, 1855. For additional detail on the political partnership of Wilkes and Broderick, see Affidavit of Charles Gallagher and James W. Coffroth, in *People* v. *McGlynn,* and the statement of Emma Theresa Maguire in *Testimony Proving the Will of David C. Broderick* (San Francisco, 1860), pp. 78–79. O'Meara, *Broderick and Gwin,* pp. 120–122, declares the difficulty between the two men arose out of a quarrel over a state supreme court position which Wilkes allegedly coveted. He is evidently incorrect, for the vacancy in question did not occur until the fall of 1854, whereas the rift between them occurred in the spring of the year; the vacancy was created by the death of Justice Alexander Wells, announced in Sacramento *Union,* Nov. 1, 1854.

[6] *Daily Evening Picayune,* Mar. 19, 1852; San Francisco *Herald,* June 29, 1852.

on matters of philosophy and program: so long as they were part of the same party there would be conflict.[7]

The two factions came face to face in the Benicia state convention in mid-July. The stakes involved control of the party's staff organization and a slate of nominees for the upcoming state election. On the opening day Broderick asked how five gentlemen, residents of San Francisco, had become the certified delegates of a number of southern counties—San Diego, Los Angeles, Santa Barbara, and San Luis Obispo. Somewhat lamely it was explained that William Smith, former governor of the Old Dominion, and Jack Hays, former Texas Ranger and onetime sheriff of San Francisco, held proxies for these counties. The discussion waxed warm, but eventually Broderick's objections were overruled.[8]

Milton S. Latham won a congressional nomination in spite of the opposition of two thirds of the delegates from San Francisco, who looked upon him as an incipient doughface. Once again Broderick sought a congressional nomination for his colleague and staunch ally in the state Senate, Thomas B. Van Buren, but the latter withdrew after a bleak appraisal of his chances. In his withdrawal speech, Van Buren candidly admitted that he had voted the Free Soil ticket in 1848. The admission came as no surprise to those who knew him well or those who had watched the battle he and Broderick had waged against the Fugitive Slave law in the legislature. It was a shock to the Chivalry, however, to find a Free Soiler flaunting his heresy in a convention of the Democracy. It was to be a long time before they forgot this incident, and they never forgot the man who sought one of the party's highest honors for a self-confessed Free Soiler.[9]

A congressional nomination was pressed on James A. McDougall, who bested Richard P. Hammond, a representative of the Chivalry. His victory and the platform indicated a rising tide of Free Soil sentiment in the party. The resolutions which made up the platform displayed this influence clearly in one formulation which pledged the

[7] *Alta California,* July 12, 1852.

[8] San Francisco *Herald,* July 21, 1852; *Proceedings of the Democratic State Convention, Benicia, July 20, 1852* (n.p., n.d.), Benjamin Hayes Scrapbooks, Vol. XVIII, Bancroft Lib.

[9] *Alta California,* July 22, 1852; Winfield J. Davis, *History of Political Conventions in California, 1849–1892* (Sacramento, 1893), p. 23.

Democratic party "to the donation of the public lands to American citizens, whether native or naturalized, who become actual settlers, in quantities not exceeding one hundred and sixty acres to each settler." Unhappy with the phrase that limited such governmental largess to citizens, Broderick moved to strike that restriction. The proposal sparked a prolonged debate in which nativist language was freely used. It came to an end when Broderick's motion to strike was laid on the table and a substitute adopted: "That all public lands of California ought to be reserved by the government from sale, and granted to citizens and actual settlers." [10]

An echo of the bitter legislative debate on the Coolie Bill was heard when John Conness introduced a resolution opposing the scheme. After some discussion, it was laid on the table. A compromise was adopted which declared, "We do not approve of the bill . . . in the legislature, providing for the introduction of serfs or coolies into California to compete with white laborers, who at the same time constitute the democracy and aristocracy of this state." Broderick was obviously reluctant to participate in this debate of "nativist" overtones. A short time before, he had castigated a delegate for his antiforeigner ideas and denounced nativism as the doctrine of the Native American party, which would mean the "death knell of the Democratic Party if adopted." [11]

As a whole, the resolutions were in accord with Broderick's political sentiments. As the convention disbanded and candidates prepared for the upcoming campaign, he had good reason to look back upon the meeting with satisfaction. In the spring of the year, the Chivalry had blocked his participation by seating the "rump" delegation from San Francisco. In the interim, between the gatherings of the party, he had met the enemy in the San Francisco primary elections and vanquished them. This time his delegation had been admitted, and his influence had shaped the deliberations of the convention. The platform and a number of the candidates were acceptable to him. When the county delegations met to select representatives to the state committee, Broderick's influence was to be seen in the selection of four pro-Broderick figures out of the five-man San Francisco contingent.

[10] *Alta California,* July 22, 1852; Davis, *Political Conventions,* p. 23; San Francisco *Herald,* July 23, 1852.

[11] *Alta California,* July 23, 1852; Davis, *Political Conventions,* p. 24; San Francisco *Herald,* July 23, 1852.

Everything considered, he was in a much stronger position when this state convention disbanded.[12]

In the campaign of 1852, Broderick worked behind the scenes. He made no public speeches in behalf of the party and did not attend the county Democratic convention held in San Francisco in October, although his friends and allies were out in force. He did not participate openly in the Free Soil convention that was staged in the same month; apparently he was still committed to the propagation of Free Soil ideas, through the Democratic party. His reluctance to identify himself with the Free Soil party reflected political realism, for it polled a sparse handful of votes.[13]

The elections were conducted in a remarkably quiet and orderly fashion and brought forth a number of appropriate comments from newspaper observers. The expected Democratic majorities in the city and county of San Francisco were accompanied by statewide victories. The margin was a small but respectable five thousand out of a total vote of seventy-five thousand. Democratic politicos rejoiced, their joy heightened by the national victory won by Franklin Pierce.[14]

Among the more significant changes in the California situation which accompanied the national Democratic victory was a change in the perspective of a number of the more important Democratic politicians on the Pacific Coast. The advent of a new national administration meant a general replacement of federal officials in California, as Whig incumbents were turned out for office-hungry Democrats. As soon as the news was known, the competition for the subordinate prizes of office and place in the new administration began. Governor Bigler, pressed by friends to look toward reelection, preferred a diplomatic appointment to the vicissitudes of another campaign. His attention focused on a minister's post in Chile, and his brother's aid was solicited. When the rumor reached the West Coast that Senator William Gwin was in line for a Cabinet appointment, Bigler's ambitious plans took more concrete shape. The governor urged his brother to push the appointment of Gwin, "the man on the Pacific Coast the people desire to see in the Cabinet as Secretary of Interior." In the event Gwin were successful, Governor Bigler informed the eastern

[12] The platform appears in Davis, *Political Conventions,* pp. 23–24; cf. *Alta California,* July 23, 1852.

[13] *Alta California,* Oct. 14, 15, 19, and 24, 1852; Election Returns, 1852, Vol. 1759, Archives of the Secretary of State, Sacramento.

[14] *Alta California,* Nov. 3, 7, and 8, 1852.

wing of the family, he would arrange his own appointment as Gwin's successor in the Senate until an election was held and "then leave for Chile." [15]

William M. Gwin was born in Tennessee, the son of a close friend of Andrew Jackson. Trained in medicine and law, he turned to politics, where his ties with Old Hickory were put to good use. He had held several major appointments, but it was not until he arrived in California that his political career began to bloom. A member of the constitutional convention who impressed the gathering, he was subsequently elected senator by the legislature of 1850. From that time on, he was a major figure in the California Democracy, a leader of the Chivalry faction who had allies and friends in both parties and on all levels of government. He was also an enduring enemy of Broderick.[16]

Broderick, aware of the possibility that Gwin might be elevated to the Cabinet, also made plans. If Gwin were to leave the Senate, Broderick intended to replace him. Wilkes was put to work canvassing the legislature and lining up prospective supporters. Preliminary findings were encouraging; but before either Bigler or Broderick could do much more than plan, it was disclosed that Pierce's Cabinet would not include Dr. Gwin. The joint disappointment of Gwin, Bigler, and Broderick was a unique feature of this decade of California's political history, for it was one of the few times when the aspirations of Broderick and Gwin coincided and worked for mutual advantage.[17]

The scramble for patronage did not include Broderick, for he had few friends at court. His enemies were well represented, however, and they profited considerably. Richard P. Hammond obtained the most powerful post—collector of customs in San Francisco—and the most significant; lesser offices were conferred on other Chivalry representatives. The Chivalry was strengthened immeasurably by garnering the

[15] John Bigler to William Bigler, Dec. 3 and 8, 1852, Bigler Coll., Pennsylvania Hist. Soc. William Bigler and his brother John were prominent Democratic politicians during the decade of the 1850's. William was a major figure in the Democracy of Pennsylvania, a close friend of James Buchanan, and, like his brother, governor of a major state (Pennsylvania). For an evaluation of them as politicians, see F. F. Low, "Political Notes," p. 25, MS in Bancroft Lib.

[16] Lately Thomas is working on a biography of William M. Gwin. Until it appears, the researcher will have to use such standard references as O'Meara, *Broderick and Gwin*, pp. 32–35, and Hubert H. Bancroft, *History of California*, Vol. VI (San Francisco, 1888), Ch. xxiii.

[17] Archibald C. Peachy to J. L. Folsom, Jan. 31 and Feb. 24, 1853, Leidesdorff Coll., Huntington Lib. Wilkes's efforts are described in *Affidavit of George Wilkes*, p. 2, Bancroft Lib.

bulk of federal patronage appointments in California; scattered throughout the state, they represented a political legion of great potential. Gwin was principally responsible for the manner in which federal patronage was distributed in California; his influence had been exerted during the Whig administration and persisted through the Pierce administration.[18]

However, while the monopoly of federal patronage tended to strengthen the Chivalry, it also had an unforeseen result. The spoils were not going to the victors but to a part of the victors. The disappointment of those who did not share soon turned to disaffection. Disaffection turned middle-of-the-road Democrats away from the Chivalry, and soon Broderick's wing of the party was strengthened by such recruits. Bigler complained bitterly of the manner in which the largess of the party was distributed: "the office holders for this state were nearly all taken from the *South* but few men from the *North* received favors." A new political milieu was in the making in California.[19]

The new alignments of this political matrix were to be seen in a meeting held on New Year's Day, 1853. Broderick, Joseph C. Palmer, and Antonio María de la Guerra met for graceful dining and friendly political consultation. Among other matters discussed was their choice of a candidate for a vacancy on the bench of the district court in Santa Barbara. Broderick was selected to make the final decision known to Governor Bigler. The participants, the discussion, and the decision illuminated the changing realities of the political scene. The Broderick-Bigler alliance was in the forge. Soon it would

[18] Bancroft, *History of California,* VI, 673–674, describes the distribution of patronage in California during the Pierce administration; William H. Richardson was appointed U.S. marshal—"with the exception of that of Collector at San Francisco . . . the most responsible office in the state." See William Gwin to Franklin Pierce, California Appointment Papers, Record Group 56, National Archives; O'Meara, *Broderick and Gwin,* p. 33. Gwin's role in patronage matters is seen in his letter to Millard Fillmore, Jan. 31, 1853, California Appointment Papers, Record Group 56, National Archives. His influence persisted into the Pierce administration; see Gwin to Franklin Pierce, Mar. 18, 1853, California Appointment Papers, Record Group 56, National Archives, which indicates that Samuel W. Inge, the preferred candidate of Gwin, is to be appointed in spite of numerous letters on behalf of other candidates. In another instance, an unsuccessful candidate had the backing of such powerful figures as John A. Dix and Montgomery Flagg but lacked the support of Gwin. See the letter of Dix and Flagg to Franklin Pierce, Mar. 14, 1853, California Appointment Papers, Record Group 56, National Archives. The significance of patronage is described in Etta Olive Powell, "Southern Influences in California Politics before 1864" (unpubl. M.A. thesis, Univ. of Calif., 1929), pp. 74–75.

[19] John Bigler to William Bigler, Apr. 14, Mar. 31, 1854, Bigler Coll.

be a firm accord of aspirations that would carry each of them along the road to power.[20]

The emphasis on a local judicial appointment reflected Broderick's interest in state, county, and city affairs and appointments. The Chivalry's monopoly of federal patronage barred him from that area but inadvertently pushed him into a field of much promise. Before long the ranks of state appointees were liberally laced with associates of Broderick and Bigler; the organization of the Chivalry, made up of federal appointees, had its counterpart in an organization of Bigler-Broderick partisans which reached into all parts of the state.[21]

Other benefits of the Broderick-Bigler alliance soon appeared. Broderick was elected chairman of the state committee of the party by a combination of Bigler and Broderick votes. When the committee met to plan the state convention, it decided that representation in the forthcoming convention would be on the basis of one delegate for each two hundred Democratic ballots cast in the preceding general election. San Francisco County, by this formula, was to have the largest delegation.[22]

The convention which met in Benicia sixty days later was called to order by Broderick. Its work was cut out for it, for the Whigs were still strong, while the California Democracy, in spite of a string of victories, was divided. A strong slate was essential if the Democratic party was to maintain its position. Governor Bigler was interested in a second term, and Broderick's wing of the party pushed his nomination vigorously. Richard Roman, onetime Texan, was the preferred candidate of the Chivalry. The chief difference between the two men was their stand on the land question—"the squatter question," as it was usually labeled by the diverse groups which championed the rights of landowners and claimants who derived their rights from Mexican and Spanish grantees. Bigler tended to identify himself with the rights of the settlers and the Free Soil position. Roman preferred a noncommittal stance. His reluctance to take a stand made him more acceptable to

[20] Antonio María de la Guerra to Pablo de la Guerra, Jan. 1, 1853, De la Guerra Coll.

[21] Governor's Appointments, 1850–1940, Drawer 1, Calif. State Archives, Sacramento, contains papers relating to the appointment of William M. Lent, R. N. Snowden, Charles H. Bryan, Edward McGowan, Moses E. Flannagan, and others drawn from the Broderick-Bigler wing of the party to fill such positions as commissioner of pilots, state prison inspector, judge of the supreme court, etc.

[22] San Francisco *Placer Times and Transcript,* Apr. 21, 1853; San Francisco *Evening Journal,* Apr. 21, 1853.

the more conservative elements of the political community, but it earned him little support among the ever increasing number of settlers in the state. Spokesmen for the latter observed: "Combinations are now at work among us to compromise the position of the party on the land question. They will not ask us to nominate an avowed enemy of the settlers but will be satisfied with some uncommitted person they think they can mould." The "uncommitted person" was Richard Roman.[23]

Broderick proved to be a towering obstacle to the nomination of Roman. Consequently, the balloting resulted in a resounding victory for Bigler: the bulk of his support came from the two urban centers, San Francisco and Sacramento, and a number of mining counties—El Dorado, Placer, and Tuolumne. The remainder of the ticket also showed the hand and influence of Broderick. Samuel Purdy, like Bigler an incumbent and ally of Broderick, was nominated for a second term as lieutenant-governor. Alexander Wells, former member of the Tammany Society and associate of Broderick from the tenth ward of New York City, was nominated for justice of the supreme court. The ticket, the organization of the convention, and the platform all showed the hand of the onetime stonemason of Washington Square.[24]

The platform was especially revealing of Broderick's values. Instead of the usual gathering of platitudes, it consisted of eight resolutions which clearly expressed the basic program of the Democratic party as it was visualized by Free Soil Democrats. The first statement declared that the party put the interests of the settler first, stood foursquare for policies whereby the public lands would be distributed in "limited quantities to actual settlers," and opposed policies that tended toward the creation of a landed monopoly. A second statement on land policy declared that "the surest and most speedy method of developing the resources of the state, promoting industry, and elevating society, is to encourage . . . ownership and cultivation of the soil in limited quantities by actual settlers." Taken together, the statements on the disposition of public land clearly indicated the strength of Free Soil sentiment in the party.[25]

[23] Davis, *Political Conventions,* p. 24; *Placer Times and Transcript,* June 20, 1853.

[24] Theodore Hittell, *History of California* (San Francisco, 1898), IV, 134; San Francisco *Evening Bulletin,* Jan. 4, 1878; Powell, "Southern Influences," p. 83.

[25] *Placer Times and Transcript,* June 21, 22, and 23, 1853; Davis, *Political Conventions,* pp. 24–25.

The resolutions on labor and monopoly that appeared might well have been written by George Evans, of the National Reform Association. Locofocos would have been delighted with a formulation which denounced laws that degraded labor and laws of special privilege that allowed "the irresponsible contraction of debts or a monopoly of privileges." "The democratic party," continued the platform, "cherishes as among the best features in the constitution of this state, those which protect the laborer from degradation and oppression." This was the rhetoric of the Locofocos of Jacksonian Democracy, painful and offensive alike to the Chivalry and conservative Democrats.[26]

It was only a matter of weeks before Broderick and his followers began to realize that their triumph and their domination of the convention had driven the Chivalry into open hostility. The disaffection soon became defection, as the magnitude of the victory of Broderick became apparent. A little more than a year had passed since they had excluded him from the state convention; now he presided over the party in triumph. The platform was a restatement of his political program; the staff organization of the party was dominated by Democrats of his persuasion; and even the candidates were his preferences. The resentment of the Chivalry smoldered for a time and then burst into a blaze of revolt.[27]

Victory was threatened by the defection of a sizable number of Democrats, for Governor Bigler had won by a razor-thin margin in 1851. Since then he had been the principal target of the opposition, which overlooked no opportunity to proclaim his instability and incompetence. If Whigs, independents, and disaffected Democrats were to unite, Bigler and Broderick might go down to defeat. The stakes were considerably more than the state offices, for a United States Senate seat was to be filled in the upcoming session of the legislature.

[26] Davis, *Political Conventions,* pp. 24–25. Broderick's dominance of the convention is graphically demonstrated by the manner in which the gathering dealt with the proposal to rewrite the state constitution, a project which was strongly pushed by proslavery interests; see above, Ch. iii. The proslavery interest in the proposal is manifested in a number of places; see David S. Terry to Cornelia Runnels, June 29, 1852, Terry Coll., Huntington Lib.; Antonio María de la Guerra to Pablo de la Guerra, Feb. 4, 1852, and Henry W. Halleck to Pablo de la Guerra, Apr. 23, 1853, De la Guerra Coll.; *Alta California,* Feb. 29, 1853; Bancroft, *History of California,* VI, 668–669; *Senate Journal,* 4th Sess., 1853, p. 633.

[27] Broderick's triumph is reflected in the membership of the state committee which was selected. Although it included Richard P. Hammond, collector of the port of San Francisco and a representative of the Chivalry, he was outnumbered, for the balance of the committee included many representatives of the Broderick-Bigler faction like Moses E. Flannagan, John Middleton, et al. See Davis, *Political Conventions,* p. 26.

As one observer saw the situation, "If Bigler is reelected, I think Broderick's chances for the Senatorship will be the best. The contest will be between Broderick and Gwin." [28]

The Chivalry of the Democratic party were in a most difficult position, for if they repudiated the choices of the convention, they would hazard the fate of other "bolters"—future exclusion from the party. Torn by indecision, most of the Chivalry eventually decided against defection and open allegiance to the Whigs. Instead they decided to sit out the election and allow their nominal compatriots to go down to defeat. "The U.S. Federal Officers are doing *Nothing* at all in this campaign," reported one observer to a friend of Chivalry affiliation. A leading newspaper commented on the same topic, "In looking around among the prominent bolters from the Democratic party . . . the fact obtrudes prominently upon us that they are of that class known as 'Southern Chivalry' men." The night before the election, a Democratic speaker pointed out to his fellow Democrats that the defectors "were all from the first families of Virginia." [29]

Not all men of Chivalric inclination were satisfied with this passive course. Solomon Heydenfeldt, longtime opponent of Broderick and sometime resident of Georgia, put aside the judicial robes of a justice of the supreme court to campaign actively for the Whigs. He joined a brigade of proslavery political figures who campaigned for the Whig ticket, which included seven southerners in a slate of nine. But while the Democrats were losing longtime members of the party to the opposition and making new enemies, they were also finding new support. When one of the more influential German language newspapers of San Francisco, the *Staats-Zeitung,* endorsed the candidacy of William Waldo for governor, Herman Wohler, a refugee of the German revolution of 1848 and an intimate friend of Broderick, promptly organized a German Democratic Association to back the Democratic ticket.[30]

The election results came as a painful disappointment to the Whigs, whose hopes for victory centered on the gubernatorial race. The

[28] Archibald C. Peachy to J. L. Folsom, Aug. 14, 1853, Leidesdorff Coll., Huntington Lib.

[29] James W. Wilson to James W. Mandeville, Aug. 21, 1853, Mandeville Coll., Huntington Lib.; *Placer Times and Transcript,* Aug. 26, Sept. 6, 1853; *Alta California,* Sept. 6, 1853.

[30] *Placer Times and Transcript,* Aug. 26, Sept. 3, 1853. Powell, "Southern Influences," pp. 83–84, describes the role of the Chivalry in this election in detail.

statewide results were slow in coming in, but Bigler's margin of victory in San Francisco was an ominous portent to Whig partisans. Such misgivings were not unfounded, for when all the ballots were counted, Bigler was the victor, his narrow margin in Broderick's stronghold determining the outcome. The Bigler vote in San Francisco confused his enemies and pleased and amazed his friends, for he failed to carry the city in 1851.[31]

The sorrow of the Whigs and the Chivalry was matched by the elation of Broderick-Bigler partisans, who had thrown themselves into a losing campaign and turned it into a victory. A few days after the election, the jubilant victors turned to what should be done about the dissident Democrats who had sabotaged the effort of the party. Among the most flagrant of the offenders was Richard P. Hammond, collector of San Francisco, member of the Chivalry and of the state committee. In the midst of the campaign, Hammond resigned as party treasurer on the grounds that private business made it impossible for him to carry on. The politically sophisticated scoffed at this transparent excuse. The fact that it was offered by the chief federal appointee in California, a man who controlled more patronage than any other individual and thus was in the best possible position to provide financial support, made Hammond's explanation completely unacceptable. Collector Hammond had turned his back on the party in the heat of battle—in its hour of need. In spite of his defection, matched by that of other members of the Chivalry, the Broderick-Bigler alliance had produced victory. Under the circumstances, it was only a matter of time until there would be an accounting. A more equitable distribution of the rewards of politics in accordance with Marcy's maxim, "To the victors belong the spoils," could not be held in abeyance long.[32]

One of the major political rewards was the United States Senate seat of William Gwin, whose term was due to expire in March 1855. In the latter part of October 1853 a number of politicos began to discuss the possibility of electing a man to fill this seat in the 1854 session of the legislature. Soon it became a matter of general discussion, editors taking positions according to their political orientation and their attitudes toward the leading contenders.[33]

[31] Election Returns, 1853, Vol. 1759, Archives of the Secretary of State, Sacramento; *Alta California,* Sept. 23, 1853; *Placer Times and Transcript,* Sept. 12, 1853.

[32] *Alta California,* Sept. 15, 1853; *Placer Times and Transcript,* Nov. 22, 1853.

[33] *Placer Times and Transcript,* Nov. 12, 1853.

A number of aspirants were mentioned in the speculation of the newspapers: Broderick, Gwin, Hammond, and James McDougall. Broderick was in the strongest position if the voting were confined to the Democratic party; but since the choice would be made in a joint legislative session, Whig legislators would play a role. As Broderick's support became more apparent, other candidates began to shy away from an election. Whigs became more vehement in their opposition, and some Democrats began to echo their objections. To offset the opposition of the Whigs and the pressure of fellow Democrats, Broderick's supporters began to push a proposal that all members of the party should be bound by the action of a party caucus. "The majority must rule," they declared, and once the Democratic members of the legislature met in caucus and made a choice, all Democrats should be bound. "Hail to the majority and long may it rule." [34]

About the middle of November, one of the leading Democratic newspapers of San Francisco reversed its stand and came out in opposition to the selection. A few days later, the Broderick-dominated state committee retaliated with a blast at the objectors to the senatorial election and the defectors of the general election. The polemic, probably the work of George Wilkes, reviewed the recent history of the California Democracy. It incorporated two documents to bolster its case: the first, the letter of resignation from Richard P. Hammond; the second, a copy of the official election returns. Hammond was accused of deserting the party and sabotaging the collection of funds. Dissident Democrats who had endangered victory were castigated and invited to leave the party they had deserted in the preceding election.[35]

The Chivalry reacted violently to this attempt to excommunicate them. In a sense, the manifesto was a stark description of the California Democracy—divided into groups that "considered each other more hateful than their related factions in the Whig party." Both parties had been fissured by the slavery question, and there was really no way to conceal these fundamental differences in philosophy and program. Superficial criticism of the polemic, couched in empty phrases of "harsh language" and a "threat to the harmony of the party" could not hide the fact that the Democratic party was breaking

[34] *Alta California,* Nov. 12 and 14, 1853.

[35] Wilkes returned from New York City, arriving in San Francisco on Nov. 7, 1853; see *Alta California,* Nov. 8, 1853. "The Address of the Democratic State Central Committee" appeared in the *Placer Times and Transcript,* Nov. 21, 1853.

up over differences in political principles. "Slavery and feeling with regard to it are at the bottom of the difference," reported a capable journalist.[36]

The contest between the two factions of the party reached a critical stage soon after the Free Soil wing led the Democracy to victory in the general election and began to eye the senatorial seat of William Gwin. Broderick apparently was soon to be fitted with the power and prestige of a senatorial toga. To prevent that calamity, the Chivalry would go to almost any length. A poll of Democratic newspapers indicated that the majority was opposed to an election, but a more direct expression of the opinion of the people indicated the opposite. In a special election to select a successor to Sam Brannan, recently resigned state senator from San Francisco, the Broderick-endorsed candidate won by a lopsided margin. The two contestants were to be distinguished chiefly because David Maloney, the victor, supported the election, while W. B. Farwell, the vanquished, opposed it.[37]

One of San Francisco's newspapers found in the result a victory "of that wing of the Democratic party that, as a party, has endeavored to preserve its identity, and has opposed conventionism and its kindred measures." "Conventionism" referred to the Chivalry scheme of revising the constitution in the interests of slavery. The writer went on to declare that Broderick's strength, manifested in this election, was not based upon personal popularity but upon "his force of character" and his identification as a champion of free labor. "He is known," the writer continued, "to represent the feelings of the people of California in their hatred of servile labor in California and encroachments on other nations for the sake of extending it." [38]

In the waning days of 1853, while some politicos looked about them in dismay, Broderick contemplated the past with satisfaction and the future with confidence. His party was divided, but he and his associates controlled it. Even in division, the party could win. Dissident Democrats of the Chivalry persuasion had been stripped of much of their power and reduced to fighting for the right to remain in the

[36] The reaction of the Chivalry to the "Address" appeared in the *Placer Times and Transcript,* Nov. 22, 1853. *Alta California,* Nov. 12 and 22 and Dec. 2, 1853, contained insightful articles on the discord of the Democratic party.

[37] *Placer Times and Transcript,* Nov. 26, 1853; *Alta California,* Dec. 16 and 20, 1853.

[38] *Alta California,* Dec. 20, 1853.

party. An analysis of the internal situation of the California Democracy went to the heart of the matter:

> The Senatorial question is now the leading topic among politicians. The removal of the Capitol and the State printing receive a due share of attention. The first and the last might easily be compromised, if there were such a word as compromise in the vocabulary of the most prominent candidate for Senatorial honors. But, unfortunately, it is not there, and a wide breach is made in the dominant party that will *never be healed.* It was the policy of General JACKSON never to desert a friend or forgive an enemy, and hence his great strength and popularity. People knew where to find him. Not unlike him in this respect is he who now stands forward as the leading candidate for the Senate. After the election of Senator at the coming session of the legislature had been urged by certain parties, and the ball set in motion by them, it was not to be supposed that they would be among the first to oppose it. But so it was, and the treachery was so apparent that the Senatorship in itself became a question of secondary importance.[39]

There was much that was valid in this analysis of the situation, but placing the emphasis on the senatorial election distorted the reality of the political matrix of California in December 1853. The slavery question and the land question were the fundamental issues that divided the party. It was the victory of the Free Soil faction and the ascendancy of the principles of "Free Labor, Free Soil, Free Men" which put Democrats into antagonistic camps—ready to do violence to opposing principles and personnel. The degree to which each was committed was soon to be revealed.

[39] *Alta California,* Dec. 30, 1853.

☆☆☆☆☆☆☆☆☆☆☆☆☆☆☆

CHAPTER SIX

Senatorial Quest: Misstep

The Broderick-Bigler dominance of the Democratic party was firmly established when the new political year of 1854 began—ushered in with the opening session of the legislature in January. Both men had worked long, hard, and efficiently to create an organization which reached into every part of the state. In the city of San Francisco Broderick used his many contacts in the business and commercial world to see that his associates were employed. He placed them in the city and county governments as well. This band of devoted followers, gainfully employed, was ever ready to do battle with the enemy in political primary or convention. Governor Bigler buttressed Broderick's effort with state patronage. The Chivalry monopoly of federal patronage was offset.[1]

The legislature that met in Benicia in the first week of January found the two antagonistic factions of the party present and girded for battle. The immediate prize was a seat in the United States Senate, for it was common knowledge that Broderick intended to force an election. The outcome of the battle for the senatorship would go a long way toward determining the ultimate question—which of the factions was to control the Democratic party. Benicia was packed with representatives of the "customhouse gentry"—patronage appointees of the Chivalry—who overtaxed the limited accommodations of the crossroads and consumed an undue amount of the equally limited supply of liquor. To the credulous the "customhouse men" explained that they had come to Benicia to lobby for a bill that would provide the federal

[1] Jeremiah Lynch, *The Life of David C. Broderick* (New York, 1911), p. 72.

government with a site for a customhouse in San Francisco. The most poorly informed resident of Benicia knew that the Chivalry was out in force to prevent the election of Broderick to the Senate.[2]

The fact that William Gwin's current term did not expire until March 1855 did not bar an election, for the legislature had never fixed a time for choosing senators. Thus it was legally entitled to elect a successor to Gwin in 1854. Experts on constitutional law were consulted, and the secretary of the United States Senate was called upon to render an opinion on the legality of the proposal. They agreed the election was legal and in accordance with the provisions of the United States Constitution, the long established practices of the United States Senate, and the practices of most of the states of the Union. None of this, however, made an election acceptable to the Chivalry of the California Democracy.[3]

From the opening day of this session of the legislature, it was apparent that this question would dominate the proceedings until it was settled. When the president of the Senate, Lieutenant-Governor Samuel Purdy, absent on the first day because of illness, forwarded committee arrangements, the Chivalry objected. Denying his right to make such assignments, the Chivalry indicated that they would combat the influence of Broderick every step of the way, for Purdy was part of the Broderick organization. The objection was met by placing the power to appoint committees in the hands of the president pro tempore. He promptly carried out the arrangements made by Purdy.[4]

Broderick determined the basic strategy of the effort to force an election, but George Wilkes also played a prominent role. The two men worked effectively, although strained relations appeared in the midst of the effort. However, personal feelings were not allowed to interfere with their productive political relationship. Wilkes's aid was important throughout the campaign and at times was nearly indispensable. On one occasion, for example, when it appeared that a Demo-

[2] *Alta California,* Jan. 9, 1854.

[3] Wilkes is often credited with the plan for the "premature" election, but he declared it was Broderick's idea; see *Affidavit of George Wilkes* (n.p., n.d.), in Bancroft Lib. Asbury Dickens, Secretary of the United States Senate, gave assurances of the legality of the proposal in a letter incorporated into *The Address of the Majority of the Democratic Members of Both Branches of the Legislature* (San Francisco, 1854), copy in Benjamin Hayes Scrapbooks, Vol. XVII, Bancroft Lib. The relevant sections of the U.S. Constitution are Article I, Sections 3 and 4.

[4] *Alta California,* Jan. 9, 1854.

cratic caucus would not be called for lack of a quorum, Wilkes rounded up the few votes that made the difference.[5]

The plan of action that was devised was uncomplicated. Since a majority of each house of the legislature was Democratic, it was simply necessary to get all Democrats into caucus where a position on the election would be taken. That position would presumably be binding on every Democratic member of the legislature, thus allowing a bill authorizing an election to pass. If such a measure could be pushed through the legislature, it would of course be signed by Governor Bigler. The election of Broderick would quickly follow. The strategy was sound, but it demanded a coordinated effort by Broderick and his associates. As they proceeded, they brought into being a coalition of all the lawmakers—Whig, Chivalry Democrat, or independent—who opposed an election. The legislature moved toward polarization—the Broderick combination bringing into being a counterpart combination.

Determined to force the passage of an election bill, Broderick organized, cajoled, pleaded, intrigued, and did whatever else was necessary to influence his fellow lawmakers. Along the way he became quite difficult at times, alienating not only Wilkes but other friends as well. When one of his associates complained of his imperious rejection of some well-intentioned advice, he declared in unequivocal language, "Leaders never take advice; leaders give direction. If it were to get whispered abroad that I ever took advice, my friends would lose their confidence in me, and leave me and go to the fountain head!" [6] He softened these remarks with a qualifying word or two, but the sting remained.

Broderick and Wilkes finally managed to get the majority of Democratic legislators to a caucus, where they were treated to a blistering attack on those who objected to an election. Published as *The Address of the Majority,* probably the work of Wilkes, it was a mélange of trenchant criticisms and constitutional arguments which reviewed the controversy. The claims of the opposition were examined and, of

[5] William H. Ellison, *A Self-governing Dominion: California, 1849–1860* (Berkeley, 1950), pp. 284–285, summarizes the involved parliamentary battle that accompanied the election fight. Hubert H. Bancroft, *History of California,* VI (San Francisco, 1888), 684–688, and Theodore Hittell, *History of California* (San Francisco, 1898), IV, 144 ff., tell the story in a similar fashion, differing only on nonessential detail. The *Affidavit of George Wilkes* describes the role that he played.

[6] *Wilkes' Spirit of the Times,* Oct. 22, 1859.

course, found wanting. The rhetoric was effective and biting. At one point the polemic declared, "The outcry of such politicians about the people's rights is too hollow to deceive. . . . such new-born love of principle . . . comes with strange grace from those who sought to cut the throat of our party over the threshold of the Benicia convention." A special outpouring of wrath was directed at those who had sat out the last election—the Democrats "who tried to betray the party on the field of battle [who] now stand breast to breast, with clasped shields to our enemies, the Whigs." It concluded with a bold attack on the Pierce administration and "the interference of the federal power and patronage with our domestic politics." [7]

This frontal assault on the Pierce administration and its partisans in California would not soon be forgotten by the administration, the Chivalry, or the signers of the *Address.* Signatures of Democratic members were difficult to acquire, but eventually a total of fifteen senators and forty assemblymen signed, a clear majority of each house. When it came time to translate this preliminary endorsement into an election bill, however, a number of the signatories fell by the wayside and repudiated their signatures. A minority address was issued to counter the Wilkes polemic, and it, too, was signed by a number of legislators. Its most telling argument declared that if the legislature of 1854 could elect a senator for the term beginning in 1855, it could also elect a senator for the next vacancy in 1857, and so on. It did not muster as many endorsements as the majority address, but eventually some eleven senators and twenty-six assemblymen signed. Obviously a number of the lawmakers signed both documents.[8]

As the proceedings dragged on through the spring of 1854 without a decision, the pressure on the lawmakers mounted. Hundreds of petitions from home constituencies were received in favor of or in opposition to the election. James W. Coffroth presented one signed by sixteen hundred residents of Tuolumne County who agreed that an election would be highly beneficial to the state and very gratifying to them. It was one of a number Coffroth received, he declared. Other petitions expressing sharp opposition to the holding of an election also came to the attention of lawmakers.[9]

[7] *California Chronicle,* Feb. 15, 1854; *The Address of the Majority,* passim.

[8] *The Address of the Majority;* Sacramento *Union,* July 15, 1875, in Winfield J. Davis Scrapbooks, XV, 34, Huntington Lib.

[9] *California Chronicle,* Mar. 7, 1854. Petitions to the Legislature, 1851–1856, State Archives, Sacramento, contain scores of such petitions.

The last representative of the old California families in the state Senate, Pablo de la Guerra, received an emotionally charged message from a relative and former member. Mariano G. Vallejo penned the appeal, which was permeated with the nostalgia of a bygone age. "I request for our friendship and our religion for you not to leave the Senate until after the election. It may be the last time that we will be represented in the legislature of California, and it is necessary for you not to abandon the position to the administration. Broderick is sincere and our friend and deserves the support of all of us." [10]

More material influences than friendship were brought into the picture. A sensational charge of bribery was investigated by the Senate. Brought by E. T. Peck, newly elected Whig from Butte County, the accusation was directed at Joseph C. Palmer, San Francisco banker of Palmer, Cook & Co. According to Peck, Palmer tried to bribe him to vote in favor of an election bill, after eliciting a promise that he would not reveal the transaction to Broderick. Peck did not observe this curious restriction or any other, but brought the matter to the attention of the entire body. After a number of witnesses had been examined, the Senate concluded that the allegations were not supported. To assuage the feelings of Senator Peck, it was added that the findings cast no reflection upon his honor or dignity. A similar charge of bribery was made by two supporters of Broderick, H. G. Livermore and G. D. Hall, but no official investigation was ever undertaken.[11]

The matter of the election was finally decided when the bill was indefinitely postponed in the state Senate. Broderick's enemies exulted in the news that the "ruffian" and "state plunderer," a man "utterly devoid of character, of honor and of every quality that should make a man worthy" had been defeated. The malignant phrases poured forth in a flood: "I am acquainted with gentlemen of high standing who knew Dave Broderick in New York as a Bullying rowdy fireman, and he kept a three cent groggery," declared one opponent. Another flung the deadly charge of abolitionism at Broderick and his associates.[12]

[10] Vallejo to Pablo de la Guerra, Jan. 26, 1854, De la Guerra Coll., Santa Barbara Mission Archives.

[11] Bancroft, *History of California,* VI, 682–683; *California Chronicle,* Jan. 19 and 20, 1854. For the Livermore-Hall charges and their disposition see Bancroft, *History of California,* VI, 685; cf. *California Chronicle,* Mar. 6, 1854.

[12] *California Chronicle,* Mar. 10, 1854; James O'Meara, *Broderick and Gwin* (San Francisco, 1881), p. 48; George W. Whitman to James W. Mandeville, Mar. 13, 1854, Andrew J. Hatch to Mandeville, Mar. 3, 1854, and Mandeville to D. A. Enyart, Mar. 15, 1854, Mandeville Coll., Huntington Lib.

A less partisan observer, who had been critical of Broderick in the past, had a different evaluation of the man, his principles, and his opposition:

> He at once [upon his entry into politics] became recognized as a leader, and the kid-gloved gentry, who had thought themselves born to rule and educated to be obeyed, were obliged to stand aside for this man of the people. Then began their tirade of abuse, and from that time to this, the stereotyped objection has been repeatedly thrown out that he was a New York shoulder-striker. Not a word is or can be said against his private life here. It is not denied that his private character has ever been above the smallest taint or suspicion; that his whole demeanor has been such that an ascetic could find no fault with it. . . . The silk-stocking gentry thought that if they could not cope with him in talents and energy, they would ruin his reputation by secretly maligning his character.[13]

The long battle for the Senate seat was ended for the present, but the repercussions from the struggle were to resound in the California political arena for years to come. The complete division of the California Democracy was almost a fact. Governor Bigler penned long letters to his brother in Pennsylvania, fixing the blame for the division on the Pierce administration, which bolstered the enemies of the "true Democracy—the men who really lead and control in the Democratic party in this state." The response to his plaintive missives is unknown, but the division he described was seen in a number of ways in California in the spring. Complete tickets put forth by each of the major factions competed in the spring elections. In San Jose, Broderick's followers won a sweeping victory. That triumph was offset when a convention in Tuolumne resulted in a clean sweep for the anti-Broderick forces. And so it went, as the factions met in conflict for control of the party.[14]

Early in the year, a new factor was introduced into the already complicated political picture of California. The new organization, the American party, was to be as ephemeral in the Golden State as in the nation at large, but for a little more than two years it was to sweep through the political arena and make a shambles of traditional alignments. Almost as rapidly as the storm gathered, it was dissipated, but

[13] *Alta California,* Mar. 1, 1854.

[14] John Bigler to William Bigler, Apr. 14 and May 31, 1854, Bigler Coll., Pennsylvania Hist. Soc.; William L. Smith to Joseph B. Wells, Apr. 14, 1854, California File, Huntington Lib.; Luther B. Curtis to James W. Mandeville, June 20, 1854, Mandeville Coll.

for a time it threatened to dominate the world of politics. Politicos of opportunistic inclination were quick to come to the banner of the Know-Nothings but equally quick to desert when the ephemeral nature of the organization became apparent.[15]

The Know-Nothings capitalized on the incipient prejudice against the foreign-born and Catholic elements of the population. Such antagonism had deep roots in the American past; the Federalists of Jefferson's day with their Alien Act represent one example, but for the most part such attitudes had been suppressed. As the decades of the nineteenth century passed in measured sequence, hostility to the immigrant and the Catholic burst forth from time to time, but for the most part it lay dormant. In the 1840's there was a brief but violent outburst of this unreasoning prejudice which resulted in widespread disorder in a number of eastern cities. Broderick himself had felt the touch of this hostility directly as his first race for a major elective office in 1846 ended in defeat when the Know-Nothings of that time split the vote by running a candidate against him—a candidate whose chief qualification was his white, Protestant, Anglo-American background.[16]

The Know-Nothings of the fifties were a resurrection of earlier political groups that attempted to capitalize on the widespread prejudice against immigrants and Catholics. The equally pervasive disillusionment with existing parties was also exploited by this party of secret and conspiratorial operations. Organized into wigwams or lodges in every community where a group could be assembled, they emphasized their purity of thought and motive and their disgust with the dishonest and opportunistic scoundrels who manipulated masses of ignorant foreign-born voters for their own ends. Unite with us, they said to the pure of thought and mind, and help us deliver the government from the wicked and designing politicians.[17]

The Know-Nothings apparently represented the wave of the future in 1854 and 1855, sweeping all before them in a number of states. In Massachusetts they achieved unprecedented victories; in Illinois,

[15] *Alta California,* May 27, 1854; Peyton Hurt, *The Rise and Fall of the "Know Nothings" in California* (San Francisco, 1930); Ray Allen Billington, *The Protestant Crusade, 1800–1860: A Study of the Origins of American Nativism* (Chicago, 1964), pp. 380–389.

[16] Allan Nevins, *Ordeal of the Union* (New York, 1947), II, 323–331.

[17] *Alta California,* Aug. 30, 1854.

Ohio, and Pennsylvania, Democrats lamented the birth of this new party that trounced them in local and state elections. The "Americans" avoided discussion of a specific program, although they were always ready to expound on the need for reform in politics and their ability to bring about rededication to honesty and civic virtue. Contending that the immigrant groups were the cause of much of the corruption of democratic processes, they advocated the curtailment of the political privileges of Americans of foreign birth. Extend the naturalization period to twenty years, restrict the privilege of holding office to citizens of native birth, limit the franchise to "true Americans," and "Put none but Americans on guard tonight"—these were the political formulations that sprinkled their rhetoric.[18]

The Know-Nothings were to be remarkably successful in California for a time. Their success reflected the internal division of the Democratic party, but it also was an indication of the secret and systematic manner in which they went about their work. Lodges were the local units of the party; membership was secret and in time became a substantial part of the community where they existed. The organization was tightly controlled and directed from the top, and political decisions were made with a minimum of discussion and participation by the membership. Once a choice had been made or a candidate put forward, all members of the lodge were expected to support faithfully the decision. Since the action taken was secret until the eve of the election, it was often difficult to counter. When the opposition was divided into warring factions, as in California, the chances of accomplishing a good deal through these procedures were enhanced.[19]

In June the two factions of the Democratic party met on the battlefield of primary elections, where delegates to the forthcoming Democratic convention were to be chosen. The huge San Francisco delegation was a major prize, since control of this group would be a long step toward control of the convention. Widespread disorder marked the election in San Francisco, where guns, fists, and knives were brought into play. The final result was a divided delegation. The Chivalry and Richard P. Hammond, collector of customs, won in a number of the wards. Broderick and his associates, however, made a

[18] Nevins, *Ordeal of the Union,* II, 342–343.

[19] Nevins, *Ordeal of the Union,* II, 326, 331; Billington, pp. 383–384; Sacramento *Union,* Aug. 4, 1854.

respectable showing; his hold on the party organization in the bay city was loosened, but he remained a major political power.[20]

While Broderick led the fight in the San Francisco branch of the Democracy, similar battles were taking place in other parts of the state. In Nevada County the Broderick forces triumphed. In other counties dual conventions were held and two delegations selected, each vociferously proclaiming its right to represent the county and vehemently denouncing the rival group as a "rump" delegation. As the reports came in from one outlying county after another, it became apparent to politicos that the forthcoming convention of the party was shaping up as the decisive battle for control of the California Democracy.[21]

As state chairman, Broderick was in a strategic position to demonstrate his mastery of parliamentary procedure and his ability to lead his faction of the party to victory. He would call the convention to order and initiate its organization. He might decide who would preside, which rival delegations would be seated and, ultimately, which factions would control the convention. And of course, control implied control of the ticket and the staff organization of the party—at least until the following year. The stakes were enormous. Preconvention speculation in the newspapers stressed the disunity of the Democracy, and one observer predicted that the Chivalry would walk out if Broderick and his associates succeeded in controlling the gathering.[22]

The stage was set for one of the most dramatic conventions in the political history of California when the delegates assembled in a church in Sacramento on July 18, 1854.[23] Broderick called the tense gathering to order and plunged immediately into the work of organizing the convention. His call for nomination of a chairman brought a number of clamoring delegates to their feet. T. L. Vermule was rec-

[20] *California Chronicle,* June 20 and 22, 1854. Irregularities allegedly involved in this election are reported in Michael Kenny Statement, MS in "Papers Relating to Ballot Box Stuffing," San Francisco Committee of Vigilance of 1856 Papers, Huntington Lib.

[21] *California Chronicle,* July 14, 1854; Sacramento *Union,* July 11, 1854.

[22] *California Chronicle,* July 18, 1854; Sacramento *Union,* July 18, 1854.

[23] There are several accounts of this convention. O'Meara, *Broderick and Gwin,* pp. 97–100, written by one of William Gwin's political aides, should be used with caution; Winfield J. Davis, *History of Political Conventions in California, 1849–1892* (Sacramento, 1893), pp. 29–34, is objective. *California Chronicle,* July 19 and 20, 1854, presents a detailed contemporary account which differs considerably from that presented by O'Meara. The accounts in the Sacramento *Union,* July 18, 1854, agree in most details with those of the *Chronicle.*

ognized by Broderick, and he promptly nominated Edward McGowan. John O'Meara quickly asked for a vote on McGowan's nomination and Broderick declared him elected. As McGowan made his way to the platform, he was joined by former Governor John McDougal, whose vociferous supporters declared he had been elected the presiding officer. The two chairmen took seats on the platform; as each began the work of selecting committees, the convention turned into bedlam.

When a measure of order was restored, the two chairmen completed the work of appointing vice-chairmen, secretaries, and committees. Each of the two committees on organization promptly reported that the chairman who had appointed it was the legitimate chairman of the convention. A bifurcated convention was the result, each of the gatherings determined to prevail. Occasionally a period of relative quiet occurred, as a speaker attempted to persuade the opposing faction to withdraw its "spurious" set of officers. Each such effort was met with a renewal of the shouting and cursing and turmoil. Governor Bigler appeared in the late afternoon and made a personal effort to restore order, but his conciliatory speech had no measurable effect. As night came on, candles were produced to offset the gathering darkness, for the trustees of the church had removed the lamps in an effort to get the disorderly mob to leave. By the fitful gleams of candlelight, the proceedings continued. Eventually it became clear that nothing could be accomplished, but neither faction was willing to leave the church before the other. Finally an agreement was reached: the two factions disbanded without formally adjourning, leaving the church in pairs of delegates, the two sets of officers linked arm in arm, leading the way. The trustees locked and barred the doors and sorrowfully surveyed the scene. The Broderick faction of the party subsequently donated four hundred dollars to repair the damage, but it was scant solace to the church trustees. Among the signs of tumult was a shattered stained glass window through which a delegate had scrambled when a gun was fired accidentally. It was to be some time before a church in Sacramento was made available to a political party again.

The next day the two factions met in separate meeting halls. Overtures from the Broderick-Bigler wing were rebuffed by the gathering in Musical Hall in Sacramento. The two conventions proceeded to the selection of nominees and platforms—once it became clear that it was impossible to reconcile the two gatherings. Broderick's wing gathered in Carpenter's Hall. The division of the Democratic party had been accomplished; henceforth the antagonistic wings would make their way independently. Two tickets, two platforms, and two campaign efforts by Democrats featured the 1854 elections.[24]

The Chivalry domination of the Musical Hall gathering was seen clearly in the platform adopted. Resolutions favoring the building of the transcontinental railroad, the donation of limited amounts of the public domain to actual settlers, and an endorsement of the Pierce administration and the Kansas-Nebraska Act were passed without debate. The latter was expressed as follows: "That we most cordially approve and sustain the passage of the Nebraska bill, and the vote thereupon shows most clearly that it was a democratic measure—one of principle, that should have enlisted in its favor every true lover of republican principles, and we only regret that among the names of those who opposed its passage we notice some few who claim to be democrats." [25]

This unequivocal endorsement of the Kansas-Nebraska Act showed clearly that the Chivalry was in full command of the Musical Hall gathering. In the long political history of the United States, few congressional acts were more thoroughly repudiated by the electorate than the Kansas-Nebraska Act. In the entire United States only one free state legislature—Illinois—endorsed this measure, and that single endorsement required a tremendous effort directed by Stephen A. Douglas, who pledged his political future to the battle. In five other free states, legislatures had not only refused to endorse the act but passed strongly worded resolutions of condemnation. California's legislature, like those of other free states, had maintained a discreet silence. Only one free state assembly of lawmakers, then, had endorsed the act, yet the Chivalry convention, which claimed to represent the Democracy of California, duplicated this endorsement.[26]

The Carpenter's Hall gathering, under Broderick's direction, made a number of overtures to the delegates in Musical Hall. When these efforts at reconciliation proved fruitless, the Broderick-Bigler wing of

[24] O'Meara, *Broderick and Gwin,* p. 103; *California Chronicle,* July 20, 1854.

[25] Davis, *Political Conventions,* p. 31.

[26] Nevins, *Ordeal of the Union,* II, 146; P. Orman Ray, *The Repeal of the Missouri Compromise* (Cleveland, 1909), pp. 15–16. When the matter came before the California legislature, Broderick's supporters opposed the endorsement of the Kansas-Nebraska Act; see Hittell, *History of California,* IV, 151; *Senate Journal,* 1854, pp. 450–451; *Assembly Journal,* 1854, p. 508.

the party turned to the selection of candidates and the writing of a platform. The incumbent congressmen, Milton S. Latham and James A. McDougall, were nominated to second terms. The writing of a platform was preceded by the composition of an "Address to the People of California," an appeal to the rank and file of the Democracy to support the Carpenter's Hall convention as the legal organization of the party. It reviewed the long history of factionalism in the party and declared that the split resulted from the attempt of one group to "divide the party and sectionalize its principles." The conciliatory language reflected Broderick's view that reconciliation was still possible.[27]

The platform adopted by this gathering was a reenactment of the platform of the Democratic party of 1853, although a resolution dealing with the rights of settlers was strengthened. Inasmuch as the Free Soil tone of the 1853 platform was its dominant feature, it was to be expected that a convention of like-minded delegates would find it acceptable in 1854. A resolution dealing with the split in the party was added. Pointing out that it was customary for the party to conduct its affairs according to the principle of "majority rule," it declared that anyone who would not observe this rule in the settlement of "all differences of opinion upon questions of party policy, expediency, or men . . . is subversive of party organization, and destructive of the harmony and dangerous to the success of the party." [28]

The two gatherings disbanded after selecting candidates and writing platforms. A short time after adjournment, the prolific pen of George Wilkes wrote an *Address of the Democratic State Central Committee.*[29] In caustic language he denounced the "bogus Democrats" who disrupted the convention and flatly declared that the Carpenter's Hall gathering contained the majority of the legitimate delegates. In the final analysis this declaration and anything else that Wilkes wrote of the split mattered little, for the outcome of the division of the party was not to be determined by speechmaking or resolution writing but by the success of each group in mustering support at the polls.

The campaign that followed the conventions was a bitterly fought contest in which epithets characterized election speeches, and fists, knives, and guns were used. A pro-Broderick candidate for the As-

[27] Davis, *Political Conventions,* p. 32; Sacramento *Union,* Aug. 3, 1854.
[28] Davis, *Political Conventions,* p. 33.
[29] In Benjamin Hayes Scrapbooks, XVII, Bancroft Lib.

sembly in Nevada County denied a charge of abolitionism flung at him in the county convention. That night he was assaulted by an opponent who walked up to him in a saloon, cursed him, then struck him with a revolver and left him lying unconscious. Another Broderick supporter who had given copies of the New York *Post* to a friend was labeled an abolitionist by a local judge before whom he practiced. On election eve an open-air political meeting was broken up by running a piece of fire equipment through the audience as a Broderick supporter was speaking.[30]

Meanwhile the Know-Nothings were busy. In San Francisco they centered their fire on the Broderick-Bigler wing of the Democratic party, although they were ostensibly hostile to the entire Democracy. The day before the election, the San Francisco Know-Nothings published a "Citizens Reform Ticket" chosen from the nominees of the Whigs and Democrats. Significantly, none of the Democrats chosen were of the Broderick-Bigler wing. The discrimination of the Know-Nothings was noted by observers who were quick to point out that Broderick had a considerable following among the foreign-born elements of the city's population.[31]

Election day dawned with scores of special police on hand to guard the polls. A goodly number of the volunteers were of Know-Nothing persuasion, and their presence seemed to indicate that this election was not to be manipulated by Democrats. A heavy turnout was expected in San Francisco, where clashes between representatives of the major factions of the Democratic party were expected to supplement the usual violent clashes of Whigs and Democrats. The electioneering of the Know-Nothings gladdened the hearts of bigots and was a challenging affront to citizens of Irish, German, French, and Hispanic background. The police served to soften and in some instances prevent violence, but before the balloting came to a close there had been a number of clashes. A leading newspaper commented on the wide-

[30] *California Chronicle,* July 18, 1854; Stephen J. Field, *California Alcalde* (Oakland, 1950), pp. 35, 61. The judge was William R. Turner of the Eighth Judicial District; the "abolitionist-lawyer" was Stephen J. Field, later appointed by Lincoln to the United States Supreme Court. *California Chronicle,* Sept. 5, 1854, carried a detailed account of the election-eve meeting and the manner in which it was disrupted.

[31] Hurt, p. 23; *California Chronicle,* Sept. 6, 1854; Bancroft, *History of California,* VI, 694.

spread violence and fraud and declared that a fundamental revamping of election laws and procedures was necessary.[32]

The statewide results were slow in coming in, but the totals of San Francisco, quickly ascertained, revealed a Know-Nothing victory of considerable magnitude. Not only had this new political organization elected the bulk of its ticket, but its most formidable opponent, Broderick, had been weakened considerably. The Whigs, in some instances running with the open endorsement of the Know-Nothings, did rather well and in fact received a plurality of the congressional vote. Broderick's congressional nominees trailed the Whigs but ran ahead of the Chivalry nominees in the county.[33]

The statewide results delighted the Chivalry. Their candidates generally outpaced the opposition, running far ahead of the Broderick ticket. Despite the split in Democratic ranks, the Chivalry's congressional nominees, Denver and Herbert, won and went off to Washington, where Herbert distinguished himself by mortally wounding an Irish waiter in a senseless fit of anger. The margin of victory for the Chivalry was decisive, for their nominees received about thirty-seven thousand votes, while ten thousand was the total cast for the leading Broderick-Bigler candidate. It was a most discouraging setback, and there was limited satisfaction in the knowledge that the Broderick-Bigler ticket had bested the Chivalry in San Francisco and Sacramento. In the beginning a great deal more had been expected, but all the high hopes of reforming the Democratic party along Free Soil lines had ended in disaster.[34]

The usual postelection analyses by pundits of the Broderick camp attributed the defeat to the last-minute withdrawal of their congressional nominee, Milton S. Latham. Such an explanation may have satisfied emotional and disappointed partisans, but—as with most political phenomena—so simple an explanation, though plausible, was unsatisfactory. Latham's withdrawal undoubtedly hurt the Free Soil Democrats, but of equal importance was the reluctance of the Broderick camp to jump into the campaign and fight a principled battle on the issues, beginning with the split of the party in Sacramento. All the

[32] San Francisco *Sun,* Sept. 11, 1854; *California Chronicle,* Sept. 7, 1854.
[33] Hurt, p. 27; *California Chronicle,* Sept. 8, 1854.
[34] Davis, *Political Conventions,* p. 66; Election Returns, 1854, Vol. 1759, Archives of the Secretary of State, Sacramento.

talk about healing the wounds within the party—all the overtures made to the dissident Democrats—muted principle and stressed expediency. Under such circumstances, the undecided voter might well conclude that there was no basic difference between the two sets of Democrats who solicited his support.[35]

The role of the Know-Nothings is difficult to assess, but there is little doubt that they centered their fire on the Broderick-Bigler faction of the Democracy. In San Francisco they avoided an independent slate for a ticket chosen from the nominees of other groups, sprinkled with candidates of Know-Nothing affiliation. Thus was support from Whig, Chivalry Democrat, and Know-Nothing groups combined to produce victory. The party of the dark lantern was probably the best-organized group of this campaign. It had observers in every polling place and representatives in every precinct. As a result, the fledgling Know-Nothings did very well in their maiden effort. Years later, a prominent Whig revealed that the Chivalry congressional candidates were elected principally because of the secret support given them by the Know-Nothings.[36]

Another factor difficult to assess was the appeal that each Democratic ticket had because of its respective stand on the Kansas-Nebraska Act. This was a clear-cut difference on a major question—an issue that was rending traditional party alignments and bringing into being new factions that eventuated in the creation of a Republican party. Ostensibly designed to bring about an organized government in the Plains area, the act was presented as a major step toward the realization of the transcontinental railroad—an objective in which all Californians were interested. Under these circumstances, the enthusiastic endorsement of the Kansas-Nebraska Act by the Chivalry did not produce the hostile reaction that such an endorsement elicited in other free states.[37]

The most important factor leading to defeat for the Broderick-led Democrats was the manner in which the Chivalry skillfully utilized the small army of federal officeholders to staff their campaign organization and muster supporters at the polls. Elections of the time required the presence of an election worker at the polls to present each prospec-

[35] Davis, *Political Conventions,* pp. 32–34.

[36] Hurt, p. 27; San Francisco *Pacific,* Sept. 22, 1854; A. P. Catlin, "Political Memoirs," in San Francisco *Post,* July 1, 1882, p. 2, col. 1.

[37] Davis, *Political Conventions,* pp. 31–33.

tive voter with a ticket or ballot. Each polling place required other personnel, unpaid representatives of each party, who supervised the election, the counting of ballots, and the posting and certification of results. The Chivalry's monopoly of federal patronage made it possible for them to mobilize the federal appointees. Scattered throughout the state, they were on the scene, ready to do battle with the enemy and safeguard the interests of their party. On election day they put aside their duties in the land offices, the postal service, or the customs service. Marshaled at polling places, they distributed tickets to prospective voters—electioneering quietly and persuasively. At other times when their services were needed they appeared in conventions or in primary meetings. While the general citizenry was absorbed in everyday affairs of business, farming, and mining—perhaps taking a short while out to vote on election day—the patronage appointees paid for past and insured future favors in payments of that most stable of political currency—effective political service.[38]

The figures from some of the outlying counties told the story of the effectiveness of the Chivalry organization. In Sutter County but one brave soul voted the Broderick ticket, while the Chivalry rang up an impressive total of 381. In San Diego County Broderick's slate received three votes to the opposition's 134. In San Joaquin the tally was 32 to 935. Only in San Francisco and Sacramento did the Free Soil slate best the Chivalry. Significantly these were areas where Broderick and Bigler had supporters who could match in numbers and energy the federal appointees of the Chivalry.[39]

The results were interpreted as a "rout" by the gleeful Chivalry representatives, who congratulated one another on the "victory, which is unparalleled in the whole history of the Democratic party and one of which we may well be proud." The results in Tuolumne County were especially gratifying, for "we thought that Tuolumne was the stronghold of the Bogusites," one reported. Another comment declared that the Broderick Democrats "may be headed by Old Bigler himself, they may have Broderick as a schemer, a Coffroth for an orator, and as many Shoulder Strikers as they can buy over but it will

[38] Mary Floyd Williams, *History of the San Francisco Committee of Vigilance of 1851* (Berkeley, 1921), p. 391; Bancroft, *History of California,* VI, 636–637; Etta Olive Powell, "Southern Influences in California Politics before 1864" (unpubl. M.A. thesis, Univ. of Calif., 1929), pp. 212–213.

[39] Election Returns, 1854, Vol. 1759, Archives of the Secretary of State, Sacramento.

avail them nothing." The results clearly showed, they declared, that no party which was opposed to the Pierce administration could be a significant factor in California, for the advocates of "Free Socialism, yes Free Socialism (for they are nothing else) cannot prosper in this young and thriving Democratic state." [40]

The political demise of Broderick was celebrated wherever partisans of the Chivalry gathered in the winter of 1854, but their rejoicing was premature. He had suffered a tremendous setback in the elections, but as forthcoming events were to show, Broderick, Bigler, and Free Soil Democrats were still forces to reckon with in California. As a newspaper editor observed, "The whole course of Broderick's political life in California indicates his sagacity in public affairs and his dauntless resolution in carrying out the ideas he advocates." [41]

When the lawmakers of California gathered in January 1855, the once powerful and influential Broderick was present. The role he played was in sharp contrast to that in the previous legislative session, when his strenuous but unsuccessful campaign for the United States Senate seat monopolized the attention of the lawmakers. The Chivalry had clipped his wings and cut him down as a chieftain in the California Democracy. His faction of the party had been tested at the polls and found wanting. He still headed a separate and independent political party, but it was a small fraction as compared with the portion of the Democratic party dominated by the Chivalry. His opponents reveled in the figures that revealed that Broderick and his followers could muster but a third of the electorate when they were pitted head to head against the Chivalry-dominated Democracy.[42]

The war between the two factions continued in the opening months of 1855. Breaches in Democratic ranks continued to exact a toll from the Democratic party and its chief leaders. Whigs had profited from that division and won new seats in the legislature. The implacable hostility of the two Democratic factions made it impossible for them to combine behind the candidacy of a Democrat. Chivalry Democrats began making overtures to Whig members of the legislature, but even Gwin, the most prominent of the prospective candidates and the incumbent senator, could muster but a part of the necessary total of

[40] Luther Curtis to James W. Mandeville, Sept. 28, 1854, and W. Ewing to Mandeville, Nov. 2, 1854, Mandeville Coll.

[41] *Alta California,* Oct. 12, 1854.

[42] Election Returns, 1854, Vol. 1759, Archives of the Secretary of State, Sacramento.

fifty-seven votes. The conflicting ambitions of James A. McDougall, Hammond, and Gwin continually threatened the unity of the Chivalry camp.[43]

The outcome of the election was foretold when W. W. Stow, a prominent Whig, was elected speaker of the Assembly. His election revealed the cleavage within the Democratic party and seemed to indicate that a Democratic-Whig combination was being forged which would result in the election of a Whig. Whig aspirant Philip L. Edwards found it difficult to curb his optimism, but there were a number of signs which indicated he should exercise caution. Democrats might very well vote for a Whig when choosing a speaker but refuse to vote for one when the larger prize of a Senate seat was at stake.[44]

Gwin and Broderick searched for a way to combine a winning number of votes in the divided legislature. Both were advised to bide their time and await more favorable conditions, but neither was inclined to exercise patience. The instability of the political situation made it difficult for them to be confident about the future. The emergence of the Know-Nothings, the upsurge in Whig strength, the fall of Broderick and his Free Soilers—all indicated the impermanency of immediate political realities and the need for vigorous action.[45]

Broderick was in no position to press his campaign for the Senate seat. Accordingly he sought the postponement of an election, with the hope that the transient scene would bring favorable changes in the political matrix. Gwin sought desperately to win reelection and put the legislature through thirty-eight ballots. He led throughout, but he could not muster more than forty-two of the total of fifty-seven that was essential. During the balloting Gwin had repeated opportunity to note the twenty-six votes cast for Free Soil Democrats which deprived him of victory.[46]

Gwin rightly blamed Broderick for the defeat. However, this assignment of personal responsibility seems to overlook the role that Gwin played in creating opposition. The Free Soil faction found much to

[43] Bancroft, *History of California,* VI, 691; *Alta California,* Jan. 3, 1855.

[44] *Alta California,* Jan. 4, 1855.

[45] Bancroft, *History of California,* VI, 694; *Memoirs of Cornelius Cole* (New York, 1908), pp. 106–107; Nevins, *Ordeal of the Union,* II, 327–331.

[46] William Gwin, Memoirs, pp. 117–118, MS in Bancroft Lib.; Bancroft, *History of California,* VI, 693; Ellison, p. 286.

criticize in the record that Gwin had compiled as a member of the Senate. In effect they declared he was proslavery, a representative of a free state, but objectively a friend of the slavery interests, a member of the cabal of political leaders which was partisan to the peculiar institution.

A sense of change permeated the gatherings of the politicos in the spring of 1855. Know-Nothings continued to exhibit vibrant and intense interest in politics, wigwams springing up in towns and settlements throughout the state. The growth of the Know-Nothings further undermined the Whigs, who continued to exhibit signs of debility. Unwilling to be displaced by this virile new party, the Whigs drifted leaderless, their great chieftains of yesterday—Webster, Clay, and Calhoun—no longer present to give guidance. The old issues of bank and tariff, which once divided the American body politic, had little significance in the United States of the mid-fifties and no meaning in the West. Attempts to breathe new life into the Whig party in the spring of the year were unavailing, for a quorum could not even be assembled by its state central committee. The Whig party was, in fact, just about beyond recall in California.[47]

The death of the Whig party portended a number of changes in California's political scene. Its demise might further the division within the Democracy and spur the formation of new parties in which the "harmonious elements" of the old would be combined in new antislavery and proslavery alignments. The fledgling American party might realize considerable benefit by attracting homeless Whigs. Exactly what lay in the political future was unclear in the spring of 1855; the only certainty was that an old order was passing.[48]

[47] *Alta California,* May 16 and 17, 1855.
[48] *Alta California,* May 26, 1855.

CHAPTER SEVEN

The Party of the Dark Lantern

The decline of the Whigs and the vibrant growth of the Know-Nothing movement brought reunification of the factions of the Democratic party. The unity which was achieved was seen in the San Francisco county convention of May 1855, where Democrats of each faction came together in harmony. It was apparent to the informed that the threat posed by the Know-Nothings was a major factor in producing reconciliation.[1] The harmony of the two wings was based upon expediency rather than principle. "An attempt will be made to preserve it until after the fall election," predicted a San Francisco newspaper, "but the great question of the day . . . the slavery extension policy of the administration" would in time make itself felt. Regardless of the nature of the accord, the fundamental fact was its existence. The once divided Democracy was united again, and in San Francisco, at least, a unified effort was to be made to insure success for the party. The most extensive campaign that had ever been staged was planned for the city.[2]

A measure of the unity that had been established was seen in a municipal election gathering where Benjamin Franklin Washington, state chairman of the Democratic party (Chivalry branch), was nominated as chairman of the meeting by Benjamin S. Lippincott, state chairman of the Democratic party (Free Soil branch). Democratic unity produced a sweeping victory in the city. Know-Nothings carried off a number of the lesser prizes, but the major offices of mayor,

[1] *Alta California,* May 26, 1855. The kind of "astounding" Know-Nothing victory which spurred Democrats to unity is reported in the Sacramento *Union,* Mar. 7, 1855.
[2] *Alta California,* May 21, 22, and 23, 1855.

treasurer, and controller went to Democrats. The election was unusually orderly. Unity was one of the major factors that produced victory; another was the "unbending hostility to Know-Nothingism that has been awakened among our adopted citizens." San Francisco's diverse population was an unpromising field for the Know-Nothings to cultivate.[3]

Broderick played a major role in uniting the divided party. As usual, his work resulted in considerable advantage to himself and his faction. Once the decision to work together had been made, the mechanics of unification became important. Broderick took full advantage of the divisions within the Chivalry camp to bring about a favorable merger of the staff organizations of the two Democratic factions. Half of each existing committee was dropped, merging the two state committees into a new committee of thirty-two. Under this procedure, Broderick's organization, which had mustered but a third of the vote of the rival organization in the preceding election, was to have half of the seats on the chief policy-making body of the Democracy. Since the Free Soil Democrats were a more homogeneous group in terms of their political philosophy and their allegiance to Broderick, while the counterpart committee of the Chivalry faction was divided into groups that looked to various leaders of the Chivalry (Gwin, Latham, Hammond, and Weller), Broderick's move was a coup. It gave him tremendous influence in the new committee of the party.[4]

The enhanced position of Broderick was seen in the state convention of June 1855. Assembling in a Sacramento theater after a number of churches closed their doors in view of the happenings of the 1854 convention, this gathering did not witness the scenes of wild disorder and discord of the previous year. On the second day, the gathering moved to a church, the minister evidently confident that the house of God would not be turned into an arena again. Such assurance was well-founded, for this gathering was not divided into fist-swinging delegates. The opening day found two delegations from San Francisco clamoring for admission. The credential committee ruled in favor of the Broderick delegation. A similar question, regarding rival

[3] *Alta California,* May 28, 29, 30, and June 7, 1855; San Francisco *Daily Town Talk,* May 30, 1855; San Francisco *Fireman's Journal,* June 2, 1855.

[4] James O'Meara, *Broderick and Gwin* (San Francisco, 1881), pp. 110–113; Hubert H. Bancroft, *History of California,* VI (San Francisco, 1888), 693. Apparently this plan of reconciliation was first proposed by George Wilkes in the previous year; see Sacramento *Union,* Aug. 3, 1854.

delegations from Tuolumne, found Broderick and Charles Scott clashing verbally and Scott receiving the favorable decision. This verbal bout was to be one of the few occasions when representatives of the two factions clashed openly.[5]

The division still existing within the Democratic party was mirrored in the selection of a gubernatorial candidate. Broderick and his associates mustered beneath the banner of John Bigler, who was completing his second term. Pleased with the working arrangements between Broderick and Bigler whereby substantial amounts of state patronage were funneled to Democrats of Free Soil persuasion, they saw no need for a change. The Chivalry and its allies, however, had good reason to be displeased with Bigler. They gathered behind Milton S. Latham, onetime congressman who had spurned a Free Soil Democratic nomination in 1854. Bigler led on the first ballot by thirteen votes, but it was not until the third day that he mustered a majority. Even then the vote was close, 157 to 125. Obviously the Chivalry and Latham had considerable support in this collection of Democrats.[6]

Once John Bigler had been nominated, the balance of the ticket was quickly chosen. Significantly, the ticket included representatives of all the major divisions of the party. Bigler and Samuel Purdy represented the Broderick faction. B. F. Keene, nominee for state treasurer, was closely associated with William Gwin. Thomas Flournoy, candidate for controller, was closely identified with James A. McDougall. B. C. Whiting and George H. Crossette, candidates for attorney-general and state printer respectively, were known to be close to Broderick. All of the discordant elements of the party were represented on the ticket, but Broderick and Bigler had secured the major prizes. A newspaper used the phrase "the age of the Chivalry is gone" in its report on the convention and its outcome.[7]

The resolutions as well as the nominations reflected Broderick's influence. The usual endorsement of the "great Pacific railroad" was included, and another declaring that "we are in favor of just legislative action, securing . . . the rights of actual settlers and miners" represented the Free Soil sentiment—a definite weakening of the stand the Broderick convention in Carpenter's Hall had taken in 1854. When it

[5] *Alta California,* June 28 and 29, 1855.

[6] Winfield J. Davis, *History of Political Conventions in California, 1849–1892* (Sacramento, 1893), pp. 41–42.

[7] *Alta California,* July 9, 1855.

came to dealing with the Know-Nothing movement, the language became stronger and more specific:

> That the democracy of California abhor and repudiate as un-American and anti-republican, the proscription of a man for the accident of his birth, or for his religious opinions; and in this crisis of American liberties, institutions, and ideas, they re-affirm and proclaim in full force the universal democratic doctrine of "equal rights to all under the constitution and laws"—and declare in the immortal words of the greatest of American patriots, that "any man conducting himself as a good citizen is accountable to God alone for his religious opinions, and ought to be protected in worshiping the Deity according to the dictates of his own conscience." [8]

When the convention adjourned, the supposedly unified party turned to the coming battle at the polls. A number of the delegates had much to explain to their constituents. In some cases an explanation was difficult to come by, since many of the delegates were confused by what had happened. It was not until they had time to reflect and compare notes that the significance of what had been done in the convention became apparent. Everything had been done so smoothly that even the most vigilant of the Chivalry had been lulled into acceptance of a new order in the party—a new order which enhanced the role of Broderick at the expense of the Chivalry. Only a year before, he had presided over a convention of a remnant of the party which was apparently repudiated at the polls, but now he was the dominant figure once more. His was the major voice in the selection of candidates and the writing of a platform, and his men were the dominant group in the state central committee. Representatives of the Chivalry shook their heads in dismay and began to search for alternatives to supporting this Broderick-determined Democratic slate in the forthcoming election.[9]

A number of alternatives were open. Since the ticket included representatives of the major factions of the party, one might vote selectively rather than the "straight ticket," endorsing those who were acceptable and "striking" those who were not. This alternative to blanket endorsement of the ticket was attractive—almost alluring to

[8] Davis, *Political Conventions,* pp. 40–41.

[9] Bancroft, *History of California,* VI, 693; San Francisco *Daily Evening Bulletin,* Jan. 4, 1878; John S. Hittell, *History of San Francisco* (San Francisco, 1878), pp. 292–293; William Henry Ellison, *A Self-governing Dominion: California, 1849–1860* (Berkeley, 1950), p. 286; O'Meara, *Broderick and Gwin,* pp. 122–126.

those who could not stomach the entire slate. The possibility of simply switching political affiliation was another alternative, but this was fraught with danger, since bolting was one of the cardinal sins of politics. Not only might a bolter find his welcome into a new political group restrained; he might also find the designation one which marked him for the balance of his political life.

In this hour of need another alternative was presented to the dissident Democrat in the form of the Know-Nothing movement. This semisecret organization had made an indelible impression on the political scene. By the spring of 1855 the Know-Nothings had lodges in almost every town and settlement in California. Dedicated, single-minded, and conspiratorial, they had become a formidable influence. The demise of the Whigs, the reestablishment of Broderick's influence in the Democratic party, and the growth of the Know-Nothings set the stage for the mass defection of the Chivalry from the Democracy to the party of the dark lantern. "The chivalry democrats went into the lodges in swarms," exulting in the opportunity to strike back at the Free Soil Democrats and their leader, who had bested them in primary, convention, and committee and driven them from their ancestral political home.[10]

The Know-Nothings gathered in convention in Sacramento in August a few weeks after Broderick had reestablished his dominance of the Democratic party. Dissident Democrats carefully watched the proceedings to learn whether this new organization might serve as a haven. The election of James Coffroth and James Churchman as president and vice-president of the convention must have given some of the representatives of the Chivalry misgivings, for both men had once been associated with the Broderick wing of the Democracy.[11]

To avoid the prolonged and divisive debate that a discussion of political program entailed and the hazards to the candidacies of the numerous aspirants which such a discussion would produce, a statement of principles was adopted before the nominations were opened. It consisted of fifteen resolutions, as revealing of the political nature of the Know-Nothings in what was omitted as in what was included. It was a collection of platitudes designed to muster as much support as

[10] Hittell, *History of San Francisco,* p. 293.

[11] Churchman had been Broderick's congressional candidate in 1854; *Alta California,* Aug. 9, 1855; Davis, *Political Conventions,* p. 42; Etta Olive Powell, "Southern Influences in California Politics before 1864" (unpubl. M.A. thesis, Univ. of Calif., 1929), pp. 92–93.

possible for the new party. The second statement declared for "the supremacy of the constitution and laws of the republic," and the seventh pledged a "stern and unqualified opposition to all corruption and fraud in high places." Corruption and fraud in low places was not noted, but prospective voters were assured that the Know-Nothings would "nominate none for office but men of high moral character and known habits of temperance." As a new organization it was to be expected that the Know-Nothings would pledge "utter disregard of ancient party names and worn-out party issues." [12]

The managers of the convention were evidently determined to avoid issues that would sink their newly launched craft as it left the outfitting dock. This was evidenced by their championing of the Constitution and the "laws of the republic." Real issues of meaning and significance were avoided. The most important such issue was the matter of slavery and the extension of slavery in the West. This was the reef that could rip the bottom plates out of the Know-Nothing clipper, and considerable political skill was required to avoid it. The Know-Nothing position was summed up in a few words: "the firmest and most enduring opposition to the agitation of all questions of a merely sectional character." The slavery issue was met by ignoring it.[13]

This was probably the most practical stand for the party if it would preserve unity. As subsequent events showed, this question could destroy the movement. Nothing was more destructive of the unity of a political organization (which included representatives of North and South) in the fifties than a discussion of slavery. On the other hand, the Whigs before them had gone into political eclipse because of their refusal to grapple with questions of importance. Perhaps a similar fate awaited this party and all others that failed to come forth with a political program that enlisted the support of significant portions of the electorate.

To broaden the base of support for the American party in California, the party moderated its hostility toward the foreign-born and Catholic elements of the population. It proclaimed in one resolution "universal religious toleration" and in another "no union of church

[12] *Alta California,* Aug. 9, 1855; Davis, *Political Conventions,* pp. 42–43.

[13] Davis, *Political Conventions,* p. 43. Allan Nevins, *Ordeal of the Union* (New York, 1947), II, 399–400, describes the manner in which the slavery question eventually destroyed the Know-Nothing movement; cf. Ray Allen Billington, *The Protestant Crusade, 1800–1860: A Study of the Origins of American Nativism* (Chicago, 1964), pp. 394–397.

and state." A "judicious revision of the laws regarding naturalization" was its cautious approach to this subject. Such resolutions were in striking contrast to those of the Know-Nothings in other states, which were much more militant and direct in their attacks on people of foreign birth or Catholic faith.[14]

The convention passed over James Coffroth and nominated a political dark horse, J. Neely Johnson, for governor. His chief political assets included an attractive wife "who did a good deal for him," pro-southern inclinations, and the fact that he was not clearly identified with established political groups. Nominations for justices of the supreme court provoked a number of heated clashes. Hugh C. Murray was attacked as a man of "intemperate habits," but this accusation was offset by the charge that his principal rival was a "Seward man" or abolitionist. The latter charge was apparently fatal, for Murray was nominated. David S. Terry, "a politician of the most ultra-Southern stamp," was nominated for the other supreme court seat. These nominations produced the greatest dissatisfaction in the convention, although the entire ticket was criticized by some delegates.[15]

There was no mistaking the influence of the Chivalry in this convention. It was to be seen in the platform as well as in the ticket. "There is not a man on it who is a candidate for an office of any importance who is not intensely Southern in all his views and feelings" was the judgment of one observer. The manner in which the cooperation of northern-minded men had been secured did not pass unnoticed. The platform, neutral in tone and content, had first been written and adopted. Only then, having disclaimed all action of a purely sectional nature, was the ticket, completely dominated by the Chivalry, selected. Adding Terry and Murray to the ticket had merely confirmed what had been apparent to informed observers. "It would be impossible, probably, to find in all California two men who more completely embody the principles of the Chivalry than these two individuals," declared the *Alta California*.[16]

However, the American party did not campaign in the fashion of

[14] Davis, *Political Conventions,* p. 43; Nevins, *Ordeal of the Union,* II, 399–400; Billington, *Protestant Crusade,* pp. 394–397.

[15] Peyton Hurt, *The Rise and Fall of the "Know Nothings" in California* (San Francisco, 1930), p. 37; *Alta California,* Aug. 9, 1855; Davis, *Political Conventions,* pp. 42–43.

[16] F. F. Low, "Political Notes," p. 27, MS in Bancroft Lib.; *Alta California,* Aug. 9 and 11, 1855; Powell, "Southern Influences," p. 94.

the Chivalry. The principal theme of the Know-Nothings as the campaign developed was the need for change and reform to bring honesty and integrity to government. It was imperative, too, said Know-Nothing orators, to quiet the turmoil over slavery. This was an effective political approach in 1855, appealing to broad segments of the electorate. Homeless Whigs, dissident Democrats, and all voters who had an interest in honesty and reform in politics and in putting an end to the acrimonious sectional quarrel over slavery, were invited to aid the American party.[17]

Soon after the Know-Nothings disbanded, the delegates of the Miners and Settlers party assembled in Sacramento in response to a call issued some time before, which included a sweeping indictment of the confirmation of "Mexican grants to lands which have been purchased as speculations, without ever having been located, or in possession of the pretended grantees." This practice, declared the manifesto, threatened "thousands of our fellow citizens in all parts of the state, in possession of a lot, a homestead, a mining claim, or a farm, who are liable to have a floating grant located upon the very places which they occupy." [18]

David Douglass was elected president of the convention. To the surprise of some delegates, a speaker denounced the election as a "sell on the honest settlers," for Douglass was an associate of Broderick and his election was an endorsement of Broderick. These remarks elicited little applause and a number of shouts urging him to depart. The Broderick-Bigler faction was clearly represented in this gathering. Its efforts were chiefly directed at preventing the convention from nominating a slate of candidates, since such a ticket would hurt the Democratic party and indirectly assist the Know-Nothings. At the close of the gathering it was apparent that the Broderick-Bigler forces had done their work well, for no ticket was nominated. Adjournment marked the end of conventioneering for this year, as a gathering of the Whigs was out of the question.[19]

Soon after the last of the conventions disbanded, the parties turned to the campaign battle. In some ways the 1855 campaign was to be typical of those staged annually in California. The young and vibrant

[17] *Alta California,* Aug. 10 and 11, 1855.

[18] *Alta California,* Sept. 3, 1855.

[19] Davis, *Political Conventions,* pp. 44–45; *Alta California,* Aug. 11, 1855. The inability of the Whigs to assemble a quorum of their state central committee was described in the *Alta California,* May 16, 1855.

Know-Nothings carried the fight to the enemy, organizing in every constituency, and advancing a candidate for every office. The Democratic party campaigned in the manner which had become its trademark. Apparently there was little real understanding of the threat posed by the party of the dark lantern. The magnitude of this error was to be revealed when the final results were recorded.

The night before the balloting took place, former Governor John McDougal presided over a tremendous meeting of the faithful in San Francisco. To the surprise of few in his audience, McDougal bitterly attacked the Know-Nothings. Milton S. Latham, Bigler's rival for the gubernatorial nomination, followed with a polemic ostensibly directed at the American party. In fact, the speech was a thinly disguised attack on the Free Soil movement, for the bulk of the address criticized the Know-Nothings because they were elevating abolitionists like Henry Wilson of Massachusetts to the Senate. When he finished, it was apparent to his auditors that Latham was antagonistic to the party of the Know-Nothings because of its effect in the political arena rather than its philosophy or platform. The nativists were strengthening the political wing of the antislavery movement, Latham in effect declared, and all good Democrats should stand against them. The audience endured his lengthy and heavy-handed oration but displayed little enthusiasm.[20]

Election day in San Francisco was marked by a heavy turnout. The usual excitement and carnival atmosphere prevailed, but there was little violence. A newspaperman who toured the city described it as the best election that had ever been held in San Francisco. This was a rather surprising turn of events, since a number of people had anticipated numerous clashes between the partisans of the American party and foreign-born voters.[21] The Democratic party registered its customary victory in San Francisco, but to the surprise of many and the shock of some Democrats, the Know-Nothings won a convincing statewide victory. The eventual margin for the nativists was just short of five thousand votes out of a total of more than ninety-seven thousand cast. In some of the outlying counties, the Democratic organization produced its usual victory: San Diego posted a margin of 204 to 17; San Luis Obispo, 118 to 45; Santa Barbara, 333 to 39; Tulare, 204 to 140. In the mining counties, however, and in the larger towns,

[20] *Alta California*, Sept. 4, 1855.
[21] *Alta California*, Sept. 6, 1855.

the Know-Nothings won. In Tuolumne, the Democrats trailed 2,391 to 2,805; in El Dorado, the Know-Nothings led 4,929 to 3,928; in Placer County the Know-Nothings' margin was 3,128 to 2,312. In San Bernardino an almost solid Mormon vote was divided 332 to 14 in favor of the Democracy. Evidently Latter-day Saints had little sympathy for these latter-day apostles of bigotry. Nowhere was there evidence that indicated voters had been selective in their balloting, distinguishing between individual members of any of the tickets.[22]

Postelection analyses of the results emphasized the desire for a change that seemed to be a prime characteristic of the California electorate in 1855. This was undoubtedly a part of the story. Another involved the defection of Chivalry Democrats who turned from their traditional allegiance in droves after the nomination of Bigler and the reestablishment of Broderick as a man of influence in the party. This was widely reported by contemporary observers. The open and wide-spread interference of federal officials in California in behalf of Know-Nothing nominees was also noted. "Men holding office under the National Administration openly and wickedly opposed the Democratic ticket," reported an informed observer, who went on to point an accusing finger at "Gift, of the Land Office at Benicia, Joseph McKibben, and Collector Mizner at Benicia, [who] worked openly against the Democratic ticket." Since all such officials of the Pierce administration owed their offices to the influence of William Gwin and John B. Weller, vigorous proponents of Chivalry persuasion, the defection of the federal appointees was to be expected.[23]

Defection of Democratic voters of Chivalry inclination and "open opposition of officials in the Federal service in behalf of the Know-Nothings" was a part of the story. The tide in the mining counties which flowed in favor of the nativists was another significant aspect of the election. The open prejudice of many miners against those of foreign birth or background was a feature of life in the mining counties throughout the fifties. The Know-Nothings tapped this wellspring of prejudice and derived considerable political advantage from it. As Governor Bigler saw it: "The prejudice in the mineral regions was great against foreigners. Many of them holding rich claims . . . the

[22] Election Returns, 1855, Vol. 1759, Archives of the Secretary of State, Sacramento.

[23] *Alta California,* Sept. 7, 1855; John Bigler to William Bigler, Sept. 12 and 15, 1855, Bigler Coll., Pennsylvania Hist. Soc.; Powell, "Southern Influences," p. 95.

opposition promised to turn them out of the mines and give their claims to Americans by birth." The impressive Know-Nothing totals in the mining counties pointed up the effectiveness of such chauvinistic appeals. Bigler also charged fraud and declared he had received a majority of the legal votes, but he failed to contest the results.[24]

The implications of the Know-Nothing victory were tremendous. They concentrated on the legislative ticket, elected a large number of senators and assemblymen, and therefore were in a strong position to elect a Know-Nothing senator to fill the vacant seat of William Gwin. For that matter, the seat of John B. Weller was not safe, for, taking a leaf from Broderick's book, some Know-Nothings began to plan for an election for Weller's seat in the coming session, although his term ran until March 1857. Prominent Know-Nothing candidates began to preen themselves in anticipation. Governor Bigler sadly wrote his brother: "As it is, they . . . have carried everything . . . and will most assuredly elect two U.S. Senators." [25]

The statewide victory of the American party was not accompanied by a collapse of the Democratic party in California. True enough, the Americans had elected their entire ticket, from governor to superintendent of public instruction, and a majority in the legislature. They had defeated the Democracy but by no means destroyed it. As a matter of fact, the California Democracy in losing had increased its total vote by seven thousand over the previous election. Its leaders could look with confidence to the next test of strength.[26]

The Know-Nothings might trumpet their triumph, but the politically informed sensed the ephemeral nature of this political party. Like a hurricane it had swept across the land, destroying the tired political arrangements of the old parties. In the name of reform and purity it had cashed in on widespread disillusionment. It had openly exploited the attitudes of intolerance that lay hidden in a great part of the American citizenry. In the interest of winning votes, it had avoided the discussion of political program—shying stubbornly away from the slavery-extension issue. Success had crowned Know-Nothing efforts, but it was highly unlikely that the peculiar combination of circum-

[24] See John Bigler to William Bigler, Sept. 17, 1855, in which he describes the "fraudulent" means used to defeat the Democratic ticket.

[25] *Alta California,* Sept. 8, 1855; John Bigler to William Bigler, Sept. 12, 1855, Bigler Coll.

[26] Election Returns, 1853, 1855, Vol. 1759, Archives of the Secretary of State, Sacramento.

stances and issues would ever reoccur and allow a duplication of the victory of 1855. On the contrary, as they administered the government of California, the discordant elements of the Know-Nothing coalition would be driven asunder in the course of the debate on candidate, policy, and program. A realignment of political groups in California was in process in 1855, but the Know-Nothings were not to be the end result of the change. The rise and fall of the Know-Nothings in California was to be as rapid as in the nation as a whole.[27]

Had Broderick taken stock after the election of 1855, he would have had good reason to be disturbed and discouraged by the events of the year. Expenses of campaigning had been a substantial burden, and he had suffered, along with most Californians, as a result of the depressed business conditions of the previous eighteen months. The preliminary victory won by him in the convention had been followed by defeat when the nativists swept the state. It meant a serious loss of political positions in the state government, as well as an end to the dispensation of state patronage by John Bigler, which had been so useful in strengthening the Broderick-Bigler faction of the party. Henceforth, state patronage, as well as federal patronage, was to be controlled by his enemies and utilized to curb and undermine the power of the plebeian Democrat and his followers.[28]

In the fall of 1855, Broderick came under fire from a new quarter when James King of William began his spectacular career in journalism in San Francisco. His San Francisco *Daily Evening Bulletin* announced in one of its first numbers that it was to be a crusading newspaper devoted to the public interest. From the beginning it was apparent that David C. Broderick was to be one of its chief targets.[29]

King introduced a new kind of journalism to California. He wielded an intensely personal pen with great skill. A Puritan set down in the midst of a raw and sinful frontier community, he pulled a cloak of

[27] *Alta California,* Sept. 7, 1855; Hurt, passim. Nevins, *Ordeal of the Union,* II, 398–402, covers the national picture. See also Powell, "Southern Influences," p. 96.

[28] San Francisco *Daily Evening Bulletin,* Oct. 16, 1855, commented on Broderick's financial problems. "David C. Broderick File" in Manuscript Collections of the Society of California Pioneers, San Francisco, contains a number of items which testify to the size of his financial burdens. They include a note for $10,000 to Thomas Fallon and a receipt signed by Sam Moss, Jr., and J. Mora Moss indicating receipt of $900 interest, July 10, 1855, on a mortgage of $30,000. Henry P. Haun to William Gwin, Nov. 18, 1855, Appointment Papers, Northern California, 1852–1860, Record Group 56, National Archives, reveals the manner in which the Chivalry continued to utilize federal patronage to strike at Broderick; cf. *Alta California,* Apr. 25, 1856.

[29] *Daily Evening Bulletin,* Oct. 13, 1855.

self-righteousness around himself and pointed an accusing finger at the transgressors. Among his targets were not only Broderick but a number of former associates from the banking community. A self-appointed spokesman for the respectable elements, he used his newspaper as a personal weapon, striking out at a long list of enemies. The *Bulletin* was almost an immediate success. Within months of its founding, it had the largest circulation of any newspaper on the Pacific Coast. The response from the city's population was mixed. King amused, intrigued, interested, angered, puzzled, outraged, alarmed, and antagonized. As each issue of the paper came from the press, it became increasingly apparent that its editor was on a collision course with a number of men and groups in the city. When and with whom the clash would take place was uncertain, but that it would take place was anticipated by many people long before the event.[30]

In the issue of October 13, 1855, a long and detailed indictment of political conditions in San Francisco appeared in the *Bulletin*. The Know-Nothings, once the party of reform, had been transformed into a party of spoils-seeking politicians and was no better than any other party. Money played too big a role in the political arena. Palmer, Cook & Co., allied with Broderick, was a political banking house that played a major role in the corruption of the democratic processes of government. The indictment piled one charge on top of another before coming to a close with an accusation which was libelous on its face: "the most conspicuous of all . . . as high over all his compeers as was Satan among the fallen angels, and as unblushing and determined as the dark fiend, stands the name of David C. Broderick."

This scorching verbal assault was but the first of a series that followed, each devoted to Broderick. No charge of political chicanery was omitted, no phrase of scorn, insult, or innuendo overlooked in these attacks on "David Catiline Broderick," as he was labeled in one editorial. The language was personal and offensive, but specific facts which would justify the accusations were not to be found in the editorials. Confessing he had never met Broderick, King declared that he would like "to be in your company and listen to the words of wisdom and cunning of Tammany Hall as they dropped from your lips." To Broderick's defense of a friend, King replied: "You said the

[30] John Denton Carter, "The San Francisco *Bulletin,* 1855–1865: A Study in the Beginnings of West Coast Journalism," (unpubl. Ph.D. diss., Univ. of Calif., 1941).

owner of the building was a friend of yours and a gentleman. Your friend and a gentleman?" [31]

In issue after issue, the arraignment of Broderick continued. Charge after charge was made in the colorful language of invective that became the hallmark of the *Bulletin.* Conceding on one occasion that Broderick had not personally done the many acts of political corruption, King went on to say, "*His* mind is the Pandora's box from whence spring all these evils. *His* is the fertile genius that creates means for every emergency." Summing up, King declared: "If, on account of the example he has set as a politician, there is one man in their community more blameable than another, or than all others combined, that man is David C. Broderick." [32]

King occasionally turned his wrath on other subjects. In the fall his paper was filled with attacks on the gambling in the city and the houses of ill fame. The latter apparently enjoyed the covert support of the authorities, and King threatened to publish a list of addresses of brothels so that they would be compelled to act. Such a list never appeared in the *Bulletin.* Judge John S. Hager felt King's lash when he failed to handle violators of the law to the satisfaction of the editor of the *Bulletin.* When Hager protested at this assumption of judicial ermine, King brushed him aside with the comment that he was known to be friendly to Palmer, Cook & Co. and a Broderick associate. The incident typified his approach.[33]

A few days later he printed a long editorial which attacked A. A. Selover, who had been associated with Palmer, Cook & Co. It closed with a thinly disguised challenge to Selover. "Mr. Selover, it is said, carries a knife. We carry a pistol. We hope neither will be required, but if this rencontre cannot be avoided, why will Mr. Selover persist in periling the lives of others?" King went on to encourage Selover to meet him, at a place where lives of innocent bystanders would not be endangered. It was an amazing spectacle—an ex-banker, turned journalist, inviting another member of the banking community of San Francisco to meet him in open combat.[34]

Toward the close of the year, Broderick's political activities came under the scrutiny of the editor of the *Bulletin.* Again reporting that

[31] *Daily Evening Bulletin,* Oct. 16, 1855.
[32] *Daily Evening Bulletin,* Oct. 17, 1855.
[33] *Daily Evening Bulletin,* Dec. 3, 1855.
[34] *Daily Evening Bulletin,* Dec. 6, 1855.

Broderick was involved in obtaining an appointment to a lesser position in the police department for a friend, King declared that Broderick promised to an unnamed official, in exchange for his support, "any office that he might wish—Mayor, Governor, or *anything*." The extravagant language made the charge ridiculous. Why Broderick would offer to exchange the governorship for the office of a petty policy official was not explained. On another occasion, King commented on two candidates who were associates of Broderick: "It does not matter how fair the past character of Mr. Campbell or Mr. Shepard may have been, if . . . these men are under the Broderick influence they should not be voted for." Obviously King's feelings toward Broderick were strong and enduring and affected many other things.[35]

As King was launching a new journal in San Francisco, the triumphant Know-Nothings were preparing to launch a new administration. The new order in which the nativists dominated all segments of the state government from the supreme court to the controller in the name of honesty, reform, and virtue was to begin officially when the Know-Nothing legislature came together for its first meeting and for the inauguration of J. Neely Johnson. As the lawmakers wended their way to Sacramento, a number of plans were being formulated.

Since the American party controlled a majority of the legislature, the election of a Know-Nothing as senator seemed assured. Such a prediction, however, did not take into consideration the internal divisions within the party. The American party was riddled with division, for it was composed of sometime Whigs and dissident Democrats who owned a "fictitious allegiance to the new party." The unifying bond of a commonly accepted set of political principles was missing, and the corrosive effect of conflicting ambitions made the American party an unstable political group. Henry Wilson had taken full advantage of this to be elected senator from Massachusetts by a legislature of almost uniform Know-Nothing affiliation. His subsequent career was eloquent testimony that his flirtation with the "Americans" in 1855 was based on naked expediency. Broderick and Gwin would find much to exploit in the division and suspicion among the Know-Nothings. While some observers were still bemused by the Broderick-Gwin rivalry, the more significant aspect of the situation was the manner in

[35] *Daily Evening Bulletin,* Dec. 19 and 27, 1855; San Francisco *Fireman's Journal,* Nov. 24 and Dec. 8, 1855, edited by Marcus D. Boruck, took issue with James King of William on the role that Broderick played in the city's political affairs.

which the two chieftains and their followers began to work together.[36]

Since both houses of the legislature had to be persuaded to enter a convention, the Know-Nothings turned to this problem first. The Assembly was easily convinced of the need to have an election—a Know-Nothing caucus blazed the way by selecting Henry S. Foote as their candidate. In the Senate an insurmountable obstacle appeared in the person of Wilson Flint, senator from San Francisco. In Flint's eyes Foote was the personification of the slave interest, and he was determined to block his election. The former senator of Mississippi, dubbed "Hangman" Foote when he had threatened a congressional speaker with hanging if he dared to come to Mississippi with his abolitionist doctrines, made a strenuous effort but eventually was defeated when a resolution to postpone the election until January 1857 was passed. Flint played a key role. The Know-Nothings stormed, but there was little more they could do, for they had been bested in the parliamentary battle. A few years later, Wilson Flint was a prominent member of the Republican party and Henry S. Foote was a senator—of the Confederate States of America.[37]

Broderick and Gwin were delighted by the outcome, for it meant that both would have another chance at the seat—perhaps under more favorable circumstances. Their elation was not shared by all of their followers. As one of Gwin's supporters put it, "I trust in God your refusal to go into the election of Senator this year may not result in his [Foote's] and Broderick's election next year. I much fear it." [38]

The unity of action between Broderick and Gwin was not to endure, for shortly after the senatorial question had been decided, the two factions of the party met in combat to see which would control the organization in San Francisco. Once more Broderick and his associates prevailed in the election to select delegates to the upcoming state convention of the party, but this time the Chivalry decided to strike back. In late February, having lost the San Francisco delegation to Broderick's organization, the Chivalry announced their position and future course in a manifesto entitled "Address of the Central Committee of the Reformed Democracy." The address spelled out the

[36] Bancroft, *History of California,* VI, 697–698; Nevins, *Ordeal of the Union,* II, 342–343; *Daily Evening Bulletin,* Jan. 15, 1856; C. L. Scott to J. W. Mandeville, Jan. 19, 1856, and Albert N. Francisco to Mandeville, Jan. 24, 1856, Mandeville Coll., Huntington Lib.

[37] Bancroft, *History of California,* VI, 698–699. *Senate Journal,* 1856, pp. 160–168, contains the official record of the debate and voting in the Senate. *Alta California,* Mar. 7, 1856, analyzes the vote in the Assembly.

[38] James Watkins to James W. Mandeville, Feb. 26, 1856, Mandeville Coll.

manner in which Broderick controlled the party, declared the reformers could no longer work with him and his associates, and announced the formation of a new party. A dozen prominent members of the Chivalry of San Francisco fixed their names to the address. James King of William endorsed the proposal.[39]

Simply announcing that a group was the legitimate and official Democratic party in San Francisco was in effect an attempt to get the fruits of victory that had eluded the Chivalry at the polls. Broderick was not inclined to concede anything. Thus when the state convention assembled in March to select delegates to the national convention, the stage was set for a showdown. The Chivalry approached the meeting with confidence, for the state committee was chaired by Benjamin F. Washington, close friend and political ally of Gwin and a prominent member of the Chivalry. It was believed by many observers that Washington would begin the process which would end in Broderick's delegation being replaced by the Chivalry delegation.[40]

To the surprise of many observers and the chagrin of the Chivalry, the committee on credentials, by a unanimous vote, seated the Broderick delegates. "The Purifiers," in a surprising show of cordiality, accepted the decision, and their magnanimity led the convention to invite them to remain as observers. A spokesman for the group, James O'Meara, political aide of Gwin, thanked the convention and announced that henceforth there would be no dissension in the Democracy of San Francisco. A number of skeptics must have found it difficult to refrain from openly airing their disbelief.[41]

The convention went on to write resolutions which were intended to reflect the views of Democrats of California on important questions. Little debate was occasioned by the collection of broad platitudes that came from the committee on resolutions. Much of it consisted of a restatement of time-honored slogans of the Democracy, little changed from the days of Old Hickory. "An undeviating adherence to the universal standard of value of gold and silver, that honest industry may receive its just reward" read one resolution that might have been framed by Old Bullion Benton himself. Another declared for the principle of "popular sovereignty . . . the sheet-anchor of our hopes,

[39] The announcement of the formation of the new group appeared in the *Daily Evening Bulletin,* Feb. 27, 1856; the text of the manifesto they issued to justify their course is in the issue of Mar. 3, 1856.

[40] *Alta California,* Mar. 6, 1856.

[41] *Alta California,* Mar. 6 and 7, 1856, carried detailed accounts of the decision of the credentials committee and the debate sparked by it.

and . . . the only sure means of perpetuating our government through all time to come." The Pierce administration was endorsed, to the obvious discomfort of some of the delegates.[42]

The matter of instructions to the delegates sparked a heated debate, and again the antagonists were drawn from the Free Soil faction and the Chivalry faction. Bigler spoke for the Free Soilers, advocating a commitment of the California delegation to James Buchanan. Volney E. Howard of the Chivalry spoke in opposition. His long speech was filled with lukewarm praise of Buchanan and included an elaborate rationalization in favor of an uninstructed delegation. As Bigler and Broderick sensed the favorable response to Howard, soon translated into votes to lay Bigler's motion on the table, they attempted a strategic retreat. Bigler attempted to withdraw the motion to instruct, but the chairman, James W. Mandeville, associate and aide of Gwin, declared it could not be withdrawn once the vote had commenced. The San Francisco delegation voted against the motion to lay on the table, but it carried nevertheless. California's delegation to Cincinnati was not to be committed to Buchanan. However, while Buchanan did not receive the benefit of an ironclad commitment, his candidacy received a warm endorsement in one resolution which declared that it was the "ardent desire [of the Convention] for the nomination and triumphant election of the Hon. James Buchanan." The election of delegates to the convention took place shortly after the last echo of the debate on resolutions had passed away.[43]

Just before adjournment, William Van Voorhies returned to the situation of the divided party in San Francisco. The competing organizations should resign, Van Voorhies declared, and a new election should be held to determine new leaders for the party. This proposal met with the heated and vociferous opposition of Broderick and his associates. Several attempts were made to adjourn, but each time the delegates refused. As the debate on the proposal continued, it became more violent and emotional. Threats to walk out were aired. Soon it was difficult to follow the debate as shouting and livid delegates competed. Van Voorhies restored a measure of order by withdrawing his resolution; shortly thereafter the convention adjourned. Broderick and his followers were still in command of the legal machinery of the Democracy of San Francisco.[44]

[42] Davis, *Political Conventions,* pp. 56–57.
[43] *Alta California,* Mar. 7, 1856; Davis, *Political Conventions,* pp. 55–58.
[44] *Alta California,* Mar. 8, 1856.

CHAPTER EIGHT

The Vigilance Committee of 1856

In the volatile city beside the Golden Gate, events were moving rapidly toward a crisis and the creation of the Vigilance Committee of 1856. The episode had a tremendous impact on the career of Broderick, the city, and the political history of California. At the outset it was not a political movement in the usual sense, possessed of a program and intent on utilizing political means to capture control of the city. In the course of its existence, however, the committee became a unique political organization.

In effect, the Committee of Vigilance was a semirevolutionary movement which seized power in the city by means of a *coup d'état.* Having gotten control, it set about the work of justifying what it had done and reforming and purifying the body politic. Utilizing freely whatever means—illegal, legal, and extralegal—were deemed necessary, the committee sought to eliminate the "political dissolute." It placed its enduring opponents in that category, pursued them, intimidated them, and banished them so that they would no longer be a political factor of importance. In effect, the committee became a "political engine" which was utilized by some of its members to strike at Broderick and his associates. Chivalry-minded politicians were prominent in this effort to smite Broderick and his Free Soil followers, and they were joined by others whom he had bested in the political arena.[1]

The chain of events which brought the Vigilance Committee into

[1] Gerritt W. Ryckman Statement, pp. 18–20, MS in Bancroft Lib.; Broderick to Pablo de la Guerra, Sept. 26, 1856, De la Guerra Coll., Santa Barbara Mission Archives; James O'Meara, *The Vigilance Committee of 1856* (San Francisco, 1887), p. 57; Etta Olive Powell, "Southern Influences in California Politics" (unpubl. M.A. thesis, Univ. of Calif., 1929), p. 97.

being began in the previous winter when Charles Cora shot and killed William Richardson, United States marshal for northern California. Cora, a well-known gambler, had been friendly with Richardson, but the two men had quarreled in public when Richardson objected to the presence of Cora's current ladylove at the theater. Several days later Richardson sought out Cora in a bar, and the quarrel was resumed. Richardson invited Cora outside. Exactly what led to the shooting is disputed, although the preponderance of objective evidence indicates that Cora was trying to evade trouble. In any case, Richardson was fatally wounded and Cora was led away to jail.[2]

Had the principals been ordinary men, the gambler would have been tried and probably convicted of manslaughter or something other than murder. They were not ordinary men, however, and these were not ordinary times. Richardson was a man of importance, a figure in the Democratic party, a leader of the Chivalry who had received his appointment to a lucrative and important position thanks to the good offices of William Gwin. Cora, on the other hand, was a professional gambler and an unsavory character generally. In spite of the evidence which seemed to indicate that Richardson was the aggressor, Cora had little chance of evading punishment. Belle Cora managed to secure for her sweetheart the services of Edward Dickinson Baker and James A. McDougall. Baker was a gifted orator and able attorney who had learned the craft of a trial lawyer from his closest friend, Abraham Lincoln. Baker prepared carefully, exploited the facts which tended to show Richardson was the aggressor, and succeeded in obtaining a hung jury. On one occasion, a plurality of the jury was bent on acquitting Cora, so well had Baker done his work. It was a moral victory of the first order for Cora's attorney.[3]

In a bitter editorial entitled "12 O'Clock Noon—Hung Be the Heavens with Black," James King of William castigated the jury, the law, the court, and the attorneys in such language as: "The money of

[2] O'Meara, *The Vigilance Committee of 1856,* pp. 12–14, reports the clash.

[3] William Gwin to Franklin Pierce, March [?], 1853, California Appointment Papers, Record Group 56, National Archives, wherein Gwin, recommending Richardson, described the office as "with the exception of that of Collector at San Francisco . . . the most important office in the state." The records of the trial were destroyed in the San Francisco Fire of 1906, but the testimony, published in detail in the *Daily Evening Bulletin,* Jan. 15, 1856, clearly establishes the fact that Richardson's aggressive conduct was directly responsible for the clash. O'Meara, *The Vigilance Committee of 1856,* pp. 14–16, reports Baker's acceptance of the case and the skillful manner in which he handled it. O'Meara knew both men, was with Richardson immediately prior to the shooting, and agrees that Richardson was the aggressor.

the gambler and the prostitute has succeeded and Cora has another respite!" The jury had been divided, four for murder, six for manslaughter, and two for acquittal. On the first ballot four had voted for outright acquittal. Conceding that the jury had been packed—with leading and responsible and honest citizens—King declared, "Gamblers and harlots will rejoice but honest men will lament what has been done by this jury." The relevance of the statement that gamblers and harlots would rejoice to the evaluation of the jury and the court was not explained. The jury was not by its nature, nor by the traditions of Anglo-Saxon jurisprudence, supposed to do anything but consider the evidence presented to it. The evidence in this case, even as edited by James King of William, clearly indicated that mitigating circumstances were involved and that Cora was not guilty of murder in the first degree.[4]

Cora remained in custody for a second trial. James King of William greeted the news of the appointment of Richardson's successor, James Y. McDuffie, as the new United States marshal for the northern district with a savage outburst. McDuffie was attacked as a onetime gambler and associate of Cora who was "an illegal brother-in-law of Cora since he had consorted with the sister of Belle Cora." Then, jumbling his opponents together, the editor of the *Bulletin* declared: "Anything that could be done to rid the city of the influence of Broderick and his followers and remove this gambler from office should be done." When the new marshal learned of the accusation, his response was in language familiar to James King: "The charge is as false and foul as the dark corruption which rankles about the heart" of the accuser. Vituperation had elicited a response in kind.[5]

Placing Broderick in the same category with his bitter and enduring enemies was typical of the editor of the *Bulletin*. Airing a charge in public print that one of the more important federal officials "consorted" with a harlot was also typical. Such an approach sold newspapers, but it did little to inform the public as to the underlying realities of the political world of San Francisco and California. To a charge by

[4] *Daily Evening Bulletin,* Jan. 17, 1856. The San Francisco *Fireman's Journal,* Jan. 19, 1856, defended the jury and its action; James King of William conceded that the jury was composed of "upright and honorable citizens" and revealed the division within the jury in the *Daily Evening Bulletin,* Jan. 18, 1856. The San Francisco *Post,* Nov. 4, 1882, p. 2, col. 1, published a list of the members of the jury.

[5] *Daily Evening Bulletin,* Feb. 13 and 14, 1856. McDuffie's response was reprinted in the *Daily Evening Bulletin,* Mar. 18, 1856.

the mayor that he edited the paper in this fashion to attract readers and to realize "pecuniary gain," King retorted in his columns: "Why, the stupid old ass, what else does he suppose any man follows business for?" [6]

In issue after issue the fighting editor flailed away at a growing list of enemies, which included Palmer, Cook & Co., A. A. Cohen, David C. Broderick, the Bowie Knife party, and Andrew J. Butler. Even Thomas Paine, of *Common Sense* fame, was castigated in a lengthy article that incorporated detailed statements by Aaron Burr, although Paine's relationship to the political situation in the city was not explained. The attacks mounted in number, frequency, and intensity. In the course of the first eight months of the *Bulletin,* King assailed a wide variety of people in language that fairly steamed. Those eight months had seen the establishment of the *Bulletin* on a prosperous basis, but they also had seen its editor acquire enemies by the hundreds. As one of King's more renowned defenders reported:

> James King of William had aroused against him not only a large class but several classes of people in San Francisco and in California. He had savagely, though most always justly castigated the class that upheld, supported or apologised for any of the excesses or irregularities in political affairs and brought a large share of the class in sharp antagonism with himself, not only officially but personally. He aroused a large Catholic influence hostile to himself in his strictures on some of the acts of the Catholic clergy. He had arrayed almost the entire Southern element against him, because of his severity on them and his denunciations of them as the Chivalry, and the unworthy Chivalry who undertook to manage the affairs of the state and the coast. All these elements, separate and combined, were really inimical to King, and he had himself, many personal bitter enemies.[7]

[6] The mayor was James Van Ness; the comment appeared in the *Daily Evening Bulletin,* Apr. 3, 1856. Charles M. Lane, "James King of William" (unpubl. M.A. thesis, Univ. of Calif., 1958), pp. 117–118, concluded: "A study of the *Bulletin* cannot but indicate that King used the newspaper more as a personal weapon than as a champion of justice and morality." His weapons "were spite, personal abuse, animosity, bigotry, rumor and emotion. Weapons which he used with impunity and with little regard where they fell or whom they hurt."

[7] William T. Coleman Statement, p. 45, MS in Bancroft Lib. The *Daily Evening Bulletin,* Mar. 29, 1856, published an attack on the Chivalry; attacked Thomas Paine, Jan. 30, 1856; printed an anonymous letter attacking Broderick, Jan. 19, 1856; printed a second attack on Broderick, Feb. 13, 1856; and turned its editorial guns on Palmer, Cook & Co., in its issue of Mar. 7, 1856.

One of the principal targets of the *Bulletin* was Palmer, Cook & Co., which was described as a political banking house that tried to obtain deposits of public funds. It used objectionable means, and the man it used, asserted King, was David C. Broderick. King wrote of banking and politics from personal experience. A pioneer banker in San Francisco as a partner of Jacob R. Snyder, former state senator, he had once been named by Broderick as a responsible member of the financial community of the city. When his venture with Snyder got into difficulty, King joined the firm of Adams & Co. In 1855, along with a number of banks, Adams & Co. was put under considerable pressure. The worsening situation of the firm was known to some in the city, who expected it to close its doors, but King reassured depositors of its solvency until noon of the day it closed forever. A great many people lost money in the failure of Adams & Co., and King's role was widely criticized.[8]

The failure of Adams & Co. was followed by prolonged litigation concerning the disposal of the assets of the bankrupt firm and the role of various people associated with it. The receiver, A. A. Cohen, came under the attack of the *Bulletin,* and a spate of charges and countercharges was exchanged. James King was one of the principal figures—accused and accuser—a member of the banking community who not only reported the news but made the news. King's dislike of Palmer, Cook & Co. colored his attitude toward anything associated with the firm. A bill to consolidate the city and county government of San Francisco received the tentative approval of the *Bulletin,* but when its editor learned that Palmer, Cook & Co. favored it, the newspaper announced its firm opposition. Although he printed an analysis which indicated that Palmer, Cook & Co. and Broderick were no longer political allies, King thereafter frequently referred to the alliance as a fact.[9]

Occasionally the attacks on Palmer, Cook & Co. took the form of appeals and warnings to depositors to withdraw their savings. A frequent feature of the *Bulletin* was a dire prediction of financial

[8] O'Meara, *The Vigilance Committee of 1856,* pp. 35 ff. See *Daily Evening Bulletin,* Mar. 7 and Apr. 5, 1856, for typical attacks on Palmer, Cook & Co.

[9] O'Meara, *The Vigilance Committee of 1856,* pp. 35 ff.; *Daily Evening Bulletin,* Feb. 27, Apr. 1 and 5, 1856, published material on the litigation that arose out of the liquidation of Adams & Co. San Francisco *Call,* May 7, 1882, p. 1, col. 1, reports the James King of William and Palmer, Cook & Co. feud in detail.

disaster for the firm—a most unusual means whereby a former banker bludgeoned his former associates. An air of tragedy hung about some of his pronouncements, and at times the audacity of the editor of the *Bulletin* was breathtaking. On one occasion the readers of the newspaper found the following in its columns:

> If these fellows (Selover, Cohen, Stillman, Broderick, Palmer, Cook and Company crowd . . . among them some of the most dastardly scoundrels this city can produce) are really determined to attack the Editor of the *Bulletin,* why don't they do it at once and be done with it? Why keep everybody in suspense? Here we have been carrying a pistol for nearly three months, because of the braggadocio bullying of this crowd, until we are heartily sick of it. We don't want to carry weapons. If the fuss must come off, let it come at once and be over with! [10]

The long-awaited clash came in mid-May, but it was not precipitated by a representative of the Broderick camp or by one of King's favorite targets. The assault was made instead by James P. Casey, a supervisor of San Francisco. Casey, onetime associate of Broderick, had changed political alliances and was a clearly identified member of the Chivalry organization in the city. The assault was provoked when Casey's criminal record was brought to the attention of the editor of the *Bulletin* by one of Casey's enemies. Casey appealed to King to suppress the matter and warned of drastic consequences if the *Bulletin* printed the story. King scouted Casey's warning and printed a story which declared that Casey had been indicted and convicted of larceny in New York City and since then had "stuffed himself through the ballot box" of San Francisco. The story was similar to dozens of others that King had printed, but unlike the others, this one elicited a violent response.[11]

In late afternoon, as King made his way homeward, he encountered Casey. Exactly what happened in the next moment may never be determined, for almost all the versions of the encounter are colored by individual animosities and allegiances. According to the story told by Casey's partisans, he warned King to defend himself, and when King moved as if to draw his weapon, Casey drew his own and shot King. According to the friends of the editor, Casey waylaid King and murdered the defenseless unarmed man whose sole offense was printing

[10] *Daily Evening Bulletin,* Jan. 6, 1856.

[11] O'Meara, *The Vigilance Committee of 1856,* pp. 24–27; *Daily Evening Bulletin,* May 14, 1856.

the truth about corrupt politics and politicians. The latter version was to become a part of the standard accounts of the period, but there is reason to believe that there was more than this to the story.[12]

Regardless of how it was accomplished, the badly wounded man was made as comfortable as possible, and while his doctors tended him, his assailant was hustled off to the county jail. Physicians applied their skill and the city waited in suspenseful quiet. The citizenry mulled over the implications of the incident while King fought for his life. Despite the best efforts of the attending physicians, life slowly slipped away, and soon the citizens of San Francisco were discussing the death of the crusading editor of the *Bulletin*.[13]

Had King been murdered in the quiet of the night and the police sent to ferret out his murderer, they would have had a difficult task, for the suspects would have been legion. There was no need to search for his killer, however, for James Casey was safely lodged in the county jail. There he was to remain until members of the Vigilance Committee assumed control of him. Together with Charles Cora, Casey was taken from the county jail and given a trial of sorts in the headquarters of the Vigilance Committee. Both men were convicted and sentenced to be hanged. As the funeral cortege of James King of William made its way through the city to Lone Mountain Cemetery, Casey and Cora were hanged outside the headquarters building of the vigilantes. Cora's last hours featured his marriage to his sweetheart, and she came forward to claim his body for burial. Casey was permitted to address the throng that witnessed the execution and made an impassioned address in which he declared that his actions were those of men of his time who were attacked in the way that he had been assailed by James King of William.[14]

The killing of the editor of the *Bulletin* was the dramatic incident which sparked the resurrection of the Vigilance Committee of 1851. In a matter of days, the efficient organization of the vigilantes had taken over the city of San Francisco—pushing into the background

[12] A version of the encounter as reported by a contemporary appears in C. E. Montgomery, "Lost Journals of a Pioneer," *Overland Monthly*, 2nd Ser., VIII (1886), 275 ff. King declared in print that he was in the habit of carrying arms; see *Daily Evening Bulletin*, Jan. 6, 1856. James M. McDonald, "Recollections of Early Days in San Francisco," p. 4, typescript in Bancroft Lib., states King was armed when he encountered Casey; see also Sacramento *Union*, May 16, 1856.

[13] Hubert H. Bancroft, *Popular Tribunals* (San Francisco, 1887), II, 50–51.

[14] Bancroft, *Popular Tribunals*, II, 226–243.

the legitimate authorities. The committee had executive, legislative, judicial, and military branches, and in effect it assumed control of the city. Having seized control, it set out to purify the body politic. The work began with the execution of Cora and Casey.[15]

The committee in 1851 had been concerned primarily with crime and criminals, but the committee of 1856 was to concern itself with other matters. The first committee pictured the city as one in which crime and criminals made it unsafe for the law-abiding citizen and his property; the committee of 1856 was primarily concerned with political crime and political criminals. The body politic was in the grip of unscrupulous operators who manipulated the government and the courts to advance their own interests at the expense of the citizenry. The body politic needed cleansing, and the processes of democratic government were in need of reformation so as to restore civic virtue.[16]

Ostensibly the committee had to be reorganized because the system of courts and law enforcement in San Francisco had broken down. The Cora trial was but one of a number of examples of the manner in which the judicial system had failed to render justice—according to the critics of the courts. In different times, the Cora trial might have been interpreted as a manifestation of the strength of the courts of the city. The trial in reality reflected little discredit on the courts, for in spite of the fact that the defendant was an unsavory character and the victim a United States marshal, the trial had been conducted in the best traditions of Anglo-Saxon jurisprudence. The evidence clearly indicated that a plea of self-defense was justified. This was apparently the considered view of the jury, which was filled with men of the highest personal reputation in the city. In the face of a press which clamored for conviction, twelve good men and true resisted. The result did not indicate a breakdown in the judicial process or a general failure of the jury system but almost the opposite. The jury's failure to

[15] Bancroft, *Popular Tribunals,* II, 267–283; Bancroft's work is one of the standard accounts of the Vigilance Committee of 1856. A different interpretation is that of James O'Meara; manifestly critical of the committee, it must be taken into consideration by anyone who is interested in a full picture. Cf. Ethel M. Tiennemann, "The Opposition to the San Francisco Vigilance Committee of 1856" (unpubl. M.A. thesis, Univ. of Calif., 1941).

[16] The political *raison d'être* of the committee is set forth in its constitution. See Henry Steele Commager, *Documents of American History* (New York, 1949), pp. 338–339, for the complete text; note especially the preamble and Article 1. Cf. O'Meara, *The Vigilance Committee of 1856,* pp. 35 ff. The political nature of the work of the committee is described in Powell, "Southern Influences," p. 97.

agree placed the prisoner in the hands of the county sheriff for a second trial, but that second trial was never held.[17]

Having initiated the work of reforming the city by hanging Cora and Casey, the Vigilance Committee turned to affairs of a political nature. The first step was the gathering of evidence on the manner in which the political processes of the city had been corrupted. The second step was the apprehension and banishment of the men who were implicated. The final step was to be left to the people. Once the shoulder-strikers, ballot-box stuffers, and wire-pullers had been removed, the good men and true of the city would resume control of the government.[18]

The members of the committee approached their tasks with crusading enthusiasm. Masses of evidence were gathered to prove that irregularities had characterized the operations of the political system of San Francisco, and a major effort was made to prove that the Broderick wing of the Democratic party was responsible. The fact that many of the Vigilance Committee members were drawn from the ranks of political groups bested by Broderick in the past may account for the anti-Broderick orientation of the committee. Many of his enemies of Whig, Know-Nothing, and Chivalry affiliation were in the ranks of the committee.[19]

In the final analysis the vigilantes failed to prove that Broderick and his associates were responsible for the alleged irregularities. The failure reflected the paucity of evidence, for much of what the committee's investigators assembled was faulty, insignificant, or not related to Broderick. More often than not, charges were made but no proof presented. For example, in 1852 it was charged by an election judge that a number of Broderick followers had destroyed the ballots cast. No proof to support this accusation was forthcoming. A special committee of the vigilantes turned to a close examination of the 1856 elections and discovered a number of irregularities. Unfortunately for those bent on blackening Broderick's reputation, the irregularities in

[17] Significantly, though denied counsel of his choosing and prosecuted, represented, and adjudged by the executive committee of the Vigilance Committee, Cora was convicted by a "bare majority." Members of the committee which conducted the trial subsequently expressed their belief that Cora acted in self-defense. See Bancroft, *Popular Tribunals,* II, 233, 241.

[18] The San Francisco Committee of Vigilance of 1856 Papers in the Huntington Library furnish abundant evidence of the nature of the attempt to change the political milieu of San Francisco.

[19] Broderick to Pablo de la Guerra, Sept. 26, 1856, De la Guerra Coll.

the stronghold of the plebeian politician were of a minor and insignificant nature. Such items were included as a difference of thirteen between the number of ballots cast and the number of ballots counted. To save themselves the trouble of recounting the hundreds of ballots cast, the officials divided the thirteen ballots between the candidates. No difference in the outcome resulted from such an irregular procedure.[20]

Another collection of documents was impressive in quantity, but a large part of it was meaningless, and the individual in question, an associate of Broderick, could not have been convicted of any crime. The voluminous file on Jacob Ritchie indicated that a major effort had been made but only limited success realized. One witness, who gave evidence that promised to tie Broderick in with a trick ballot box, was a trying disappointment when it was reported that his wife had accused him of incest. An investigating committee looked into the matter and recommended that he be dropped from membership in the Vigilance Committee.[21]

Another affidavit filed with the committee met some of the requirements of a legal deposition and seemed to furnish evidence upon which the committee could base an action against Broderick. Upon examination it was discovered to be a summary of a conversation overheard in a bar, in which the chief participant was laboring under the stress attendant to being notified by the committee that he was to leave California subject to execution if he returned. In other words it was hearsay, and a court observing the most rudimentary rules of evidence would have barred its presentation and perhaps rebuked the member of the bar who offered it in evidence.[22]

The committee, of course, was not bound by rules of evidence or the niceties of legal procedures. The objective was to change the political system that had brought one victory after another to Broderick. There was no mistaking the political orientation of the committee and its members, for its concentration on Broderick and his associates left little doubt as to what the committee was out to do. The men

[20] Houseman Statement, MS, Report of W. C. Phelton, C. S. Biden, and J. C. Flanders in "Papers Relating to Ballot Box Stuffing," San Francisco Committee of Vigilance of 1856 Papers.

[21] Jacob Ritchie File, San Francisco Committee of Vigilance of 1856 Papers; B. F. Moses to the Committee, July 26, 1856, in the same collection. Moses was dismissed from the committee on Aug. 15, 1856.

[22] Affidavit of Anthony J. Sansoni and L. A. Degroote, MS in "Papers Regarding Ballot Box Stuffing" in San Francisco Committee of Vigilance of 1856 Papers.

banished by the committee, under threat of execution if they returned, were principally the followers of Broderick and Democrats to a man. The fine distinctions made by the vigilantes that enabled them to ferret out wire-pullers, shoulder-strikers, and ballot-box stuffers only among Democrats were never explained. To direct accusations only at Democrats reflected the political animus of the accusers. As one of the better-informed observers of the committee reported, "It was a noticeable discrimination; no reason for it was apparent or expressed on the part of the Executive Committee." [23]

Broderick was not inclined to concede the battleground to this new organization, however formidable its power and influence. He had for a time hesitated, apparently uncertain of his response to the vigilantes. Time was running out for him, for one by one his political aides in the city were being caught up in the dragnet of the Vigilance Committee. Others cringed before the awesome power of the committee, which successfully defied the city, county, and state authorities, but Broderick was inclined to fight back.[24]

While Broderick considered a course of action and aided in the escape of Judge Tom McGowan, one of the men the committee was especially interested in finding, the committee struck down a number of his associates. "The intelligence, the respectability, and the weight of the city were with the committee" and evidently determined to end the system which brought victory to Broderick and his associates in one election after another. Terence Kelly pleaded for fair play, pointing out that the bulk of the testimony against him was given by a single unsavory character. "It is unfair that I should be deprived of liberty by reason of any statement which such a fellow might make," Kelly declared, and once more he asked for a hearing: "I again solicit an examination." The terse notation on his letter, "Convict on evidence," indicates that his efforts were unavailing.[25]

[23] O'Meara, *The Vigilance Committee of 1856,* p. 45; *Alta California,* July 10, 1856, and July 17, 1857; Powell, "Southern Influences," p. 97.

[24] Bancroft, *Popular Tribunals,* II, 324. It was reported to the committee that Broderick shielded James King of William; see H. M. Snyder Statement, MS in San Francisco Committee of Vigilance of 1856 Papers. Theodore Hittell, *History of California* (San Francisco, 1898), IV, 194, describes the clash of Broderick and the committee; cf. John S. Hittell, *A History of the City of San Francisco* (San Francisco, 1878), p. 295.

[25] Kelly to Members of the Executive Committee, June 19, 1856, in "Papers Regarding Ballot Box Stuffing," San Francisco Committee of Vigilance of 1856 Papers.

Among other men who ran afoul of the committee were Martin Gallagher, Billy Carr, and Billy Mulligan. Gallagher and Carr were boatmen who earned a precarious living on the waterfront carrying passengers and cargo to and fro. They were husky men, usually to be found in the service of Broderick. Their brawn was utilized in political meetings, conventions, and elections in the interests of Broderick and his faction of the Democratic party. Every major political group in the city had a number of such men who performed in a similar capacity. Mulligan was "the incarnation of fearlessness, fight and frolic." His loyalties were real and lasting, and "the world's wealth couldn't seduce or bribe him from the support of the men he liked." He had once served as city treasurer and "fully accounted for every dollar that he received." There was nothing in Mulligan's background to justify banishment except his association with Broderick.[26]

The trial or hearing accorded by the Vigilance Committee was that in name only, and in some cases banishment was decreed without the formality of a trial. Thomas Maguire, a prominent member of the theatrical community in San Francisco, was banished without a trial or hearing. He and his wife had shared their home with Broderick and were among the closest of his friends. Maguire complained bitterly of his conviction in a letter to the committee, pointing out that he had lived in the city since 1849 and had never carried weapons or been anything but a law-abiding citizen. "I have been a hardworking, industrious man, endeavoring in all things to deal justly with my fellow men," he wrote. Maguire's deadline was extended for two weeks to July 20, 1856, but then apparently forgotten, for he remained in the city for years to come as an important figure who gave such thespians as David Belasco and William O'Neill their start. When the committee struck at Maguire, they were coming close to Broderick himself.[27]

The committee moved against one after another of the lesser figures in the Broderick camp, but the chieftain himself escaped unscathed. It was well known that he was the spearhead of the opposition, the tireless organizer who attempted to put iron in the backbone of the authorities and sought to consolidate opposition. For weeks the committee and its chief opponent fought at arm's length, the vigilantes

[26] O'Meara, *The Vigilance Committee of 1856,* pp. 47–49.

[27] Maguire to Executive Committee of the Committee of Vigilance, June 28, 1856, Investigating Committee Files, San Francisco Committee of Vigilance of 1856 Papers.

leaving no stone unturned in their efforts to prove that Broderick was chiefly responsible for the political corruption that allegedly characterized the city government. Apparently the diligence of the committeemen was rewarding, for on July 19, 1856, an order for Broderick's arrest was issued.[28]

Broderick's arrest was to be but one of a number scheduled for that time. It was a fateful moment in the career of Broderick, for if he were to be arrested and subsequently handled as so many others had been, his political career might be irrevocably damaged. In his hour of need, Broderick turned to Gerritt W. Ryckman, a prominent leader of the Vigilance Committee of 1851, who had played a lesser role in the Committee of 1856. Exactly what passed between them is unknown, but as Ryckman later recalled, Broderick pointed out the damage to his political career that would ensue from summary arrest, trial, and punishment by the vigilantes. Ryckman was asked to intervene in Broderick's behalf, for if he were to be arrested and "manhandled by the Committee, it would destroy his popularity as an aspirant for senatorial honors." [29]

Ryckman proceeded to committee headquarters, where he met with a number of policy makers of the group and demanded that they rescind the order for Broderick's arrest. "I told you you were going to make a political engine of it. If you don't countermand that order for the arrest of Broderick, I will tap the bell and order an opposition and arrest every damn one of you" were the imperious directions of Ryckman. Broderick's fate hung in the balance while this threat was weighed. The decision to revoke was finally reached, and thereby the various serious disturbances, inside as well as outside the committee, which an arrest of Broderick would have precipitated, were avoided.[30] Broderick did appear at the Vigilance Committee headquarters, however, for interrogation. He stayed but a short time and later explained that he had gone voluntarily to give evidence relating to the character of one of the prisoners of the Vigilance Committee. Apparently the committee handled him with care, for "any harm to him, by that body, would have been the occasion of very serious trouble." [31]

[28] Gerritt W. Ryckman Statement, pp. 18–20, MS in Bancroft Lib.; Hittell, *History of California,* III, 618.

[29] Ryckman Statement, pp. 18–20.

[30] Ryckman Statement, pp. 18–20; O'Meara, *The Vigilance Committee of 1856,* pp. 53–56; Hittell, *History of California,* IV, 194.

[31] O'Meara, *The Vigilance Committee of 1856,* pp. 53–56.

Sometime after his interrogation, Broderick came to the conclusion that his efforts could be better spent in this presidential election year on the political hustings in the interior of California. The committee was in full control of the city, and despite Broderick's efforts, no serious opposition to it had appeared. City and county officials had confined their opposition to the committee to refusing the demands made on them to resign their offices. The governor had taken several positions toward the committee and demonstrated in the process a kind of inept leadership that strengthened the committee. The vigilantes apparently constituted the only organization with a sense of purpose and the means of executing its will. Under the circumstances, there was little to keep Broderick in the city and a number of reasons that called him to the countryside.[32]

It was not the time for a political leader to retire from the field and await results, for the air was thick with political change. A presidential election was in the offing, and important political matters were to be decided. A legislature was to be chosen which would in turn select two United States senators. State and county conventions were to be held where the preliminary battles within the party would be fought. The political leader who would strengthen his wing of the party and enhance his own chances for a bright political future could not afford to remain in San Francisco.

The political situation in California in the summer of 1856 was fluid, complex, and bright with promise for the Democratic party. The Know-Nothings still clung to their positions of power in the state government, but it was apparent that they were treading on the heels of the Whigs, who had shortly before passed into oblivion. For a time, the party of the dark lantern had displayed surprising strength. It had capitalized on the internal disunity of the California Democracy and widespread disillusionment with the old parties to win surprising triumphs in 1855. The situation had changed sharply in the intervening year, for now Democrats were united, the question of the extension of slavery momentarily quieted. The same question was at work in the Know-Nothing organization, dividing it into hostile factions, tearing it asunder. When the national convention of the party tried to

[32] Most accounts of the committee emphasize the ineptitude of the governor, J. Neely Johnson, elected as a Know-Nothing in 1855, as well as the unity and single-mindedness of the leading members of the committee. See Bancroft, *Popular Tribunals,* II, Ch. xx, for a picture of Johnson's reaction to the committee, and Ch. xix for a detailed description of the manner in which the committee operated.

sweep the issue of slavery under the rug by refusing to take a stand on it, the northern wing of the American party walked out of the convention. Thereafter, Know-Nothings drifted into the newly formed Republican party in the nation as well as in California.[33]

The unity of the Democratic party doomed the Know-Nothings to impotence in the election of 1856. Unity had been strengthened when James Buchanan was nominated for the presidency, for he was a "national Democrat"—not committed to either branch of the party. He was, instead, a conservative and cautious man who had walked the thin line that divided the Democracy into antagonistic camps for years. To an astute observer of the California scene, his nomination was an important move which would unite the two wings of the party and allow the suppression of the "element of Republicanism in their party so as to carry the state." [34]

Eventually the "element of Republicanism" was to join with other political groupings to create a victorious Republican party in California. In 1856, however, these incipient Republicans marshaled behind the presidential banner of Buchanan. But the process of effecting a union of all antislavery elements continued. "We have all the elements here for a powerful opposition to Slavery aggression. The only difficulty is in concentrating and combining them and this we hope to do under the Republican flag," wrote one of the founders of the new party. Another suffered the indignity of being pelted with rotten fruit when he attempted to speak in behalf of the fledgling Republican organization in Sacramento. The timely intervention of a Know-Nothing leader, Henry S. Foote, prevented even rougher treatment. The violence of the response to the new party measured the threat to existing political organization which it posed.[35]

The American party displayed a good bit of vigor in the summer of 1856. At its state convention, delegates came from all parts of California, a large segment demanding a clear-cut stand in behalf of the expansion of slavery into the West. Another faction strongly opposed slavery extension, while a third group looked with dismay on the

[33] Powell, "Southern Influences," p. 94; Peyton Hurt, *The Rise and Fall of the "Know Nothings" in California* (San Francisco, 1930), p. 51.

[34] Cornelius C. Cole to Edwin Morgan, May 3, 1856, Cornelius Cole Coll., Univ. of Calif., Los Angeles. Milton S. Latham announced his opposition to a "rump" anti-Broderick Democratic organization in the *Alta California,* May 6, 1856.

[35] Cornelius Cole to William F. Seward (n.d.), quoted in *Memoirs of Cornelius Cole* (New York, 1908), p. 87; Winfield J. Davis, *History of Political Conventions in California, 1849–1892* (Sacramento, 1893), pp. 59–60.

controversy and favored a stand which would unite rather than divide and alienate. The possibility of straddling the issue was appealing, but even this course had its share of hazards. "The Southern members will either have a direct avowal or will leave," reported one observer. Antislavery members of the organization were likely to be equally disenchanted with dodging the issue and to be completely alienated if the party were to endorse the views of the proslavery ultras. The state committee satisfied neither faction when it tabled a resolution endorsing the "measure known as the 'Kansas-Nebraska bill' . . . as a finality, so far as congressional action on the subject of slavery is concerned." [36]

When Know-Nothings came together to select candidates, it was obvious to many people that there was considerable life left in the party. The first sign that harmony and fellowship were superficial came when a number of Chivalry delegates introduced a resolution which was unmistakably hostile to the Vigilance Committee of 1856. A wave of hissing and booing rose in a mighty chorus and almost drowned out the voice of the secretary. When order was restored and the reading finished, the resolution was buried by an avalanche of votes in favor of laying it on the table. It was obvious to all that while the Vigilance Committee had a number of enemies in the convention, it also had a full measure of supporters. They included the president of the American party, J. G. McCallum, senator from El Dorado County.[37]

The Know-Nothing platform was remarkably brief. The mantle of civic purity and reform was clutched by its framers, who modestly declared that "the American party, being essentially a reform party . . . pledge themselves . . . to lend their energies in the aid of the great and essential reform movements of the day." Among the reform movements they advocated was purity of the ballot box. They also thought it desirable to elevate "none but pure men to positions as local officers," and all who shared in their enthusiasm for such innocuous stands were welcomed to the fold as "co-laborers with us in the glorious cause of union and regeneration." Such hollow and fulsome pledges of devotion to the "glorious cause of union and regeneration" found a welcome place in the rhetoric of Know-Nothing politicians.

[36] Davis, *Political Conventions,* pp. 63–64.

[37] *Alta California,* Sept. 3, 4, and 5, 1856, carried detailed accounts of the American party convention.

However, the failure to tackle the most serious and vital of questions —the extension of slavery in the West—eventuated in the alienation of men who felt strongly one way or the other on the slavery question.[38]

While Broderick observed the Know-Nothing convention and mused over the significance of its failure to take a stand on the slavery issue, he continued to work actively in Democratic fields for both personal and party victory. In the interior he traveled from county to county, attending conventions and influencing primary elections. The objectives to be realized were many. In the first place, influencing the selection of candidates to legislative office was obviously an effort to build support in the legislature in anticipation of the senatorial election of January 1857. A secondary objective was the selection of delegates to the upcoming state convention who would be representative of the Free Soil faction of the Democracy. His enemies kept careful track of his activities with rising apprehension.[39]

In San Francisco the primary elections for delegates to the county and state conventions revealed that Broderick was still a force, in spite of everything the Vigilance Committee had done to strip him of political power. The election was conducted quietly, although the "old feud of Broderickites and Gwinites" raged fiercely in some of the wards. One newspaper suggested that the orderliness of the election was due to the absence of some of the characters banished by the Vigilance Committee. In any case, when the results were tabulated it was revealed that Broderick was still a power and capable of dominating the San Francisco delegation to the state convention by exploiting the divisions which arose out of the ambitions of Gwin, Hammond, Latham, and Weller.[40]

While Broderick remained a power in San Francisco's Democracy, his wings were apparently clipped in the state, for he played a minor role in the convention of 1856. The convention was called to order by Benjamin F. Washington, a ranking member of the Chivalry. In the process of selecting nominees Broderick's men were bested one after another. Charles Scott, of Chivalry affiliation, became the nominee for the congressional seat of the northern district, and Charles S.

[38] The text of the platform is in Davis, *Political Conventions,* pp. 69–70.

[39] L. B. Curtiss to James W. Mandeville, Aug. 21, 1856, Mandeville Coll., Huntington Lib.; James O'Meara, *Broderick and Gwin* (San Francisco, 1881), p. 145.

[40] San Francisco *Daily Town Talk,* Aug. 24, 1856; *Alta California,* Aug. 24 and 25, 1856.

Fairfax, of similar affiliation, was nominated for clerk of the supreme court. None of the presidential electors was an associate of Broderick. The ticket as a whole and in each of its parts was anti-Broderick, leading one newspaper to comment, "Matters look as though Mr. Broderick has been outgeneraled this time." Others found the whole business somewhat puzzling, for it was thought that "he had it in his power, as usual, to dictate the nominations and sweep the Chivalry out of existence," at the start of the convention.[41]

The convention's handling of the platform also reflected a subtle touch by the Chivalry. Under the guidance of the chairman, John P. Hoge, a platform was written which used broad platitudes to say much that was designed to appeal to everyone and offend as few of the electorate as possible. The construction of the Pacific railroad was urged and the ticket of John C. Breckinridge and James Buchanan hailed as a combination of the statesman "who has grown gray in the service of his country" and "a younger laborer in the political field, a man of unquestionable ability." Economy was pledged, and old-line Whigs were invited to join the "great conservative party of the Union." Such a platform was almost meaningless. It was accepted by the convention in a single vote.[42]

Some of the assembled delegates were dissatisfied with the manner in which the platform avoided issues. One such issue was the San Francisco Vigilance Committee, and a number of delegates were determined to get the state convention to adopt a resolution condemning it. When it was offered, however, the chairman ruled it was out of order, since the tenth resolution of the platform, adopted a moment before, was a resolution in favor of adjournment. Hoge's ruling brought the San Francisco delegation to its feet. As the shouting and livid delegates objected to the manner in which they had been outmaneuvered and prevented from registering their objections to the vigilantes, the chairman's gavel announced the adjournment of the convention.[43]

At the close of the 1856 convention the Chivalry was apparently in full control. They had selected a ticket, written a platform, and chosen

[41] Sacramento *Daily Times,* Sept. 13, 1856; *Alta California,* Sept. 11, 1856; *Daily Town Talk,* Sept. 11, 1856.

[42] Davis, *Political Conventions,* pp. 70–73.

[43] *Alta California,* Sept. 13, 1856; *Daily Town Talk,* Sept. 13, 1856; Davis, *Political Conventions,* p. 73.

a new state central committee which was thoroughly anti-Broderick in its membership. The plebeian politician had apparently been shorn of power in the California Democracy. Observers of the political scene speculated in print on the manner in which this had been done. The presence of Broderick in the convention city and his failure to play a direct role in it stimulated speculation. "Why was he not there as usual, and with his great parliamentary tactics, scattering in dismay and wonderment his ancient foes?" queried one editor.[44]

The answer to this question was found by some in an arrangement made by Broderick and Gwin. According to this report, the two men had arranged political matters between them so that Gwin was to choose the congressional nominees and Broderick was to have a fair chance at the Senate, by getting enough of the nominations in county conventions to legislative seats. The union of the forces would mean "a preponderance on joint ballot in the next Legislature, and thus secure two United States Senators," declared a reporter of the political arena.[45]

All of this was speculation, and no announcement or convincing evidence was made public to sustain it. The objective conditions permitted—even demanded—an accord which would be in the interest of both men. Such an arrangement was possible, perhaps likely, and it began to haunt the dreams of other senatorial aspirants. Such a *rapprochement* would tend to explain Broderick's failure to participate in the convention and his encouraging report to a friend in late September that "three fourths of the nominations for Senate and Assembly, thus far, are my friends." [46]

However, the political situation in California was not simplified by an accord of Broderick and Gwin. On the contrary, the political matrix continued to be a confused welter of faction and personal ambition complicated by the rise and fall of major political groups. The decline of the Know-Nothings was accompanied by a spectacular growth of the Republican party; the two events were directly related. The Know-Nothings followed the example set by the Whigs and refused to take a stand on the issues related to slavery; straddling cost them a sizable bloc of voters who moved into the ranks of the fledgling

[44] *Alta California,* Sept. 13, 1856; Sacramento *Daily Times,* Sept. 13, 1856.
[45] *Alta California,* Sept. 11, 1856; Sacramento *Daily Times,* Sept. 13, 1856.
[46] Broderick to Pablo de la Guerra, Sept. 26, 1856, De la Guerra Coll.

Republican organization. The Know-Nothings were preparing to follow the Whigs into political oblivion.[47]

The California voter was to be presented with a number of options by this unstable political situation. Proslavery electors of Democratic persuasion could vote for the Chivalry candidates on the congressional and state level; were they of the party of Jefferson and Jackson but of Free Soil inclinations, they might concentrate their support on nominees for local and county offices. Were they of Whig antecedents and antislavery views, they might well turn to the fledgling Republican party. In sum, they had many choices and therefore were little inclined to muster beneath the American party banner in support of a synthetic platform built of outworn political platitudes.

When the Republican party held its first state convention in late August, it provoked a violent response from the populace and a part of the press. It took considerable fortitude to face down the opposition which "denounced the convention of nigger worshippers," but backbone was plentiful in the founding organization. The unity of this meeting was in sharp contrast to the divided conventions of the California Democracy. Candidates were selected and a surprisingly moderate platform of nine crisply written resolutions adopted. The national platform and the national ticket of John C. Frémont and William L. Dayton were endorsed.[48]

Violent language and action did not prevent Republicans from vigorous campaigning, especially in San Francisco. Here the picture was complicated by the appearance of the People's party, the political arm of the Vigilance Committee of 1856. Somewhat self-consciously, this new group dedicated itself to the "political purification" of the city and the completion of the work begun by the vigilantes. Through banishment it had eliminated a large number of "shoulder-strikers" and "wire-pullers" from the political arena. Having purged the body politic, the committee now turned to the problem of furnishing the city with candidates who would keep the city on a straight course. The People's party, like the Vigilance Committee, did not follow the usual

[47] Hurt, pp. 51 ff. Catherine Coffin Phillips, ed. *Cornelius Cole, California Pioneer and United States Senator* (San Francisco, 1929), pp. 82–97, describes the spectacular growth of the Republican party in 1856. Sacramento *Daily Times,* Oct. 23, 1856, printed a detailed analysis of the party affiliation of the press in 1856; cf. San Francisco *Newsletter,* Oct. 5, 1856, in Mariano G. Vallejo Papers, Huntington Lib.

[48] Davis, *Political Conventions,* pp. 65–66; Sacramento *State Journal,* Aug. 28, 1856; Phillips, ed. *Cornelius Cole,* pp. 83–84.

forms. Instead of a primary or a convention, the new party chose a slate by a nominating committee. Usually the announcement of such a slate was accompanied by a notice of a ratification meeting where the citizenry would assemble and endorse the ticket, but no ratification meeting was to be held on this occasion.[49]

The People's party ticket was not to remain in the field, however, for a short time after Broderick's organization displayed surprising strength by trouncing the opposition in a primary election to select delegates to the county convention of the Democracy, the People's party ticket was withdrawn. The Broderick triumph was quite unexpected, for it was thought that the Vigilance Committee had smashed his organization. Apparently instead of being weakened, he emerged stronger than ever. Broderick reported to a political friend: "The efforts of my enemies, Gwin, Foote, and Bailie Peyton, etc., to direct the aim of the Vigilance Committee against me, have signally failed, to their great discomfiture." But the failure was to be a temporary one, and if the primary victory encouraged Broderick, it also demonstrated to his enemies that a coalition of anti-Broderick forces was necessary. Such a coalition was to be a reality before the election, when the Know-Nothings, the Republicans, and the nominees of the People's party joined hands.[50]

The rising tide of interest in politics continued through the election itself. In Sacramento a friend reported to the former banking partner of James King of William the intense interest of the people in the election and predicted a victory for Broderick. He also predicted defeat for the Chivalry candidates on the state and congressional ticket. His cryptic comment on some of the figures involved, "They are unreliable and unsafe men, sound and safe for Broderick but damned unsafe on property rights and other important questions," sheds light on his image of Broderick and his associates.[51]

The mechanics of this election effort were to be much the same as those of previous campaigns. The usual assessments were made on incumbent officeholders—those of major importance paying a flat ten percent of their salaries into party coffers. The faithful were exhorted

[49] *Alta California,* Sept. 18, 1856.

[50] *Alta California,* Oct. 22 and 24, 1856; Broderick to Pablo de la Guerra, Sept. 26, 1856, De la Guerra Coll.

[51] Pierre B. Cornwall to Jacob Rink Snyder, Oct. 31, 1856, cited in *A Calendar of the Major Jacob Rink Snyder Collection in the Manuscript Collections of the Society of California Pioneers* (San Francisco, 1940), p. 107.

to get out the vote on election day and to scrutinize the activities of campaign workers around the polling places. One news story, to emphasize the importance of each vote, declared the Kansas-Nebraska Bill was passed by a single vote, its author was elected to the Senate by a single vote, and the legislator who cast the vote for that senator was himself elected by a single vote.[52]

But there were to be no close elections in California in 1856 where the outcome would be decided by a small margin, let alone a single vote. The voters marched to the polls in ranks, those in San Francisco casting their ballots in a quiet, orderly manner. A new set of inexperienced judges and inspectors slowed the election machinery somewhat, but on the whole they performed well. By midafternoon of election day, trends in the voting were observed; and before the close of the polls, the more knowledgeable political observers sensed a major change in the city's political picture.[53]

The change was the result of impressive victories by the Republican party and the People's party. The latter swept the local field, although one or two Democratic candidates survived, while the Republican party elected assemblymen and state senators in both San Francisco and Alameda counties. Winning three assembly seats and a seat in the upper house of the legislature was an auspicious beginning for the fledgling party. Republicans in the interior counties were not so successful. The "Mariposa estates hung like a millstone around his neck," and the "West's greatest pathmarker," John C. Frémont, did not get a single vote in some of the mining-county precincts. In Fresno County one voter cast a ballot for Frémont, and in Stanislaus and Tulare counties less than two dozen supported him. In the larger centers of population, San Francisco and Sacramento, Frémont and the Republicans did rather well, but the state picture was one of Democratic victory.[54]

California went Democratic by a substantial margin; both the American party and the newly launched Republican party were bested. Know-Nothings castigated the Republicans for dividing the

[52] Election rallies of the Democratic party in San Francisco are described in colorful detail in the *Alta California,* Oct. 26 and Nov. 1, 1856. Sacramento *Daily Times,* Oct. 10, 1856, reported the plans of the state finance committee of the Democratic party. *Alta California,* Nov. 4, 1856, reported the incident in Illinois which revealed the importance of voting.

[53] *Alta California,* Nov. 2 and 4, 1856.

[54] *Alta California,* Nov. 5, 6, 7, and 11, 1856; cf. Election Returns, 1856, Vol. 1759, Archives of the Secretary of State, Sacramento.

vote that would have defeated the Democracy, but there was little they could do beyond that. Soon the Know-Nothings were to be a thing of the past—a part of California's political history which occasionally attracted the attention of the historian. This election marked the demise of the American party as an organized political force in California.[55]

The San Francisco *Herald* could not allow the election to pass without noting that the results showed that all the charges of ballot box stuffing which the Vigilance Committee alleged to be characteristic of the previous election were exposed as empty and meaningless talk. The newspaper pointed out that the election this year was supervised by a new set of officials selected from among the "most honest and responsible men in the city." The "ballot-box stuffers, the shoulder-strikers and ruffians" who previously ruled the roost had been driven from the city by the Vigilance Committee. However, pointed out the *Herald,* the vote in the two elections differed by less than two hundred out of more than twelve thousand cast in each election. The insignificant one percent difference in the two election totals probably reflected the San Francisco–San Mateo County boundary change, which shifted a small number of voters to the latter county. The conclusion was inescapable: "After this test, all that has been trumpeted forth to the world of ballot-box stuffing at the last election falls to the earth." [56]

Broderick emerged from this election in a formidable position, despite the setback in San Francisco. The newly elected legislature was overwhelmingly Democratic, and it was likely that it would confer a senatorial toga on one or more of the Democratic aspirants at the coming session. The conclusion that Broderick had been stripped of power by the Vigilance Committee through the deportation of his political aides in San Francisco was obviously in error. "He does not seem to have been shorn of a single lock by the Vigilance Committee, but on the other hand, he appears to be rendered stronger by their work," commented an observer.[57]

For the balance of the year, the aspirants for the Senate seat

[55] Reaction of the Know-Nothings to Republican achievements in the election of 1856 is described and analyzed in Hurt, pp. 52–53.

[56] San Francisco *Herald,* Nov. 5, 1856; *Daily Town Talk,* Nov. 5, 1856.

[57] Sacramento *Daily Times,* Nov. 9, 1856. *Alta California,* Nov. 8, 1856, analyzed the composition of the legislature and predicted the choice of a pro-Gwin senator and a pro-Broderick senator in the forthcoming election.

maneuvered for position in the political arena. Gwin analyzed the legislature and found the picture reassuring. His correspondents were optimistic, and one pointed out that "the pure Broderick has been defeated in every county in which it has been run," citing the results in San Francisco, Santa Clara, and Sacramento. He went on to declare that Gwin could easily best Broderick in a rough and tumble political battle. Gwin expressed great confidence: "We have the materials to achieve a complete and brilliant triumph in this campaign if we use them properly." A spokesman for the Chivalry indicated the basis for the hostility to Broderick: "I notice that every man who has quit the Democrats for the Republican Blacks has been a Broderick wire-puller." [58]

There were other candidates interested in a senatorship. John B. Weller's term was to end in March 1857, and he made no secret of his wish to be reelected. Milton S. Latham, collector of San Francisco, was another strong contender. A former congressman who had declined to run for reelection as the candidate of Broderick's Free Soil Democracy of 1854, Latham had a number of political assets, which included a substantial private fortune and the extensive patronage of the customhouse in San Francisco. His defection in 1854 and his identification with the Chivalry wing of the party had earned him the enduring enmity of Broderick, but he was still hopeful of arriving at some sort of an understanding with the plebeian politician. A most fearful thought troubled Latham: the possible union of Broderick and Gwin forces—in Latham's words, "What I have feared is a fusion between Gwin and Broderick friends which would shut me out of the Contest." [59]

The victory of the Democrats in 1856 had created a new set of problems. Unity of preelection days had been based upon the need for a victory by each of the factions of the party. Once the victory had been won, "the ghosts of Musical Hall and Carpenter's Hall began to stare them in the face." The two wings of the party were as "inharmonious as fire and water," and nothing less than political extermina-

[58] Anonymous to William M. Gwin, Nov. 10, 1856, in Gwin to James W. Mandeville, Nov. 11, 1856; A. C. Blaine to Mandeville, Nov. 11, 1856, all in Mandeville Coll.

[59] Latham to James W. Mandeville in Albert Dressler, ed. *Letters to a Pioneer Senator* (San Francisco, 1925), pp. 22–23; Sacramento *Evening Times,* Dec. 18, 1856.

tion of one by the other would end the contest, predicted an editor.[60]

Latham was not discouraged by the situation. Recognizing the basic importance of Broderick as a factor in the political equation, Latham turned to the task of increasing his support in the Chivalry faction of the party while he sought to arrive at an understanding with Broderick. The latter had thirty-odd followers in the legislature who clung to him. "You know he has the peculiarity of tying to him his supporters in the most wonderful degree," Latham plaintively commented to a leading supporter of Gwin. With this base of thirty votes, Broderick was in an excellent position to trade and negotiate for the small number he needed to put him over the top. Ten more would be enough to produce a nomination. The fact that two seats would be filled made for a flexible stance on the part of each aspirant. The possibilities and dangers inherent in this fluid situation were to be seen in the defection of Charles Scott, newly elected congressman, from Gwin's camp to the standard of Latham.[61]

Gwin, Latham, and Weller had similar problems, for each was competing from the same general group of lawmakers, while Broderick, the single Free Soil Democratic aspirant, had no serious ideological competitor. Each of his Chivalry-oriented competitors was pushed by objective conditions toward reconciliation with Broderick. Rumors began to circulate that a Gwin-Broderick accord had been made; these were followed by suggestions that Latham and Broderick would effect an understanding. Weller was in Washington, but his agents were actively engaged in tracking down the rumors and negotiating for the benefit of their principal.[62]

As the year closed, Broderick was in the midst of a tour of the inland counties—shoring up sagging walls and strengthening weak points in the organization. Gradually he picked up newspaper support until he had more of the press in his corner than any other candidate. A veritable ovation greeted him upon his arrival in Sacramento, and throngs of people, true and professed friends, came to receptions honoring him. Among those who attended were "some of the promi-

[60] Sacramento *Daily Times,* Nov. 14, 1856.

[61] Latham to James W. Mandeville, Nov. 18, 1856; Gwin to Mandeville, Dec. 13, 1856, Mandeville Coll.

[62] B. D. Wilson to Gwin, Dec. 5, 1856, J. S. Watkins to James W. Mandeville, Nov. 22, 1856, and P. L. Solomon to Mandeville, Dec. 28, 1856, Mandeville Coll., reveal part of the complicated story of the attempts of the aspirants to bring their ambitions to realization.

nent Democrats who have been his bitter enemies, and in fact, persecutors." Their presence was a clear indication of Broderick's growing strength.[63]

Other signs of that growing strength were to be seen. Gwin put it bluntly in a letter he penned on Christmas Day, 1856. Virtually conceding Broderick's election to the Senate, he went on to describe his own plans. In such phrases as "I care not who my colleague is if I am elected," he displayed his longing for a second term. The die was cast: "I do not think Broderick can be defeated, and if elected who so important to our section of the party to be his colleague as myself?" The letter closed with a pliant truism: "A half a loaf is better than no bread." [64]

While Gwin was committed to a union of his forces with Broderick, the latter made no reciprocal commitment. On the contrary, while Gwin was coming painfully and reluctantly to this position, Broderick was receiving overtures from the other aspirants. Weller's agent conversed with him and sought an understanding, and Latham's aides tried to ascertain if there was a basis for accord. Had these three rivals combined against the stonemason politician, they would have had the power to best him again. They might have humbled him as they had on previous occasions. At this juncture, however, the coalition of Gwin, Latham, Weller, and Washington was impossible in view of their conflicting ambitions and their animosities. A much more likely possibility than coalition against Broderick was the negotiation of an understanding between Broderick and one of his rivals.[65]

A newspaper which supported John B. Weller did little toward bringing about an accord with Broderick when it printed a bitter attack on him in one of its final numbers of 1856. Posing the question, "Is Mr. Broderick a Black Republican?" the article answered with a resounding affirmative and the editor marshaled the evidence to establish the validity of the charge. In a detailed examination of

[63] Joseph Walkup to Gwin, Dec. 23, 1856, Gwin to James W. Mandeville, Dec. 19, 1856, Mandeville Coll. An analysis of newspaper support for the various candidates appeared in the Sacramento *Daily Times,* Dec. 9, 1856. Broderick's reception in Sacramento is described and analyzed in the *Alta California,* Nov. 19, 1856. Sacramento *Evening Times,* Nov. 28, 1856, reported the results of his tour of the mining counties.

[64] Gwin to James W. Mandeville, Dec. 22 and 25, 1856, Mandeville Coll.

[65] Sacramento *Daily Times,* Dec. 12, 15, 18, 19, 20, and 27, 1856, printed perceptive articles on the forthcoming election. See also Gwin to James W. Mandeville, Dec. 29, 1856, Mandeville Coll.

Broderick's record in the political arena of California, proof was offered to sustain the indictment, beginning with his opposition to the Fugitive Slave Act of 1850. Broderick therefore, concluded the editorial, was not entitled to the support of the California Democracy.[66]

The article was intended to label Broderick with a damaging political epithet, and to some extent it may have hurt him politically. On the other hand, such an assault underscored the source of much of Broderick's strength in the legislature. His antipathy to slavery and its spread to the West was a matter of record. That antipathy was shared by many other figures in the political arena, although the other significant aspirants to senatorial honors were either out-and-out Chivalry figures or "doughfaces" of the western variety. Weller and Latham were pliant politicians of the latter category; Gwin and Washington were well-known defenders of the peculiar institution. The only serious contender for the Senate who could expect to receive the support of every adamant opponent of the spread of slavery into the West was Broderick. That he was aware of the implications of his position is indicated by the words he put to paper as the year came to a close, assuring his friends that he would "have a majority on the first ballot." [67]

[66] Sacramento *Evening News,* Dec. 30, 1856—a reprint of an article taken from a recent issue of the San Francisco *Globe.*

[67] Broderick to Pablo de la Guerra, Dec. 16, 1856, De la Guerra Coll.

CHAPTER NINE

Triumph and Defeat

Sacramento was a cold, gray, and dismal city the first week of January 1857, its hotels jammed with hundreds of lawmakers and politicos who had come for the opening of the California legislature. The mountains nearby were buried from base to peak ranges with record drifts of snow as the great and near-great of the political world gathered. A moment of truth was at hand for the political community —a time of trial and imminent triumph or defeat. The stakes were two seats in the United States Senate; their disposition would go far in determining the locus of power in the California Democracy for some time to come.

A full complement of federal placeholders was on hand to do what it could to avert the political catastrophe that the election of Broderick represented. Richard P. Hammond, W. P. Dameron, and James Y. McDuffie were but three of the prominent members of the Chivalry who were present. The chief candidates for the seats, Broderick, Gwin, Latham, and Benjamin Franklin Washington, were there, although the incumbent, John B. Weller, was in Washington. His interests were to be safeguarded by a lieutenant, Solomon Heydenfeldt. The other aspirants rightly considered the matter too important to be entrusted to subordinates.[1]

The Chivalry was elated when a "Gwin man of the deepest dye" was elected speaker of the Assembly. Realistic observers noted that the Broderick candidate mustered twenty-five votes in a losing cause. These votes, coupled with twelve in the Senate, portended victory for Broderick. To emphasize the significance of Broderick strength in the

[1] *Alta California,* Jan. 3, 4, and 6, 1857.

legislature came the election of one of his supporters as president pro tempore of the Senate. The Chivalry had good reason to be apprehensive.[2]

Had the anti-Broderick forces in the legislature been united, they could have prevented his election. Had there been but one seat to be filled, they might have achieved the unity of action that was essential. However, there were two seats and a number of aspirants. Broderick was ten votes shy of a majority and in an excellent position to negotiate with his rivals. The negotiations would lead to an exchange of support—Broderick to obtain enough votes to be elected to one of the seats and the other seat to be conferred on the aspirant who received Broderick's support. Having carefully examined the reality of the situation, Broderick began the process of assuring himself not only a Senate seat but the more desirable of the two to be filled.[3]

One seat had remained empty since 1855, when Gwin failed to be reelected. That seat entailed a four-year term in the Senate, two years having already run. The other post was that of Weller, whose term expired in March 1857. It provided a full term of six years, and Broderick decided that it should be his. This arrangement involved an understanding with one of his rivals, since the usual procedure would have been to fill the short term first. However, the majority of the Democratic legislators could, by vote, reverse the order of election.

The first sign that an accord had been reached on this matter came in the Democratic caucus, when a motion was passed to reverse the usual order of election. The change followed the usual motion binding all members of the caucus to abide by its decisions. It was passed by a combination of Broderick and Latham supporters and was strongly resisted by Gwin and Weller representatives, who vainly used substitute motions and motions to adjourn to prevent this action by the caucus. Every delaying tactic was put down, and then the caucus turned to the selection of a nominee to the long term. Within a few moments Broderick was elected by a vote of forty-two to thirty-four votes scattered among his opponents. The vote was then made unanimous, but this was largely a mechanical and ritualistic gesture in which some of the lawmakers participated grimly. The group then

[2] William Holden to James Mandeville, Jan. 4, 1857, Mandeville Coll., Huntington Lib.; *Alta California,* Jan. 6 and 7, 1857; Sacramento *Evening Times,* Jan. 6, 1857.

[3] Hubert H. Bancroft, *History of California,* VI (San Francisco, 1888), 706; James O'Meara, *Broderick and Gwin* (San Francisco, 1881), p. 158.

turned to the selection of a nominee for the short term, but after two ballots failed to produce a result, the caucus adjourned.[4]

Partisans of the various aspirants spilled out of the caucus room, Broderick's supporters flushed with victory, the stalwarts of other camps worried and wary. While Broderick's friends gathered to celebrate their triumph, the supporters of Gwin, Latham, Weller, and Washington assembled to exchange recriminations and warnings. The voting clearly revealed the disunity of the anti-Broderick forces. As they looked balefully about in search of a culprit, they came eventually to Milton S. Latham. It was his defection on the agenda question that led to disaster. Not only had he provided Broderick with the chance to be elected, but he had also placed him in the powerful position of deciding which of his co-aspirants he would take to the Senate with him. Little wonder that the representatives of the Chivalry found strong words insufficient to describe the perfidy of Latham.[5]

A leading Republican newspaper hailed Broderick's victory in a glowing tribute to his principles, his record, and his masterful tactics. To its editor, James McClatchy, he was "the staunchest of the many good and true Republicans" in the Democratic party. Broderick's record revealed clearly that he had incurred the enduring hostility of the Chivalry because of his animosity to slavery. "The battle had been long and hotly contested. Federal power and patronage—money and the promise of it—office and the promise of it—slander, secret misrepresentation and open calumny—all have been used against him but he has triumphed," was a part of this joyful response of a leading member of the Republican party of California to Broderick's election.[6]

Meanwhile the formality of electing Broderick to the Senate was undertaken by a joint meeting of the legislature. At the outset an attempt was made to invalidate the action of the caucus in changing the agenda, but James W. Mandeville, a subaltern of Gwin, led the defense. The sight of Gwin's lieutenant leading the battle to prevent

[4] Bancroft, *History of California,* VI, 704–706, and William Henry Ellison, *A Self-governing Dominion: California, 1849–1860,* pp. 289–290, rely heavily on O'Meara, *Broderick and Gwin,* pp. 157–160, and do not reflect the caution that should be exercised in the use of this account, which was written by one of Gwin's political aides. The Sacramento *Evening Times,* Jan. 8, 1857, lists the votes that were cast; cf. "Balloting of Caucus for U.S. Senator, Jan. 8, 1857," MS in Milton S. Latham Papers, Calif. Hist. Soc., San Francisco; F. Amyx to James W. Mandeville, Jan. 16, 1857, in Albert Dressler, ed. *Letters to a Pioneer Senator* (San Francisco, 1925).

[5] O'Meara, *Broderick and Gwin,* pp. 161–164; *Alta California,* Jan. 10, 1857; Sacramento *Evening Times,* Jan. 8, 1857.

[6] Sacramento *Weekly Times,* Jan. 10, 1857, and Dec. 10, 1856.

any attempt to forestall the election of Broderick was astounding. To those who were privy to the inside story, it merely revealed the aptness of the old saw, "If you can't lick 'em, join 'em." There was another Senate seat to fill, and Broderick's aid and support was essential; it was no time to antagonize him. The galleries, filled with "sturdy yeomanry who were chock-full of enthusiasm for Broderick," looked down on the lawmakers as the voting was completed. The call of the clerk announcing Broderick's election was greeted with a tremendous burst of applause and cheers.[7]

Broderick's election was a tremendous personal achievement. The years of striving which had begun more than a decade before in a congressional race had been capped by his election to one of America's highest political offices. The young man born in obscurity to Irish Catholic working-class parents was to return to his birthplace in a senatorial toga. From obscurity to eminence, from setback to triumph, and now much more was possible. Thrust onto the national stage, guaranteed six years of the political power and prestige of a senator, Broderick was given new perspectives and horizons. In these years of crisis, America's embattled antislavery leaders were to be reinforced by a unique figure from the Pacific Coast. A number of observers wondered if he would measure up to the new challenges, new opportunities, and new responsibilities. In the offing was another triumph. When it took shape, those who questioned whether Broderick would measure up to new opportunity had their doubts quieted.

Broderick's influence was amplified by his election; the maneuvering of the principal aspirants for the second seat—Gwin, Weller, and Latham—reflected that fact. Each sought to circumvent his rivals; each sought an understanding with Broderick. The latter preferred former Congressman Joseph C. McCorkle, of Free Soil persuasion, to all others, but when it became apparent that he could not be elected, Broderick turned to other possibilities. Each of the other aspirants was equally objectionable and therefore equally acceptable. Faced with such options, Broderick decided to support the individual who could be used to strike a crippling blow at the Chivalry. His identity was not immediately known, even to Broderick, but in the course of the negotiations, he stepped forward.[8]

[7] San Francisco *Daily Town Talk,* Jan. 11, 1857; *Alta California,* Jan. 11, 1857.

[8] Sacramento *Evening Times,* Jan. 10, 1857; Sacramento *Daily Times,* Jan. 8, 1857; J. M. E. [James M. Estell] to Honorable M. S. Latham (n.d.), and J. McCorkle to Latham (n.d.), Latham Papers, Calif. Hist. Soc.

For a time it appeared that Latham was Broderick's choice of colleague and bludgeon with which to strike at the Chivalry. Two events decided that he would not receive Broderick's support. The first was Latham's refusal to sign an agreement to relinquish his share of federal patronage (in the event of his election) to Broderick. The second was the disappearance of a similar agreement—specifically a letter by Latham to Frank Tilford promising the latter the collectorship of the port of San Francisco if Latham were elected.[9]

Latham's refusal to sign a patronage agreement with Broderick was taken on the high grounds of honor and integrity and "my word is my bond." That ground was eroded from beneath him by Tilford's accusation that Latham had purloined the letter when he wished to escape his commitment of the collector's post. Tilford subsequently explained that the letter had been misplaced, but by this time the damage had been done. Broderick, unable to make a patronage accommodation with Latham, interpreted the "purloined letter" incident as evidence of his duplicity. In reality the fact that Latham would not sign such an agreement (although, as the disappearing letter indicated, he would execute other written patronage agreements) cost him Broderick's support and a Senate seat.[10]

Broderick's real concern was not which of the three aspirants would accompany him to Washington but was with a radical redistribution of power in California's political world. That objective was to be realized by stripping the Chivalry of its monopoly of federal patronage. For years that monopoly brought great political power to a group which was committed to the notion that the society of the slaveholding South was a superior society. It was described by one of its champions as a society erected on the mudsill of servile labor but nevertheless the finest civilization the world had seen since the grandeur of Rome. The political representatives of this static, anachronistic society came

[9] Gwin described that arrangement, putting it in the best possible light, in "William M. Gwin to the People of California, January 13, 1857," O'Meara, *Broderick and Gwin,* p. 192.

[10] Numerous manuscripts in the Milton S. Latham Papers, Calif. Hist. Soc., deal with the senatorial election of 1857: see D. Mahoney Statement, Jan. 13, 1857; Charles S. Scott Statement, Jan. 14, 1857; J. M. Pindell Statement (n.d.); J. M. Estell to Latham, Jan. 17, 1857; Frank Tilford to Latham, Jan. 17, 1857. A few days after the election, Latham resigned as collector of San Francisco and recommended Tilford as his successor; see Latham to James Buchanan, Jan. 20, 1857. The mass of letters and manuscripts gathered by Latham to refute the charge that he had stolen Tilford's recommendation evidences the seriousness of the charge and the possible damage to his political career.

under increasing attack by the representatives of the emerging new order of liberal capitalism. Placing the power of federal patronage in the hands of the Chivalry strengthened its attempt to stay the clock and forestall the demise of the sick society of slavery. It meant, as well, enduring conflict between the two groups. As Roy F. Nichols observes: "Power, therefore, can invite conflict to secure it; but . . . the fear of losing power may be a stronger influence to conflict than the desire to obtain power." [11] The conflict in California mirrored a similar battle on the national stage.

The small army of federal appointees who came to office and remained in office at the pleasure of a superior official—whose tenure reflected past or future political service—represented a legion which carried spears as convention delegates or as distributors of ballots at the polls. Scattered throughout the state, they distributed election materials during campaigns, made the necessary arrangements for the printing and distribution of ballots at the polls, served as inspectors and polling officials who encouraged the turnout of friendly electors and discouraged the participation of the opposition. These were the vital ligaments of political muscle which a monopoly of federal patronage represented. Broderick would not destroy the monopoly but would assume control of it.

If Broderick could not deal with Latham or Weller, he could with Gwin. He later declared that he decided to support Gwin to unite the Democratic party, but most of his contemporaries believed more material considerations were involved. Gwin, who had declared only a few weeks before that Broderick could not be defeated and that he was determined to be his colleague, signed the written agreement that Latham allegedly spurned. Shortly after the document changed hands, and on the fourteenth ballot of the Democratic caucus, William M. Gwin was selected as the nominee for the short term. The following day the legislature made the matter official, electing Gwin to a term which expired in March 1861.[12]

The sophisticated immediately began to search for an explanation of this curious outcome which found one of the leading members of the Chivalry, a dedicated enemy of Broderick, going to the Senate thanks

[11] *The Stakes of Power, 1845–1877* (New York, 1961), p. x.

[12] *Alta California,* Jan. 12 and 13, 1857; Sacramento *Evening Times,* Jan. 13, 1857; "Balloting for U.S. Senate, January 12, 1857," MS in Latham Papers; O'Meara, *Broderick and Gwin,* pp. 186–187; Theodore Hittell, *History of California* (San Francisco, 1898), IV, 205.

to the magnanimity of the politician from Washington Square. No word of the patronage arrangement had leaked out, but the politically informed searched for the quid pro quo that aligned them. Californians did not have long to wait for a plausible explanation, for before the week was out the press published an unusual letter written by Gwin.[13]

Gwin's letter to the "People of California" contained five carefully composed paragraphs. In precise words he declared he had been deserted by a number of his friends and supporters in the election. Their wavering support and wandering allegiance grew out of his involvement with the distribution of the patronage. Patronage had been a curse; he would no longer concern himself with it. The letter closed with an expression of thanks for "the timely assistance of Mr. Broderick and his friends," for to their support and aid, he said, "I conceive, in a great degree, my election is due." The arrangement which Broderick and Gwin had made was not spelled out, but it took little imagination to visualize the missing details.[14]

Newspaper editors commented upon the letter according to their own predilections. The *Alta California* described it as "a rare production, a singular compound of inexplicable charges, scathing rebukes, and personal justification." Another writer, obviously enjoying the rout of the Chivalry, commented: "If Broderick's thrall, Gwin, sticks to his sale, and Broderick uses the power he has thus grasped, the only thing left in the hands of the Chivalry is the Stockton Insane Asylum. They will need it for their own use." A third newspaper confined its comment to: "Died—At Sacramento, on the 12th instant, of political bargaining affecting his honor, W. M. Gwin, the relict of David C. Broderick, aged about 60 years. His obsequies will take place from the Capitol, at Washington, in 1860. The body is carefully embalmed." [15]

Spokesmen for the Chivalry were astounded by the implications of the deal and gave vent to their alarm and grief in strongly worded missives that crossed the continent. A prominent Chivalry representative wrote to an ultra of South Carolina: "We are fighting the old war of the Cavalier and the Puritan. . . . Our opponents have just triumphed over us by the election of Broderick to the Senate. . . .

[13] The *Evening Times,* Jan. 13, 1857, stated flatly: "It is self-evident that Gwin has been elected by Broderick."

[14] "William M. Gwin to the People of California, January 13, 1857," in O'Meara, *Broderick and Gwin,* p. 192.

[15] *Alta California,* Jan. 15, 1857; San Francisco *Daily Town Talk,* Jan. 14, 1857; Sacramento *Evening Times,* Jan. 14 and 15, 1857.

Gwin obtained his reelection by a surrender to Broderick of all the Government patronage." Another expressed his dismay to a sympathizer in the South as follows: "Politically the long agony is over. David C. Broderick is elected U.S. Senator for the long term and Gwin has sold his friends for the sake of being elected." A few writers who were close to Gwin interpreted his letter and its implied arrangements as an accord which would initiate a "constructive period," saying, "no longer will our legislators and politicians be distracted from their normal work." [16]

Republican James McClatchy saw the matter more clearly than most. He predicted future discord in spite of any agreement between Broderick and Gwin and pointed out that Broderick had nothing but an unenforceable agreement. Already, he asserted a few days after the election, representatives of the Chivalry were combing the files of California newspapers in search of evidence of Broderick's anti-slavery convictions. When the Chivalry in Congress was given the proof of Broderick's enduring animosity to slavery, it might turn on him, and "he will not have a single appointment except by sufferance." Future events were to illustrate McClatchy's grasp of the realities of the American political scene.[17]

For the moment, Broderick and his friends reveled in the astounding victory he had won. He had taken over two of the major seats of political power in California after years of striving. True enough, one of the seats was to be filled by a representative of the Chivalry, but he was to be a figurehead, deprived of power and reduced to the status of a pawn. Henceforth the largess of federal patronage in the state was to be distributed along the lines laid down by the Free-Soil Democrat. The hundreds of appointments to federal service in California, which had once given strength and vitality to the Chivalry, were now to be distributed by its enemies to strengthen its enemies. The Chivalry had good reason to be alarmed as the chasm of political oblivion yawned.[18]

[16] C. T. Botts to R. M. T. Hunter, Jan. 15, 1857, Calif. State Lib.; John C. Hyatt to Dr. C. M. Hitchcock, Jan. 20, 1857, Hitchcock Family Correspondence, II, Bancroft Lib.; San Francisco *Daily Evening Bulletin,* Jan. 12, 1857; *Daily Town Talk,* Jan. 21, 1857.

[17] Sacramento *Evening Times,* Jan. 12, 1857.

[18] The Chivalry monopoly of the federal patronage is described in Bancroft, *History of California,* VI, 709. The magnitude of federal patronage in California is clearly shown in *United States Official Register, 1859;* compare the number of positions in California to those of other states. In his Memoirs (pp. 131–132, MS in Bancroft Lib.), Gwin declared his renunciation of patronage was a "voluntary surrender" of a privilege that had only brought him ingratitude and anxiety.

In late January the two senators left for Washington via the Panama route. Broderick carried in his baggage letters and petitions soliciting his assistance in securing federal appointments. Apparently a great many people in California believed that the new distribution of patronage was a reality.[19]

A hundred guns on the evening of February 13, 1857, announced to New York that Broderick had arrived in the city of his youth. The vessel had no sooner touched the wharf than crowds of friends and well-wishers hurried aboard, anxious to bid him welcome. Later, at a reception in his honor, dozens of the great and near-great of the New York Democracy came to hear and participate. The onetime Locofoco listened patiently to the tributes, which stressed themes of humble birth and the rise to eminence of the poor but honest man of ability. His response was disappointingly brief. Pleading fatigue, Broderick thanked the group, then retired to a smaller gathering of intimate friends.[20]

Gwin hurried off to Washington, but Broderick lingered in the city, renewing old friendships and basking in the homage. The New York *Times* reviewed his career and described him as a striking illustration of the saying of Talleyrand, that "nothing is successful in this world but success." The *World* used less equivocal language to express its opinion: "All recognize in him what every unprejudiced mind must acknowledge, that he has incessantly laboured for justice and honest legislation." The language was in sharp contrast to that used by New York editors on former occasions.[21]

Broderick's arrival in Washington was eagerly awaited by many people who had heard of the peculiar circumstances of his election and the manner in which he had humbled a leading member of the Chivalry and brought him to the capital in "chains." Gwin was already on the scene, making whatever explanations he could to those who had known him in his time of political greatness. Preparations for the inauguration of James Buchanan were in full swing, and the turmoil attendant to the change of administration created a number of problems for the junior senator, but he was soon settled in a private boarding home and ready to enter the political arena of the capital.[22]

[19] Petition to Broderick, MS, Jan. 26, 1857, Application Files, Customs Service, San Francisco, Record Group 56, National Archives.

[20] *Alta California,* Mar. 18, 1857; San Francisco *Morning Call,* Mar. 18, 1857.

[21] New York *Times,* Feb. 17, 1857; New York *World,* Mar. 15, 1857.

[22] *Congressional Directory,* 1st Sess., 35th Cong.

In a matter of days Broderick met with the new President, the way having been prepared by an introduction which John W. Forney wrote to his longtime political associate and friend. It began "I hope I do not presume in calling your attention to the most important man from California, Senator Broderick, and to the case he may present to you." Buchanan's reaction to the subtle downgrading of his intimate friend Gwin, implied in the phrase "most important man from California," is not recorded. Forney continued, "He is a man of the people and was your devoted friend in the last struggle. He feels most anxious to see you. But for my regard for you I would not ask your attention to this case." The closing implied that Broderick was having trouble in arranging a meeting with the new chief executive.[23]

From the outset, the odds were stacked against the establishment of a warm and friendly relationship between Broderick and Buchanan. Part of the difficulty was Broderick's treatment of Gwin, for the latter was a close friend of the Sage of Wheatland, and his humiliation was vicariously shared by the President. The friendship of Gwin and Buchanan was deep and enduring. It survived secession and the alignment of Gwin with the Confederate States of America. It also produced resentment toward the man who had humiliated the senior senator from California.[24]

Complementing the strained feelings growing out of this situation was the personality clash of the two men. Buchanan's exaggerated sense of the proprieties, his pretensions to breeding, his acute sensitivity in matters of decorum and social rank made it difficult for him to look with favor upon this roughhewn ex-porterhouse-keeper who had battled his way into the inner circles of power in the Democratic party. Buchanan was almost ponderous in his thinking, while Broderick was quick to seize upon the essence of a complicated situation and act on it. The Sage of Wheatland was inherently conservative, a man who had spent a lifetime in public service, inching his way to his present pinnacle by never taking a stand on any question before he ascertained the drift of important opinion. Broderick was almost the opposite, ever ready to express his opinion vigorously, never overly concerned with the pitfalls to career that identification with the minority view represented. He had made his way to the rank of a senator and

[23] Forney to Buchanan (n.d.), 1857, Buchanan Papers, Pennsylvania Hist. Soc.

[24] Buchanan to Mrs. W. M. Gwin, May 4, 1861, in John Bassett Moore, ed. *The Works of James Buchanan* (Philadelphia, 1908–1911), XI, 187.

along the way had never avoided the unpopular position. Both men were of the same party, but they represented widely different political viewpoints. The gap between these men who represented the radical Free Soil wing of the Democracy and the conservative national Democratic view was never to be bridged.[25]

That there would be no accord between these representatives of the Democracy was ensured by Buchanan's situation. As President he was faced with unprecedented problems of Cabinet construction, factionalism, and patronage. While the nation stumbled toward disaster, Buchanan wrestled with his manifold burdens and found his modest talents quite inadequate. The tired formulas of yesteryear were no longer workable. Each day the pressure mounted; each day brought a new batch of troubles to his desk. When California appeared on the agenda, there was little wonder that Buchanan turned to his intimates for counsel.[26]

Broderick was evidently interested in a working relationship with the new administration. There was reason for him to believe that such an accord could be worked out. The record would show, for example, that not only had Broderick been among the first to come to Buchanan's standard as he sought the nomination, but he was also among the most effective campaigners of the Democratic party in California during the 1856 election. Ostracized by the Pierce administration and vehemently opposed to the presidential aspirations of Stephen A. Douglas, Broderick evidently saw in Buchanan a man of national reputation who was the best of the potential candidates for the presidency. Accordingly he came to Buchanan's camp early, supported him through the thick of the battle in California, and rejoiced in his victory.[27]

The fact that John Bigler was the right bower of the Broderick-Bigler faction of the California Democracy was an additional reason to believe that the new administration would work out a cordial relation-

[25] Roy F. Nichols, *The Disruption of American Democracy* (New York, 1948), pp. 74–78; Allan Nevins, *The Emergence of Lincoln* (New York, 1951), I, 61–65.

[26] Nichols, *Disruption of American Democracy,* pp. 74–75.

[27] Winfield J. Davis, *History of Political Conventions in California, 1849–1892* (Sacramento, 1893), p. 58; *Alta California,* Mar. 7, 1856. The failure of the Democratic convention of September 1856 to censure the California delegation for its tardy support of Buchanan in the Cincinnati convention despite strong support from the Broderick-Bigler faction is described in Davis, pp. 70 ff. The Sacramento *Union,* Feb. 25, 1856, reported Broderick support of Buchanan in advance of other groups in the Democratic party.

ship with Broderick. John Bigler, like his brother William, was a close personal as well as political friend of James Buchanan. "One word from him will be worth half a dozen from as many State Senators and Assemblymen," declared a California political observer. All these things seemed to indicate that Broderick and Buchanan would meet no insurmountable problems in working out a satisfactory political relationship.[28]

Such an accord of mutual advantage was not to be, for within a month of his arrival in Washington, Broderick was estranged from the President. The immediate cause of the break was the distribution of the patronage in California. Many observers felt that a struggle for the spoils of office led to the rupture and that the President, in declining to honor the arrangement that Gwin and Broderick had made, was acting in the best traditions of statesmanship. This interpretation, assiduously propagated through the years by the Chivalry, became widely accepted.[29]

The break between the two men was of more than passing moment and academic interest, for Buchanan's treatment of Broderick and his section of the Democratic party had far-reaching effects. Buchanan's reputation as a "National Democrat," a representative of the broad middle ground of opinion within the Democracy, was destroyed in large measure in the course of his clash with Broderick. In the opening hour of his administration, he endorsed the Dred Scott decision—then known only to the members of the Supreme Court and a few insiders. Thereby he indicated the course that his administration would follow in the difficult question of the extension of slavery. In the first month of his administration, he cast Free Soil Democrat Broderick into outer darkness. This pious and premature support of the Dred Scott deci-

[28] Nichols, *Disruption of American Democracy,* p. 55; Sacramento *Evening Times,* Dec. 20, 1856; William Bigler to Buchanan, Mar. 11, 1857, Buchanan Papers.

[29] Nevins, *The Emergence of Lincoln,* I, 67–79, describes the process of selection that Buchanan followed to put together a Cabinet which was dominated by proslavery interests. The Broderick-Buchanan break is frequently attributed to Broderick's refusal to submit his patronage recommendations to Buchanan in writing because he had made so many conflicting promises to supporters; see such interpretations in Ellison, *A Self-governing Dominion,* p. 294, Jeremiah Lynch, *The Life of David C. Broderick* (New York, 1911), p. 163, Hittell, *History of California,* IV, 211, O'Meara, *Broderick and Gwin,* pp. 196–198. The existence of a number of letters from Broderick to Buchanan in the National Archives recommending candidates for federal appointments in California demolishes this version of events; see Broderick to Buchanan, Mar. 8 and 11, 1857, both in Treasury Dept. Applications, Record Group 56, and Broderick to Buchanan, Mar. 19, 1857, in Dept. of Justice Appointment Papers, Record Group 60.

sion, coupled with his break with Broderick, gave credence to the charge that he was a doughface and a captive of the proslavery figures that surrounded him.[30]

The battle for the California patronage began even before Buchanan's inauguration, with the defeated Milton S. Latham bypassing both Broderick and Gwin. He was apparently unsuccessful. Gwin, too, was approached by office-hungry associates, although it was well known that he was bound by the arrangement with Broderick. At first he indicated a reluctance to become involved. One of his associates described him as "utterly powerless by reason of the contract that he had entered to relinquish the patronage of the state." Later he exhibited greater interest, and eventually he played a major role.[31]

Gwin's failure to plunge into the fray from the beginning puzzled some of his associates. "Old Gwin has been merely a looker on and [Broderick] seems to hold him by some spell or chain," wrote one of his associates. The battle went ahead without him, a phalanx of the Chivalry, "Denver, Weller, Bradford, De la Torre, Herbert, and myself [Scott] uniting in opposition to Broderick." They reported their prospects differently from time to time. "We are sanguine of success" were the cheering words sent to a supporter, but later in the day the following was written: "I am in hopes we shall beat Broderick on the Collectorship, but I consider it a matter of very considerable doubt." [32]

The picture was complicated by the aspirations of John Bigler, for he had set his eyes on the collector's post—the most powerful federal office in California. Broderick from the beginning committed himself to Bigler. The Broderick-Bigler alliance had been productive of much political power for them, and there was little reason to end that alliance now. Broderick's support of Bigler was direct and complete:

[30] William Bigler to Buchanan, Mar. 11, 1857, Buchanan Papers; *Alta California*, Apr. 30, 1857. Rose O'Neal Greenhow, *My Imprisonment and the First Year of Abolition Rule* (London, 1863), p. 196, said of her intimate friend, Buchanan, "By a fatality of birth . . . thrown on the wrong side."

[31] Latham to Buchanan, Jan. 20, 1857, Treasury Dept. Applications, Record Group 56, and Latham to Buchanan, Feb. 14, 1857, Dept. of Justice Appointment Papers, Northern California, Record Group 60, National Archives; Charles Scott to James W. Mandeville, Mar. 18, 1857, Mandeville Coll.; Paschal Bequette to Howell Cobb, Secretary of the Treasury, Mar. 17, 1857, Treasury Dept. Applications, Record Group 56, the latter endorsed by Weller, Scott, McKibben, Denver, and William M. Gwin.

[32] Charles Scott to James W. Mandeville, Mar. 18, 1857, Mandeville Coll.; Charles Weller to Jacob R. Snyder, Mar. 18, 1857, Jacob Rink Snyder Coll., Soc. of Calif. Pioneers Lib., San Francisco.

"It affords me great pleasure to express the utmost confidence in the principles, ability, and integrity of Governor Bigler." [33]

Broderick had candidates for Buchanan to consider for other offices of importance. Elliot J. Moore, longtime friend and political ally, was commended as a "consistent and reliable Democrat and a worthy citizen." The office sought was that of marshal for the northern district of California, one of the more significant posts in federal service. Herman Wohler of San Francisco, who had fled Germany at the close of the abortive revolution of 1848 and whose right to sit in the California legislature had once been challenged on the grounds he was not a citizen, was also recommended for a major position as superintendent of the mint in San Francisco. Broderick closed his unqualified endorsement: "His appointment would be acceptable to the people and serviceable to the Government." [34]

As the days passed without a decision from the President on California patronage, the pressure mounted. The Biglers became more insistent. William pushed the claims of his brother vigorously. "John Bigler has set his heart on it . . . and his brother has set his heart on it," but the appointment was not to be made. In spite of all the support he could muster, Bigler went down to defeat at the hands of Benjamin Franklin Washington, a stalwart of the Chivalry faction. There was no mistaking the significance of that decision; the Buchanan administration had weighed the factions of the party in California and found the Bigler-Broderick division wanting. The tremendous power of the collector's office was to be placed in the hands of the enemies of the Free Soil wing of the Democratic party.[35]

The disappointment of Bigler was moderated by his appointment as Minister to Chile, a position he had sought some years before. The appointment of his onetime secretary Charles Hempstead as superintendent of the mint in San Francisco was a sop to the Biglers and the Free Soil wing of the California Democracy. Neither appointment offset the damage that was inflicted on the Broderick-Bigler wing by the final and fateful division of the patronage decided in a lengthy

[33] Broderick to Buchanan, Mar. 8, 1857, Treasury Dept. Applications, Record Group 56, National Archives.

[34] Broderick to Buchanan, Mar. 11, 1857, Treasury Dept. Applications, Record Group 56; Broderick to Buchanan, Mar. 19, 1857, Dept. of Justice Appointment Papers, Record Group 60, National Archives.

[35] William Bigler to Buchanan, Mar. 11, 1857, Buchanan Papers; *Alta California*, Apr. 30, 1857.

Cabinet meeting. A quick analysis of the division of the spoils revealed that they were bestowed not on the victors but on the Chivalry of California. The "Chivs" manned the posts of real political power. Not only was the Broderick-Bigler wing of the party stripped of its political assets, but Bigler himself was removed bodily from the political scene.[36]

The dangers of an open rupture with Broderick were appreciated by some of Buchanan's advisers. Accordingly they extended themselves to placate this politician of quite certain ability and uncertain influence. Robert J. Walker conferred with Broderick and Gwin, evidently searching, without success, for a *modus vivendi.* Howell Cobb, Secretary of the Treasury and moderate voice of Georgia, joined in the effort but to no avail. However moderate their voices and realistic their views of the political situation, they were more than offset by the strident declarations of others closer to Buchanan. The Sage of Wheatland exhibited his own unique brand of ignorance of California affairs by remarking to Broderick that since two of his friends had been appointed to the customs service in San Diego and Stockton, it was only right that the post of collector of San Francisco should go to another faction of the party. Broderick's response to this devious or naïve explanation is not recorded, but his reaction to the distribution of the patronage was sharp and clear. Typically he made no secret of his displeasure but expressed it in imperious language. The words indicated a final break with the President: "I will not cross the threshold of the White House while the present incumbent occupies it." [37]

"Washington's appointment was the fatal stab," reported Gwin gleefully and then added, "His [Broderick's] denunciations of the President are gross in the extreme." Soon additional letters were being sent west to alert the Chivalry of the return of Broderick to California. He left in the first week of April, departing, said Gwin, "in a great rage. . . . His object is to carry the state convention, nominate his friends for the state offices and censure the Administration." He

[36] Broderick to Charles H. Hempstead, Apr. 4, 1857, telegram, Treasury Dept. Applications, Record Group 56; John Bigler to Buchanan, Mar. 8, 1857, John Bigler to Howell Cobb, Apr. 3, 1857, and Andrew Jackson Butler to Benjamin Franklin Butler, July 20, 1857, Treasury Dept. Applications, Record Group 56, National Archives; *Alta California,* Apr. 30, 1857; *Daily Town Talk,* Apr. 21 and 30, 1857; Bancroft, *History of California,* VI, 711.

[37] *Alta California,* May 1, 1857; Gwin to James W. Mandeville, Apr. 3, 1857, Mandeville Coll.; *Daily Town Talk,* Apr. 21, 1857.

piously added, "I don't think I shall hereafter be charged with bargaining of the patronage of the government to Mr. B. [Broderick]." [38]

Broderick lost no time upon his arrival in San Francisco but plunged into a round of conferences with his associates. Plans for the forthcoming campaign began to take shape as he again took "the destinies of his party under his wing, and the war of the factions," the *Town Talk* predicted, would become "as virulent and vindictive as the long feud" of the past. The preliminary work in San Francisco done, Broderick hurried off to Sacramento for similar conferences with members of the legislature. His arrival in Sacramento was marked by a festive gathering of his friends and supporters. Salvos of artillery notified friend and foe alike that the "Field Marshal" of California politics was back on the battleground. The cheers of his friends greeted him at the wharf when the steamer docked. Wasting little time on ceremony, he hurried off to the Magnolia Hotel for another round of political conferences. Much of the night was consumed in celebrating his return before the serious work of planning the future course of the Free Soil Democracy began. Sober faces mirrored the concern of some of the celebrants. Some reflected on the manner in which the political wheel of fortune had turned. A few months before, Broderick had earned a Senate seat and capped his triumph by stripping his political enemies of patronage, the chief weapon with which they had resisted the growth of the Free Soil branch of the Democracy. Now the triumph was a hollow victory, for not only had Broderick been deprived of its fruits, but his enemies had been strengthened by a renewal of their long-held monopoly of federal patronage.[39]

Three thousand miles away, another Democratic senator turned to a troubled analysis of the Buchanan administration and the future of his country and his party. In a letter permeated with anguished predictions of "utter destruction" of the Democratic party in the Northwest, he declared that the party must be an antislavery party if it would avoid catastrophe. "Although," Senator Charles E. Stuart continued, "there is a strong feeling in certain quarters of the great strength of this administration . . . my opinion is, it cannot sustain itself, throughout its term." The letter closed with a troubled phrase, "I wish

[38] Gwin to William J. Anderson, Apr. 5, 1857, in O'Meara, *Broderick and Gwin,* p. 199; C. L. Scott to James W. Mandeville, Apr. 2, 1857, Mandeville Coll.; *Daily Town Talk,* Apr. 30, 1857; Gwin to Mandeville, Apr. 3 and 5, 1857, Mandeville Coll.

[39] *Alta California,* Apr. 30 and May 1, 1857; *Daily Town Talk,* Apr. 30, 1857.

to God it was unnecessary for me to report this . . . but it will prove true as holy writ." Stuart's analysis was the work of a mind which reflected the realities of the American political scene. Soon he was joined by Stephen A. Douglas and Broderick in the work of checking the process that was making the Democratic party into a sectional proslavery organization.[40]

The process had already advanced far in California. The Chivalry had recovered much of the ground it lost in the senatorial election of 1857 and was now ready to press its advantage over the Free Soil wing of the party. The political picture was somewhat simplified by the disappearance of the Know-Nothings as a major force. Their demise reflected the restoration of the Chivalry to power and the movement of their political kindred back into their ancestral Democratic home. A formal dissolution of the order followed a meeting of some of its more prominent members in Sacramento. They joined Henry S. Foote, who publicly announced that Buchanan's Cabinet and "such political views as are announced in the inaugural" made unnecessary a "distinctive organization of the American party." While some members resisted its dissolution, it was obvious to political realists that the heyday of the party of the dark lantern was past. Henceforth, the state political arena would feature the Democratic and Republican parties.[41]

The smoldering factionalism within the Democracy was fanned into flame from time to time. As the state convention approached, the apprehension of the Chivalry became more apparent. There was much strong talk of "bolting" if the principal candidates of the Free Soil wing of the party, John Conness and Joseph C. McCorkle, should be nominated. John B. Weller's followers began to boom him for governor. Soon their efforts began to show results in the form of support from various parts of the state. Broderick's role in the forthcoming election was a matter of much speculation.[42]

A few weeks before the opening of the state convention, Broderick issued a lengthy political statement to the press in response to a set of inquiries made by several friends. Four questions were asked: (1)

[40] Stuart to Douglas, Mar. 29, 1857, Douglas Coll., Univ. of Chicago.

[41] *Alta California,* May 1, 1857; *Daily Town Talk,* May 1, 1857; F. B. Murdock to Douglas, Jan. 7, 1858, Douglas Coll.; Peyton Hurt, *The Rise and Fall of the "Know Nothings" in California* (San Francisco, 1930), p. 66. Foote's letter is in Davis, *Political Conventions,* pp. 79–80; see also Hurt, p. 58.

[42] *Alta California,* May 6, 7, 9, and 22, 1857.

Had Broderick broken with the Buchanan administration and decided upon open war with it in the forthcoming campaign? (2) Did Broderick have a specific course of action in mind for the forthcoming convention? (3) Was Broderick aware of the fact that Gwin had publicly declared he had secured several patronage appointments "against you" in spite of his expressed declaration to refrain from patronage matters? (4) What basis was there for the charge that Gwin gave up patronage to secure Broderick's support in the senatorial election? [43]

Broderick took full advantage of the opportunity to set forth a detailed picture of the California political scene. In the first place, he declared, he did not intend to "make war on the administration of President Buchanan." This was a false report, stated Broderick, circulated assiduously by the friends of the Vigilance Committee of 1856 who conspired with the Know-Nothings to bring about the defeat of twenty Democratic legislators in the last general election. He went on to declare that his election to the Senate had been done "without bargain, contract, alliance, combination or understanding with anyone." His decision to support Gwin had been made in the interests of party unity. As for the report that Gwin dabbled in patronage, Broderick referred to Gwin's unequivocal renunciation of patronage announced in his "Address to the People of California." The Broderick response went on to review the manner in which he and his supporters had been maligned, and he challenged his enemies "to produce a man in the length and breadth of the State, whom I ever deceived, or to whom I ever falsified my word." [44]

There was more to this letter, but the substance of it was the announcement that Broderick and his supporters did not intend to organize a separate and distinct political organization in the immediate future. Apparently he clung to the opinion that he could influence the course of the California Democracy. Evidence was mounting to indicate that this was an unrealistic view, for the political conflict between the two factions escalated. As violence became more prevalent in the contest, each side was put on notice that the other was determined to triumph. The usual primary to select delegates to the state convention was preceded by one of the biggest brawls in the

[43] Alfred Redding and J. P. Dyer to Broderick in *Alta California,* June 9, 1857, and New York *Times,* July 14, 1857.
[44] *Alta California,* June 9, 1857.

history of San Francisco's politics. Supporters of the Chivalry and of Broderick turned from rhetoric to muscle and fists. When the police arrived on the scene, they made no arrests but simply consoled the injured. The election results: Broderick retained control of the San Francisco delegation, although the Chivalry made strong inroads.[45]

Weller continued to pick up support. In one county after another, he and his backers carried the day. Sacramento's first ward, a stronghold of Broderick, was the scene of another combat, with knives and fists and ballots deciding the outcome. On the eve of the convention, it was generally understood that Weller had enough delegates to win a first ballot nomination. Apparently Broderick and his supporters were not doing well in this contest for supremacy in the Democratic party.[46]

On the eve of the convention, Broderick met with Gwin's chief political aide, probably to explore the possibility of a reconciliation, but no accord was produced by this meeting. The stonemason politician who had exploited the divisions within the Chivalry in the past was to be denied another opportunity. The united Chivalry, emboldened by the strong showing its preferred gubernatorial candidate made in party primaries, would settle for nothing less than outright capitulation. While some warned of the hazards to the party of a renewal of the "War of the Roses," as the split of 1854 had been labeled, the Chivalry was apparently determined to crush the opposition.[47]

For the first time in years, Broderick was not on the scene when Democrats gathered for their annual state convention. Joe McCorkle led the Free Soil delegates, evidently unwilling to concede defeat in spite of the massive strength of the Chivalry. On the opening day, Free Soilers offered a resolution which would have barred delegates who had not voted for James Buchanan. The objective was to bar the door to the hundreds of erstwhile Democrats who had mistakenly taken the Know-Nothings as the wave of the future in 1856 and now wished to reenter the Democracy. William Van Voorhies, Chivalry Democrat, offered a substitute which was found more acceptable. It extended a "welcome to all national men, of whatever party heretofore, to unite

[45] *Alta California,* May 24, June 26, 27, and 30, July 3, 12, and 14, reported the details of the political conflict that preceded the Democratic convention of 1857.

[46] *Alta California,* July 12 and 14, 1857.

[47] *Alta California,* June 20, 1857, reported the arrival of Gwin and Weller. William B. Norman to James W. Mandeville, June 24, 1857, Mandeville Coll., reported the meeting between Gwin's aide, Mandeville, and Broderick.

with us in finally and forever destroying within the limits of our state, the fell spirit of disunion and sectionalism." The substitute was adopted by a vote of 224 to 81, and thereby the Chivalry's strength as well as its affinity to sometime Know-Nothings was revealed.

As predicted by informed observers, John B. Weller's nomination for governor came on the first ballot. John Nugent, editor of the San Francisco *Herald,* withdrew to avoid being flattened by the Weller forces. The business of selecting candidates was temporarily disrupted when Nugent initiated a discussion of the Vigilance Committee of 1856. The acrimonious talk became more heated when Congressman Philip Herbert followed Nugent to the podium. Herbert assailed the committee but could scarcely be heard above the uproar. The committee obviously had its share of supporters in the convention.

When the nomination process was renewed, only Weller and McCorkle remained as candidates, and when the ballots were counted, it was discovered that Weller had bested his rival by a count of 254 to 61. Once again the Chivalry proved its power and control. It demonstrated its ruling hand repeatedly as each of the candidates endorsed by the Chivalry was selected.[48]

The committee on resolutions produced two reports. Both advocated the reenactment of the platform of 1856, but the minority report recommended as well the censure of the California delegates to the 1856 national convention who failed to come to the support of Buchanan in the Cincinnati convention, despite their instructions. Presented as a motion, this portion of the report was postponed indefinitely. A second resolution of the minority, which was an indictment of the Vigilance Committee of 1856, sparked a renewal of the debate that John Nugent had initiated earlier. Supporters and defenders of the committee rallied to its standard, castigating those who attacked the vigilantes. The uproar finally made it difficult for even the chairman to make himself heard. One speaker turned to statistics to indicate the basis for Democratic hostility to the committee, stating that four men were hanged, twenty-eight banished, and two hundred and sixty arrested, all Democrats. Vincent E. Geiger, stalwart of the Chivalry wing, responded with an observation that with the single exception of Congressman Herbert all who were in favor of the resolution were against John B. Weller. Both men indicated that the Vigi-

[48] Davis, *Political Conventions,* p. 77; *Alta California,* July 14, 15, and 16, 1857.

lance Committee in San Francisco had directed much of its fire against Democrats of Broderick affiliation.

The Chivalry brought an end to the discussion when they rallied around a substitute which pledged the Democratic party to the "support of the constitution and laws of their state and of the United States . . . and that priceless legacy of our fathers contained in the bill of rights and the writ of habeas corpus." The final vote was 181 to 104 in favor of the substitute. It indicated that the Chivalry maintained their control of the convention even when an issue that cut across factional lines was under consideration.

The final humiliation to the Free Soil wing of the party came when the Chivalry jammed through a state central committee that was completely anti-Broderick. Geiger, a longtime associate of Gwin and experienced in the ways of parliamentary bodies, guided the massive steamroller that overcame all resistance by moving immediate adoption after the list of proposed members was read. As the opposition frantically sought ways to delay and amend, the question was put to the convention by the chairman and declared passed. The uproar that followed this high-handed procedure was almost sufficient to drown out a delegate's move to adjourn, but the sharp-eared chairman picked up the motion, repeated it to the assembly, and then with a fall of the gavel announced the adjournment of the convention.[49]

Free Soil Democrats left the convention in a smoldering rage. They had been permitted to sit in the gathering and ostensibly participate, but their voices had been muted and they had been overwhelmed by the opposition whenever a significant decision was made. The candidates, the platform, and the staff organization of the party were controlled by the Chivalry. In terms of power and influence within the party, Free Soil Democrats had been reduced to an impotent faction. They had good reason to look again at the decision that had been made earlier in the year to remain within the Democracy instead of launching an independent organization.

The choice of the California voter was made more complete in the summer of 1857 with the addition of American and Republican tickets. Attempts to dissolve the Know-Nothings met with limited success, although the party of the dark lantern was seriously weakened by the movement of Chivalry-minded nativists into Democratic ranks.

[49] Davis, *Political Conventions,* p. 79; *Alta California,* July 16 and 17, 1857.

A substantial body of nativists clung to the organization, declaring that reorganization rather than dissolution was in order. In convention in late July, they dropped tests, oaths, and obligations of secrecy and patterned themselves after the Democratic party. Their platform remained a collection of platitudes distinguished by its flexibility and the light it failed to cast on significant political issues. Attempts to block the nomination of candidates, masterminded by Bailie Peyton, who sought thereby to aid the Chivalry-dominated Democratic ticket, failed, but choosing a slate proved to be difficult, for nominees were uncommonly shy. As an observer pointed out, this was one convention where the office truly sought the man—hardly characteristic of a healthy and confident political party.[50]

Unlike the Know-Nothings, Republicans were members of a growing and vibrant organization in 1857. Its vitality further weakened the Free Soil faction of the Democracy, for just as proslavery adherents tended to gather around the Democratic standard, antislavery Democrats tended to move toward the Republican banner. In each case, the interparty movement of partisans tended to weaken the Free Soil wing of the Democracy. The vitality of the Republican party was demonstrated repeatedly during this convention. Its political future was bright with promise, and there was no need for the fledgling party to search for candidates. The platform drew heavily upon that of the previous year but added a condemnation of the Dred Scott decision, "a palpable violation of the principles of the declarations of independence, a falsification of the history of our country, subversive of state rights, and a flagrant injustice to a large portion of the people of the United States." [51]

The campaign of 1857 proceeded in a tedious fashion through the long, hot summer that followed the conventions. Broderick and his close associates were conspicuous by their absence, but Weller, Scott, Gwin, and Washington traveled the campaign trails in eager search of the approval of the voters. Long before election day many people were eagerly looking forward to the respite from politics that the balloting would bring. The results came as no great surprise to those who were not blinded by wishful thinking. The Democrats won an impressive statewide victory. They carried their traditional strongholds in the mining counties and the cow counties of the agrarian hinterland by

[50] Davis, *Political Conventions*, pp. 79–83; *Alta California*, July 29 and 30, 1857.
[51] Davis, *Political Conventions*, pp. 74–76.

substantial margins. In San Francisco they trailed the Republicans, but in the other major urban center, Sacramento, they edged the opposition. Weller received a total vote of over fifty thousand, which was more than the Know-Nothing and Republican totals combined.[52]

The Chivalry celebrated, but it was anything but a joyous occasion for Broderick and his supporters. They had been all but pushed out of the party, and then, as if to demonstrate their insignificance, the Chivalry-led Democracy had won an impressive victory. The process of recovering some of the political ground lost by the Chivalry in the senatorial election of 1857 was proceeding handsomely. It entailed curbing Free Soil sentiment and cutting down the chief leader of the Free Soilers. The man who once mastered the Chivalry by a sort of political magic found his legerdemain ineffectual. The plebeian senator who had humbled his enemies at the beginning of the year was now humbled by them. It was a time of rejoicing for the victors and a time for the vanquished to take a long, hard look into the political future.

[52] *Daily Evening Bulletin,* Jan. 4, 1878, p. 4; Davis, *Political Conventions,* p. 84; *Alta California,* Sept. 3, 1857; Election Returns, Vol. 1759, Archives of the Secretary of State, Sacramento.

CHAPTER TEN

The National Political Arena

In early October, Broderick left San Francisco for Washington and the December meeting of Congress. His return to the city of his birth was heralded in letters which alerted the friends of the Chivalry of his coming and his plans. Governor-elect John B. Weller wrote to his old friend Stephen A. Douglas and solicited his assistance in preventing Broderick from blocking some of the nominations to federal service that would come before the Senate for confirmation.[1]

The first session of the Thirty-fifth Congress began in December 1857, and it soon became common knowledge that the break between Broderick and Buchanan was irrevocable. The immediate issue was the President's policy in Kansas—that troubled territory where the controversy over the status of slavery in the West had gone beyond the realm of debate, and guns had been brought into use as a final arbiter. In his maiden speech, heavily larded with stark nouns and vigorous adjectives, Broderick reviewed the situation in Kansas. When he had finished, there was no question in the minds of his fellow senators that Broderick was a vigorous and enduring enemy of the administration.

Broderick began with a simple statement which identified him as an ally of Douglas and Senator Charles E. Stuart of Michigan in the battle over the admission of Kansas under the Lecompton constitution. Once there had been two Democratic senators in open opposition

[1] *Alta California,* Oct. 6, 1857; C. H. Hempstead to William Bigler, Aug. 1, 1857, Garrett W. Ryckman to Bigler, Sept. 21, 1857, and Hempstead to Bigler, Oct. 4, 1857, Bigler Coll., Pennsylvania Hist. Soc.; Weller to Douglas, Nov. 18, 1857, Douglas Coll., Univ. of Chicago.

to the administration on this issue; henceforth there would be three. The President, and the President alone, was responsible for the disorder that prevailed in Kansas, declared Broderick. Buchanan's own appointees, Robert J. Walker and Frederick P. Stanton, he said, had labored to bring peace to Kansas only to be overwhelmed by the lawless and disorderly—emboldened by the President's failure to support his appointees. Both had resigned in disillusionment and despair, but still the President endorsed the Lecompton constitution, which made a mockery of the doctrine of popular sovereignty. The President was indicted in phrases that steamed with hostility. Buchanan was personally responsible for the prevailing disorder, having "stepped down from that exalted position . . . to coerce the people into a base submission to the will of an illegalized body of men." Broderick added, "I do not intend, because I am a member of the Democratic party, to permit the President of the United States, who has been elected by that party, to create civil war in Kansas." [2]

While some were shocked by the vehemence of his language, there was little doubt that Broderick's indictment of the President aired opinions held by many. A review of the events leading up to Broderick's speech tended to establish the logic and validity of his position. A year before, Governor John W. Geary sounded public opinion and declared that the majority of the population of Kansas favored the establishment of a free state. Geary had been replaced by Walker, who accepted the post only after long consultation with the President and an agreement that the principle of popular sovereignty would be utilized to settle the question of slavery. Shortly after his arrival, Walker found himself frustrated and threatened by the proslavery politicians on the ground. To complicate his problems, he found the President and his retinue of proslavery advisers in Washington cutting the ground from under him, until he too left Kansas in disgust. The overwhelming majority of the population of Kansas was opposed to the extension of slavery, but a minority had foisted on its people a constitution which established, supported, and defended the institution of slavery. The President, expressing his views in a miasma of legalisms and technicalities, had endorsed the odious work of the Lecompton convention. "Seldom in the history of the nation has a

[2] *Cong. Globe,* 35th Cong., 1st Sess., pp. 163–164. The San Francisco *Daily Evening Bulletin,* Jan. 30, 1858, praised the speech.

President made so disastrous a blunder" is the considered judgment of Allan Nevins.[3]

Douglas, Broderick, and Stuart comprised the small band of senators who opposed the President openly. Other leaders of the Democratic party pleaded with him to heed the advice of the territorial officials. The Democracy had few figures of greater stature and integrity than George Bancroft. A few days before Buchanan made the fatal endorsement of the Lecompton constitution, Bancroft pleaded with the President to reject it. His words left little doubt of his concern for the welfare of his party and his country if the President placed the prestige of his office on the side of the cabal which was attempting to subvert the principle of popular sovereignty. Bancroft declared that Buchanan was a powerful figure and implored him to avoid the fate of Pierce, whose administration of "doughfaces" had been repudiated. Buchanan's "very powerful position could be made impregnable if you choose to make it so," he wrote. The Pierce administration, declared Bancroft, had "died of Jefferson Davis and Caleb Cushing; the nullifiers never were in their palmiest days able to storm the government, and are less able than ever." [4] Bancroft and Broderick alike put the burden on the President, who had the power to determine how this momentous crisis in national affairs would be resolved. The decision of the President to endorse the Lecompton constitution was followed by Broderick's indictment.

A few days after the President announced his decision, Douglas unfurled the banner of popular sovereignty in the Senate in a smashing attack on administration policy. Only Broderick, Stuart, and George E. Pugh of Ohio stood with Douglas, but a flood of mail from all parts of the nation indicated that Broderick and Douglas had struck a responsive chord in the conscience of the Democratic party. Gideon Welles joined in the chorus of acclaim.[5]

The question of admission of Kansas under the Lecompton constitution dominated the Thirty-fifth Congress. All other matters were colored by it. As a newcomer, Broderick was assigned the customary

[3] Roy F. Nichols, *The Disruption of American Democracy* (New York, 1948), pp. 159–163; Allan Nevins, *The Emergence of Lincoln* (New York, 1951), I, 239–249.

[4] George Bancroft to Buchanan, Dec. 5, 1857, Buchanan Papers, Pennsylvania Hist. Soc.

[5] C. H. Knapp to Douglas, Dec. 10, 1857, William Hull to Douglas, Dec. 5, 1857, and Gideon Welles to Douglas, Dec. 12, 1857, Douglas Coll.

role of the freshman senator—that of observer. The pressure of events, however, made it impossible for him to sit as a mute observer in the distinguished company of Judah P. Benjamin, John J. Crittenden, Stephen A. Douglas, Lyman Trumbull, Charles E. Stuart, William H. Seward, Sam Houston, and Robert M. T. Hunter. As the days passed, Broderick came to play an ever more prominent role. Described as "one of the quietest and most unassuming members of the Senate," he "rarely took the floor in debate, but when he did speak he was always heard with respect." By his bitter denunciation of the President, Broderick attracted national attention. His maiden speech was widely reported, and almost overnight he was transformed from a somewhat obscure antislavery politician from California into a national figure whose political future was bright with promise.[6]

The administration made the Lecompton question a party test—those who rebelled were subjected to discipline through the distribution of patronage or committee assignments in the Senate. Both forms of the party lash were applied to Broderick, Douglas, Stuart, and their allies within the Democracy. Disciplining the Little Giant was a formidable task, however, for he was a major figure with a tremendous national following. His backbone stiffened through association with Broderick, Douglas was soon casting about for allies. Before long, joint strategy meetings with Republican members of Congress were being held.[7]

The bill to admit Kansas under the Lecompton constitution was introduced in early February, and its passage by the "ides of March" was confidently expected by the administration. This schedule was not kept, however, for with each passing day came additional evidence, in the form of letters, telegrams, and delegations, that public opinion was opposed. Robert J. Walker's successor in Kansas, James W. Denver, the President's handpicked choice, personally reported to his chief that an honest election in Kansas would be won by Free State men. Denver recommended discarding the Lecompton constitution and assembling a new convention which would accurately reflect public sentiment in the territory. Buchanan ignored this latest evaluation from his chief-

[6] *Colonel Alexander K. McClure's Recollections of Half a Century* (Salem, Mass., 1902), p. 30; Jeremiah Lynch, *The Life of David C. Broderick* (New York, 1911), pp. 174–175.

[7] Henry Wilson, *History of the Rise and Fall of the Slave Power in America* (Boston, 1874), II, 562; Joe McCorkle to Douglas, Dec. 13, 1857, Douglas Coll.; Broderick to John W. Forney, Dec. 14, 1857, Pennsylvania Hist. Soc.

tain in the field and disregarded, as well, every sign that public opinion, especially in the North, repudiated the administration's Kansas policy.[8]

While leaders of the administration maintained that the bill would be passed eventually and the controversy quickly forgotten, Broderick predicted soon after it was thrown in the legislative hopper that it would be defeated. Fervently he expressed himself: "God grant it may be defeated. For it will break up the Democratic party in the free states if it passes." His aides did not share his views; Andrew Jackson Butler, younger brother of Benjamin F. Butler, advised a friend that Broderick "had let his passion and bitterness run away with him, against the wishes and counsel of his best friends." [9]

Everywhere the Democratic party was divided, and leaders sought a way out of the dilemma that found them caught between the national leadership of the party and a substantial part of its rank and file. A politician in San Francisco, when asked where he stood on the issue, declared that he did not exactly know but he was with the party. Douglas, veteran of scores of difficult political situations, found himself in a quandary. To his embarrassment, Republicans began to woo and caress him. His opposition to the administration cost him dearly, and an informed observer commented: "No matter what turn the thing now takes, he is politically dead for a long time. It is not within the range of possibilities that he should receive a Southern vote for many years." The fact that without Southern votes no Democrat could be nominated or elected to the presidency was not unknown to the ambitious Little Giant of Illinois.[10]

In late March, the Senate voted to admit Kansas under the Lecompton constitution, only Douglas, Broderick, and Stuart breaking the solid Democratic ranks. A week later, a roadblock in the form of an amendment which would resubmit the constitution to the people of Kansas appeared and prevented further progress in the House. The balance of the month was consumed in a futile effort to cope with this

[8] Denver to Buchanan, Jan. 16, 1858, Buchanan Papers. Nichols, *Disruption,* pp. 155–175, presents a detailed analysis of the Lecompton battle.

[9] Broderick to John A. McGlynn, Feb. 4, 1858, Broderick File, Soc. of Calif. Pioneers Lib., San Francisco; C. H. Hempstead to William Bigler, Feb. 19, 1858, Bigler Coll.

[10] H. Fellows to Douglas, Feb. 4, 1858, and L. M. Mizner to Douglas, Feb. 5, 1858, Douglas Coll.; S. L. M. Barlow to "Dear William," Feb. 13, 1858, Barlow Coll., Huntington Lib.

problem, but the impasse was not broken until the English Bill was devised.[11]

The English Bill, carefully drawn to muster maximum support, resubmitted the Lecompton constitution to the electorate of Kansas. If it was ratified, the new state was to be enriched by a grant of about four million acres of public land and five percent of the net proceeds from the sale of an additional two million acres. If it was rejected, the admission of Kansas was to be delayed until a census indicated the state had the population required for a congressional representative. The appearance of this measure threatened the unity of the anti-Lecompton group in Congress. Republicans were generally ready to stand firm, but Democratic members of the strange alliance, still searching for a graceful manner to rejoin and reunify their party, looked with hesitant approval on the English Bill.[12]

Douglas analyzed the bill carefully before he took his stance in a long speech in the Senate. He was especially conscious of his precarious position. A reelection campaign impended, and division of the Illinois Democracy portended defeat and political oblivion. On the other hand, his long political career might be capped with election to the presidency if he could surmount the political obstacles that lay in his immediate path. Circumstances pushed him in the direction of compromise, especially if that compromise would reunify the party in Illinois and allow him to continue carrying the banner of popular sovereignty. This was the background of his suggestion that Democratic foes of Lecompton might now accept the English Bill, "because they could claim that it did virtually submit the question at issue to the people." [13]

Broderick did not agree. Undoubtedly he was aware of the pressure that events and the administration were exerting on Douglas, but he "indignantly denounced any sacrifice of the principle on which they had hitherto fought the Lecompton Constitution." Stuart was equally vehement in his objections to such a compromise. John B. Haskin, anti-Lecompton Democratic congressman from New York, expressed the objections of the group in an evaluation of the English Bill which included: "Its passage would enable the administration to retreat by a

[11] Nichols, *Disruption,* pp. 176–180.

[12] Nevins, *The Emergence of Lincoln,* I, 297–298; Nichols, *Disruption,* p. 179.

[13] Wilson, II, 562; Nichols, *Disruption,* pp. 168–173; Nevins, *The Emergence of Lincoln,* I, 299.

back-door passage from its support of a nefarious scheme and infamous legislation which President Buchanan and his heads of department should never have favored."[14]

The leaders of the administration, now in a desperate situation, brought all their forces into play in an attempt to push the English Bill through Congress. California Representative Joseph McKibben was offered the choice of supporting the measure or of seeing his father removed from his position as naval agent in Philadelphia. His father and brother joined in appeals to McKibben, but he refused. Haskin reported that a township of land was offered if he would change his views and support the Lecompton policy. Studies were made of the constituencies of stubborn congressmen to ascertain what could be done to influence them. One analysis that crossed Buchanan's desk declared that "we must make major changes in appointments, Marshall, U.S. Attorney, Postmaster & etc." in Michigan in order to bring Senator Stuart to heel.[15]

In California it was apparent that Broderick and Douglas represented the bulk of popular opinion. A newspaper which had vigorously supported the administration suspended publication when Douglas and Broderick supporters began a boycott, and the sorrowful publisher conceded that "this state, at present, is [for] Douglas." Another California observer reported "four-fifths of the Democracy support Stephen A. Douglas." A study of the state's newspapers indicated that of "twenty-five Democratic papers in the State, there are but five that sustain the Administration."[16]

Fully aware of the difficulties that Douglas faced, the administration continued to negotiate with him. Robert J. Walker met with the Little Giant and reviewed the political realities that demanded his support of the English Bill. Walker pointed out that it represented a feasible way out of the impasse in which Douglas and the administration were locked. Douglas paced the floor with large drops of sweat springing from his forehead—"they were almost drops of blood"—as

[14] Wilson, II, 562; Nevins, *The Emergence of Lincoln,* I, 299–301; George Fort Milton, *The Eve of Conflict* (Boston, 1934), p. 275.

[15] Henry Ledyard, "Memorandum on Matters in Michigan" to Buchanan, March 1858, Buchanan Papers; Jere McKibben to William Bigler, Feb. 19, 1858, Bigler Coll.; Wilson, II, 565; Nevins, *The Emergence of Lincoln,* I, 299; Philip Shriver Klein, *President James Buchanan: A Biography* (University Park, Pa., 1962), p. 311.

[16] R. Schoyer to William Bigler, Mar. 3, 1858, Bigler Coll.; C. J. Whitney to Douglas, Mar. 21, 1858, Gideon Welles to Douglas, Mar. 16, 1858, and H. B. Payne to Douglas, Apr. 9, 1858, Douglas Coll.

Walker ticked off the arguments designed to get him to change his mind. The hammerlike blows of Walker's logic made deep impressions. Slowly, reluctantly, fearfully, Douglas responded. The decision finally came; he would vote for the English Bill, and the news would be telegraphed around the country to alert his supporters.[17]

Douglas' ordeal was not over, for now another set of imperious demands was served on him. The day after his conference with Walker, Douglas met with Broderick and other representatives of the anti-Lecompton congressional bloc. The freshman senator demanded to know the truth of the report that Douglas had changed his position. "Mr. Douglas, I understand you proposed to abandon this fight," was his opening gambit. Douglas explained, "I see no hope of success. They will crush us and if they do there is no future for any of us, and I think we can agree upon terms that will virtually sustain ourselves." Broderick's heated reply left little room for equivocation: "You came to me of your own accord and asked me to take this stand and I have followed you. I have committed myself against this infernal Lecompton constitution. If you desert me, God damn you, I will make you crawl under your chair in the Senate." The full exchange is not recorded, but there is little doubt that this meeting with Broderick and his associates determined the final stand that Douglas took on the English Bill. The meeting and the outcome were reported to the President.[18]

Despite a major effort, the anti-Lecompton coalition was unable to prevent the passage of the English Bill. Shortly before the final ballot in the Senate, Broderick summed up the objections of advocates of popular sovereignty. He conceded the bill submitted the Lecompton constitution to the electorate of Kansas but pointed out that the bill

[17] Edgar E. Robinson, ed. "The Day Journal of Milton S. Latham," *Calif. Hist. Soc. Quart.*, VI (1932), 14; Nevins, *The Emergence of Lincoln,* I, 299; Nichols, *Disruption,* p. 173.

[18] Nichols, *Disruption,* pp. 173–174; Nevins, *The Emergence of Lincoln,* I, 300; F. F. Low, "Political Notes," pp. 53–54, MS in Bancroft Lib.; Wilson, II, 562 ff. L. E. Fredman, "Broderick: A Reassessment," *Pacific Historical Review,* XXX (1961), airs his doubts as to the authenticity of the accounts of this incident. In addition to the foregoing, and perhaps the best single piece of evidence that it took place, is the memorandum in the Buchanan Papers, Pennsylvania Hist. Soc., dated Apr. 30, 1858, which declares: "Senator Gwin informed me that Governor Walker had told him that on last Saturday night (24th) he, Douglas, Stanton and Forney had held a consultation on the English programme. They agreed to accept it and Douglas was to advance $100 to telegraph that determination over the United States. On Sunday, another meeting was held at which Broderick, Montgomery, McKibben and others were present and they prevailed upon Douglas to change his mind."

hinged the voting rights of the people to a base condition. Admission of Kansas, in the event of rejection of the constitution, was to be postponed until a census taker, appointed by the administration, certified the population had reached the congressional ratio of 93,420. In effect, Broderick declared, the admission of Kansas was being postponed indefinitely by the bill. The imputation of want of integrity to a "census taker" appointed by the Buchanan administration was not lost to his audience.[19]

In the most striking speech Broderick made during the Lecompton crisis, he scored the South for its pretensions to greatness.[20] He began with an allusion to a recent speech by William H. Seward in which the senator from New York expressed regret that the Kansas-Nebraska Act and the revocation of the Missouri Compromise had been passed. Republicans, Broderick declared, had little reason to regret its passage, for it laid the basis for the rise of the Republican party. No opponent of slavery should grieve over the revocation of the Missouri Compromise, for that event "made the Territories a common battlefield in which the conflicting rights of free and slave labor might struggle for supremacy." The North felt that a great wrong had been done, but that was a mistaken view of things.

The North should have applauded, and the South mourned, the removal of that barrier, for "In the passage of the Kansas-Nebraska Bill, the rampart that protected slavery in the southern Territories was broken down." In the ensuing contest there could be little doubt of the eventual outcome. "How foolish for the South to hope to contend with success. . . . Slavery is old, decrepit, and consumptive; freedom is young, strong, and vigorous." He went on to point out that there were but six million people interested in the extension of slavery, but "there are twenty million freemen to contend for these Territories, out of which to carve for themselves homes where labor is honorable."

Broderick reviewed the arguments marshaled to establish the constitutionality of the Missouri Compromise and the right of Congress to regulate the spread of slavery into the territories of the United States. He incorporated extensive quotations from the congressional debates which dealt with the Compromise and showed that the views of such authorities as Henry Clay, Reverdy Johnson, and James Buchanan

[19] Nevins, *The Emergence of Lincoln,* I, 301; Nichols, *Disruption,* p. 175; *Cong. Globe,* 35th Cong., 1st Sess., p. 1892.

[20] *Cong. Globe,* 35th Cong., 1st Sess., App., pp. 191–193.

had defended the right of Congress to regulate the institution of slavery in the territories. Buchanan and Johnson, however, had taken new ground and joined with the Supreme Court in its belated discovery that Congress did not possess the right to regulate slavery in the territories.

Turning to a recent speech by Senator James M. Hammond of South Carolina—the "mudsill" speech—Broderick began the reply to Hammond which brought him national acclaim. Hammond declared that the South had built the greatest civilization the world had seen since the Roman Empire. Like all great civilizations, it was erected on a mudsill, a servile class of laborers—the slaves of the South. The North too had a mudsill, Hammond declared, a servile class, but it was white, not black. Every civilization is built on such a mudsill, contended Hammond, and if northern agitators continued to stir southern slaves into discontent and rebellion, the South would retaliate by sending agitators among the nothern servile class. The mudsills of the North would be informed as to their rights and grievances and directed in the mighty weapon that was available to them in the form of a ballot.

If servile revolt by the mudsills would not restrain the provocations of the North, Hammond went on, perhaps economic warfare would. The northern economy could be brought to a shattering decline by a withdrawal of cotton from the export trade. "Cotton is king" was his graphic phrase, and its export could be manipulated to trigger a commercial panic in the North similar to the panic of 1857.

Broderick began his reply on a personal note. He assumed that the senator from South Carolina was not referring to anyone personally in stigmatizing the free laborers of the North as mudsills. His own origin as the son of a mechanic, Broderick declared, was well known. Pointing to the intricate sculpturing on the columns of the Senate chamber, he said they were the work of his father. Were he inclined to forget his origin, he went on, this was not the place he could do it. Five years he had labored in stonework, following in the footsteps of his father. Unlike others, he would not gloss over the harsh bleakness of his life as an apprentice stonemason. A life of toil in stonework was not to be envied, but on the other hand, he was not ashamed of the fact that he was a mudsill—and the son of a mudsill.

As for Hammond's threat to send agitators among the mudsills of the North—let them come. The mechanics and artisans of the North

—the mudsills, Broderick acknowledged—tended to forget the political power they held in the form of a ballot. If agitators from the South could awaken them to a sense of their power and responsibility, let them come. He admonished his listeners to remember that these mechanics of the North held the future of the United States in their hands. As for Hammond's proud boast that "Cotton is king," Broderick quoted in rebuttal one telling fact: California alone produced annually the equivalent in gold of the value of all cotton exported by the South in a year.

As his fellow senators began to shuffle papers in anticipation of adjournment, Broderick brought his speech to a close by an examination of Buchanan's role in the present crisis in government. His final statement was a scathing indictment of the President: "I hope, in mercy, sir, to the boasted intelligence of this age, the historian, when writing a history of these times, will ascribe this attempt of the Executive to force this constitution upon an unwilling people to the fading intellect, the petulant passion, and trembling dotage of an old man on the verge of the grave."

The sharp language brought no immediate reaction in the Senate, which quietly resumed its usual routine. The failure of anyone present to rise to the President's defense was significant. The personal language of Broderick was also significant and extraordinary, not so much for the Senate as for the senator. Broderick was customarily a man of vehement opinion, but he did not usually utilize the language of personal vituperation. On this occasion the language reflected Broderick's conviction that Buchanan's policy in Kansas was destroying the Democratic party, advancing the interests of slavery, and creating civil war in Kansas. Moreover, the President was immediately and personally responsible.

The will of the administration finally prevailed, and the Lecompton crisis passed into the limbo of other crises. The effects of this struggle on the American political scene, however, were visible long after the final vote on the English Bill had been tallied. The administration won a Pyrrhic victory that destroyed James Buchanan as a national political figure. The controversy cleaved the Democracy, separating the proslavery wing from the antislavery wing and destroying the middle ground between them. Walls of animosity were erected that were never breached; henceforth the two wings of the party were locked in deadly combat. While Douglas remained a powerful figure in the party, his stand in favor of popular sovereignty in Kansas destroyed him in the South. Southern ultras and the spokesmen of the administration rejoiced in their victory, little realizing that this triumph, like the earlier one of the Kansas-Nebraska Bill, was to strengthen their political enemies. Perhaps the most tragic consequence was the destruction of the Democracy as a national organization unified enough to cope with the forces of disunion that were destroying all national organizations in the United States of the 1850's.[21]

While the Lecompton question dominated the proceedings of the Thirty-fifth Congress and Broderick's role in it, a number of other legislative matters interested him. He took steps, for example, to have the Civil Fund of California turned over to the state, supported legislation which would have refunded duties paid on goods destroyed in a series of fires in San Francisco, and pushed a bill which would have compensated California for sums expended in suppressing Indian uprisings—a responsibility assumed by the state in the absence of federal action. In general, he was concerned with the routine duties which his office imposed on him, as well as matters of larger scope and significance.[22]

Broderick's commitment to the Free Soil position and the agrarian dream of a free society of landed yeomen based upon a distribution of public lands to frontier settlers was seen in a Senate resolution which he introduced. Typical of hundreds of such statements, passed in innumerable meetings of the National Reform Association and similar groups, it stipulated that the federal government should survey the public domain and distribute it "for the free and exclusive use of actual settlers not possessed of other lands." A portent of the Homestead Bill of the future, the resolution was referred to the Committee on Public Lands, where it was assured a friendly hearing because its author was a member.[23]

A resolution of the California legislature calling for the donation of segments of public land to each state and territory for the establishment and support of colleges was also brought to the Senate's attention by the freshman senator. It, too, was referred to the Committee on

[21] Nichols, *Disruption,* p. 175; Nevins, *The Emergence of Lincoln,* I, 301–303; Buchanan to William Bigler, Feb. 25, 1858, Bigler Coll.; Philadelphia *Press,* Apr. 20, 1858.

[22] *Cong. Globe,* 35th Cong., 1st Sess., pp. 428, 377, 329.

[23] *Cong. Globe,* 35th Cong., 1st Sess., pp. 492, 623. Gwin subsequently joined with the southern bloc to defeat the measure. See Nichols, *Disruption,* p. 232.

Public Lands, where it languished. A succeeding Congress enacted it into law under the title of the Morrill Act, several years after Broderick introduced it to the Senate.[24]

On a number of occasions, Broderick struck at his political enemies. A resolution which advocated the termination of the existing contract between the government and the Pacific Mail Steamship Company and the establishment of "two distinct weekly mail contracts, on separate routes, to two distinct companies" was introduced by Broderick.[25] It was, among other things, an unsubtle thrust at Gwin, for the senior senator was widely known as the chief representative of the Pacific Mail in the United States Senate.

Broderick clashed repeatedly with Gwin. Efforts to push a Pacific Railroad Bill through the Congress tended to unite the two men, but as the session unfolded it became apparent that this measure, too, would divide them. As chairman of the special committee to which the bill had been referred, Gwin was in a strategic position and Broderick deferred to him; however, differences developed over the nature and scope of the bill and the parliamentary tactics that should be utilized to guide it through Congress. Gwin advocated the construction of three railroads to link the East with the Pacific Coast. Each of the three would follow a specific route—northern, central, or southern—and the three would be linked by north-south lines. All of the proposed construction would be supported by subsidies from the federal government. However pleasing at first blush, it was an impractical program, for a large part of the Senate was reluctant to support a single road, let alone three.

Broderick became increasingly restive and critical of Gwin's leadership. At one point he criticized Gwin's refusal to allow the admission of Minnesota to be considered by the Senate. The admission, he declared, could be handled expeditiously, and the support of Minnesota's two senators would strengthen the advocates of the Pacific Railroad Bill. Gwin made a sarcastic rejoinder to this observation, beginning, "When he has been here as long as I have," and went on to compare the experience of the two men. Broderick was, of course, found wanting in the comparison. The two men supported a proposal

[24] *Cong. Globe,* 35th Cong., 1st Sess., p. 2157. Gwin voted for a bill which incorporated the principle, but Buchanan vetoed the measure; see Nichols, *Disruption,* pp. 232–233.

[25] *Cong. Globe,* 35th Cong., 1st Sess., p. 1400.

that contractors be allowed to determine the difficult question of the route, but a short time later the whole question was postponed to the second session by "administration votes." Californians were uniformly disappointed, for this was an issue that cut across most party lines. Perceptive observers noted that Gwin's allies in the Senate blocked the measure.[26]

Of all the great problems that confronted the California politician of the 1850's, none was more troublesome than the question of land titles. A matter which became increasingly complex as the years passed, the problem began during the Mexican period, when huge swaths of land passed into private hands under casual procedures which were in sharp contrast with Anglo-Saxon traditions. A number of grants were made in anticipation of American acquisition; others were steeped in fraud. Substantial amounts of land were involved, and individuals or groups stood to lose or gain a great deal. To the land-hungry American settler, the rich golden land was—as it had been in other areas of the Trans-Mississippi West—public domain, subject to preemption. To the long-established resident possessed of such property, the land or a substantial part of it was owned by private individuals, and anyone who attempted to settle on it and exercise preemption rights was a trespasser and a squatter.[27]

The land commission established by the federal government in 1851 to examine and validate California titles was a unique organization. Its work was reviewed and supplemented by the courts. A morass of complicated procedures and legalistic technicalities eventually emerged which provided the unscrupulous with opportunity. Lawyers were provided with work to last for years. The manufacturing of

[26] *Cong. Globe,* 35th Cong., 1st Sess., pp. 902, 1297–98; Broderick to E. J. Moore, Apr. 19, 1858, Broderick File, Soc. of Calif. Pioneers Lib., San Francisco; Nichols, *Disruption,* pp. 231–233, 326.

[27] W. W. Robinson, *Land in California* (Berkeley, 1948), is the best single book on this complex subject. Paul Gates has made exhaustive research and written a series of articles on aspects of the topic; see his "California Agricultural College Lands," *Pacific Historical Review,* XXX (1961), 103–122, and "The Adjudication of Spanish and Mexican Land Claims in California," *Huntington Library Quarterly,* XXI (1958), 213–236. Josiah Royce, *California, from the Conquest in 1846 to the Second Vigilance Committee in San Francisco* (New York, 1948), Ch. vi, is a useful account, and Robert Glass Cleland, *The Cattle on a Thousand Hills* (San Marino, 1941), pp. 46–71, is brief but excellent. John Walton Caughey, *California* (Englewood Cliffs, N.J., 1961), Ch. xx, is a clearly written review of the subject. A survey of the literature reveals the lack of a definitive account. Andrew Rolle, *California, a History* (New York, 1963), pp. 298–307, is a summary based upon a recent study and review of the relevant published materials.

evidence to satisfy the arbitrary requirements that had been set became an established procedure. Interested parties suppressed adverse evidence, altered, destroyed, and forged documents, suborned perjury —in short, committed every offense known to courts which had been concerned with such things through the years. As apparently dubious and worthless titles successfully passed the scrutiny of the commission and courts, many people became increasingly intolerant of the findings and the manifest injustice that was sometimes accomplished.[28]

From the beginning of his career in California, Broderick had come into contact with some of the people involved and was generally familiar with the subject. As a Free Soil Democrat, he was interested in the distribution of the public lands so as to bring about the reality of the Jeffersonian dream of a land of free and independent yeomen. Not only did his philosophy lead him in this direction, but the fact that he drew a considerable amount of his support from like-minded people made him sensitive to the needs of the settlers. On the other hand, although he was denounced as the "squatter candidate" by a member of a legal firm which fattened on land case fees, he enjoyed the support of the representatives of the old California families. Apparently he was determined to see justice done but unwilling to see the bold and unscrupulous speculator enrich himself through the validation of specious claims.[29]

For years the uncertainty of land titles in California troubled its people, burdened its courts, and factionalized its parties. In some instances it required a generation of lawyers, judges, and courts to settle the difficult questions that had been raised. The public peace was repeatedly sacrificed when men turned from the courts and resorted to violence to establish their right to land. The economic well-being of the state was adversely affected as this uncertainty of title put a brake on its entrepreneurs and investors.[30]

Broderick made a tremendous contribution, which has generally gone unnoticed, to the effort to bring a degree of order and justice into

[28] Rolle, *California,* pp. 300–301; Caughey, *California,* pp. 306–318; Ivy B. Ross, "The Confirmation of Spanish and Mexican Land Grants in California" (unpubl. M.A. thesis, Univ. of Calif., 1928).

[29] Gates, "California's Agricultural College Lands," p. 103; Sacramento *Times and Transcript,* Jan. 27, 1852; Henry W. Halleck to Pablo de la Guerra, Jan. 29, 1852, De la Guerra Coll., Santa Barbara Mission Archives.

[30] Rolle, *California,* pp. 303–306; Herbert W. Drummond, "Squatter Activity in San Francisco, 1847–1854" (unpubl. M.A. thesis, Univ. of Calif., 1952).

this area. It took the form of three federal laws which he introduced and guided through the Thirty-fifth Congress. The first provided for the systematic collection and preservation of archival material that would facilitate the process of establishing titles. It provided heavy penalties for the concealment of such materials and made the surveyor-general of California responsible for the work of collection and preservation. A second law permitted parties at interest in the district courts to subpoena witnesses, books, papers, and so forth in other jurisdictions if they were material to a land case. A third measure made the forgery or alteration of documents a federal offense; not only was the fabrication of spurious documents made a federal offense but the establishment of a false claim also became a federal crime. All of the bills were adopted and a badly needed framework of law provided whereby the involved and difficult land title problems in California could be approached.[31]

Broderick's battle with his political enemies frequently spilled over onto the Senate floor, although most of those enemies were thousands of miles away. On one occasion he pointed out that John B. Weller's brother, Charles Weller, postmaster of San Francisco, collected special charges from patrons of his post office and retained the income. A series of acrimonious exchanges resulted in a resolution of inquiry. The investigation revealed a number of irregular practices but nothing justifying the removal of the postmaster. The incident alerted federal officials in California that the Chivalry had an enemy in the Senate who was quick to spot irregularities and eager to expose those responsible.[32]

In the Senate, Broderick revealed some of the activities of appointees of the Chivalry that disturbed him. He made a number of charges: "When I arrived here in 1857 I was present at an interview which took place between the then Secretary of the Treasury, Mr. Guthrie . . . and I heard him inform my colleague [Senator Gwin] that the

[31] The bills in question were S. Nos. 312, 313, and 314; see *Cong. Globe,* 35th Cong., 1st Sess., p. 1960. These Broderick-backed measures were passed, and the collection of "all papers, documents, books, etc., of every description belonging to or pertaining to the former government of California" was undertaken, the "United States surveyor-general for California" appointed custodian, and his superior, the Secretary of the Interior, given the responsibility "to collect said documents wherever they might be found and place them with the custodian" (Zoeth Skinner Eldredge, *The Beginnings of San Francisco* [San Francisco, 1912], II, 758–759); cf. Ross, "The Confirmation of Spanish and Mexican Land Grants," pp. 87–89.

[32] *Cong. Globe,* 35th Cong., 1st Sess., pp. 2070, 2108.

collector of customs at San Francisco in 1854 and 1855, was a defaulter to the amount of $430,000." This sort of thing was continuing, Broderick declared. "Last year, the melter and refiner and assayer of the Mint in California was discovered to be a defaulter to the amount of about one hundred and seventy-five thousand dollars." These were but two instances of the manner in which the "officers in California have a way of getting outside fees, besides the salaries they receive from the Government," he concluded wryly. The last comment was at the expense of Gwin, who was vigorously pushing an increase in California surveyor allowances. Broderick went on to point out that such allowances in Minnesota, Wisconsin, Iowa, and Kansas were much less than those paid in California. When the matter finally came to a vote, however, he cast an affirmative ballot, after explaining he did not wish to bring surveying in California to a halt by blocking the appropriation.[33]

Broderick's probing for a vulnerable spot was annoying to the representatives of the Chivalry, but it was not until he touched on the Lime Point matter that they became obviously unhappy. The affair began innocently enough when a Broderick-introduced resolution directed the Secretary of War to inform the Senate "what contracts, if any, have been entered into by the Department for the purchase of Lime Point, in California, for military purposes." A week later, Secretary John B. Floyd reported that the site had been purchased for $200,000. Gwin supplemented the explanation of the Secretary of War, declaring that the land, which lay at the mouth of San Francisco Bay, was essential to the fortification of the bay. Broderick rose to the attack. The land, he declared, was not worth $200,000 and would not bring more than $7,000 at auction. The contract was an "enormous fraud." Senator William B. Fessenden joined the fray with a comment which stripped the contract of a major defense when he pointed out that the land could have been acquired by condemnation proceedings if it were, in fact, essential to the government. The Senate passed on without making a final disposition of the question, but the matter was only to lie dormant. The Lime Point scandal was to haunt the Chivalry, for it was a palpable steal—fraudulent on its face.[34]

Toward the close of the session Broderick interrupted Senator

[33] *Cong. Globe,* 35th Cong., 1st Sess., pp. 2902, 2455–56, 2643, 2645.

[34] *Cong. Globe,* 35th Cong., 1st Sess., pp. 1907, 2068–69; Philadelphia *Press,* June 5, 1858.

Douglas, as the latter reviewed the political situation in Illinois and skirted the issue of the use of federal patronage by the Buchanan administration, in an effort to bring about Douglas' defeat. Having broken with the President and his retinue, Broderick sought to have Douglas publicly fix responsibility on the President. Douglas refused to go so far, although he indicated that the patronage lash was being applied by men acting in the name of the President. Broderick had crossed the Rubicon, but Douglas refused to join him, still lingering on the near side, anxious to avoid a final and complete rupture with the administration.[35]

Douglas still hoped for a *rapprochement* with Buchanan and the Democracy of the South—responding to the overtures that came via spokesmen for the administration. He was told that the leaders of the administration regarded him as one who "desired to conciliate and strengthen the Democracy of the Union," as an overture. The negotiations went on for some time, but the reconciliation was not to become a reality. Warned that Douglas was planning to switch parties in 1860, the administration continued to bludgeon the Douglas organization. Hampered in his battle for reelection, Douglas clung to the middle ground between the proslavery and antislavery wings of the Democracy. That middle ground was being eroded from beneath him by the welter of political currents that operated in the American political scene—dividing it into Republicans and Democrats.[36]

In midyear the session came to a close, and Broderick took ship for California via the isthmus route. The annual political battles were at hand, and he was anxious to participate. The situation was rife with danger but also bright with promise. A majority of the Democratic press lined up with Broderick and Douglas on the Kansas question. The spring elections had been marked by a string of setbacks for supporters of the administration. The fact that the "anti-Lecomptonites and Black Republicans" united in the campaign did not make the rout of the administration Democrats more palatable.[37]

[35] *Cong. Globe,* 35th Cong., 1st Sess., p. 3057.

[36] James May to Douglas, June 21, 24, and 25, 1858, Douglas Coll.; Isaac B. Sturgeon to Buchanan, May 17, 1858, Buchanan Papers; Nichols, *Disruption,* pp. 210–215.

[37] *Alta California,* June 25, 1858; B. B. Redding to William Bigler, June 4, 1858, Bigler Coll.; J. B. Sutherland to Thomas Sutherland, Buchanan Papers; Henry J. Sabette to Douglas, May 7, 1858, and J. H. Ralston to Douglas, May 8, 1858, Douglas Coll.

Broderick arrived late on the scene of the fray; soon after, the tactics and strategy of the contest had been set. Primary elections in San Francisco and the interior counties were over, and the division of the Democracy into separate and independent organizations was well under way.[38] Broderick's memory of the disastrous outcome of the 1854 election, when he had led a separate and distinct organization of Democrats, gave him reason to pause and consider carefully before embarking on a similar course. On that occasion he had suffered a smashing defeat, the Chivalry-led Democrats outpolling their Broderick-led rivals by a margin of three to one. On the other hand, Douglas had a tremendous following in California, and if it could be marshaled under an anti-Lecompton banner in an independent organization, the result would be quite different. However, there was no guarantee that Douglas supporters could be persuaded to join an independent organization. Without the support of the Douglasites, a new organization was foredoomed to defeat. The Little Giant clung to the regular organization; his followers in California might well follow his example.[39]

On the other hand, the manner in which the Chivalry had ridden roughshod over the opposition in the 1857 state convention had left a lasting and distasteful memory. There was little reason for Broderick and his followers to remain in a party that allowed them no voice in the formulation of policy or the selection of candidates. The treatment accorded Broderick and his followers in 1857 was a powerful argument in favor of an independent organization.

The decision to launch an independent party was made by events as well as by Broderick and his lieutenants. In one county convention after another, the hostility of the two wings of the party severed the bonds that joined them. By the time of the state convention, the delegates were divided into three distinct groups. Supporters of the administration held the largest number of seats, the Broderick group was substantial, and more than a third of the delegates were contested. Control of the convention would be decided by the credentials committee, and since the Chivalry controlled the staff organization of the party, there was little doubt that Broderick would lose in any contest

[38] *Alta California,* July 30, 1858.

[39] *Alta California,* July 17 and 25, 1858; J. H. Ralston to Douglas, May 8, 1858, Douglas Coll.

decided by the credentials committee. The Chivalry announced through friendly newspapers that they would walk out of the convention if Broderick controlled it. A separate organization would then be formed—one devoid of Free Soil contamination.[40]

Broderick and his followers took the initiative in organizing independently, apparently convinced that there was no place for them in a Chivalry-dominated convention. It was a fateful decision, for it meant that all the problems attendant to the launching of a new political party would have to be dealt with in a few weeks. The new party was to go forth under the awkward designation of the anti-Lecompton Democratic party; its reception by the electorate of California was uncertain.[41]

The effectiveness of the Kansas question in rallying a significant portion of the California Democracy to the anti-Lecompton banner was yet to be seen. The issue had been blunted since the passage of the English Bill, and California supporters of the administration stressed the theme that there was no major issue dividing the followers of Douglas and Buchanan. The presence of a Republican ticket was a threat to the anti-Lecompton movement, for if voters were looking for a clear-cut alternative to the Democracy of Buchanan, they had it in the form of the fledgling Republican party.

The two Democratic conventions met in separate churches in Sacramento. In each gathering the preliminaries were handled without controversy. Lecompton Democrats listened to speeches praising loyal Democrats and castigating dissidents. Eventually they came to the adoption of a platform of seven resolutions which had been skillfully written to minimize the divisive issue of Lecompton and the administration's role in trying to engineer the admission of Kansas under the proslavery constitution. The platform began with a fulsome tribute to popular sovereignty and followed this gambit to Douglas-minded delegates with a defense of the English Bill. The latter had referred the problem to the people of Kansas and said "we do, without regard to former differences of opinion, accept and abide by that reference." This theme was to be stressed throughout the campaign that followed.

[40] *Alta California,* July 22 and Aug. 4, 1858; Winfield J. Davis, "Notes on the History of California," pp. 340–342, MS in Huntington Lib.

[41] Winfield J. Davis, *History of Political Conventions in California, 1849–1892* (Sacramento, 1893), pp. 88–90.

The Lecompton constitution was conspicuous in its absence: the term itself did not appear in the platform. In essence, the platform was a complete vindication of the administration's Kansas policy.[42]

Across town, in the anti-Lecompton convention, a different set of resolutions was being considered. The expected support of Broderick, Douglas, and McKibben was written into the platform along with a resolution recommending the passage of the Homestead Bill, forerunner of a similar plank in the Chicago platform of the Republican party in 1860. The bulk of the platform dealt with the Kansas question. "All just powers are derived from the people," stated the platform, and then went on to declare that "all attempts by the administration and congress to coerce and bribe the people into the adoption of a particular constitution . . . are subversive of the principles of pure democracy." Another section condemned the attempt of the "executive and congress to force upon the people of Kansas a constitution which they have rejected," and this was made even more explicit with an expression of "detestation [of] the passage . . . of the . . . 'English bill' . . . an attempt to bribe a free people into the indorsement of an odious constitution." [43]

The perennial complaint of the Free Soil faction of the party concerning the interference of federal officeholders in the internal political affairs of California was aired. The resolution specifically condemned the interference "with the primary affairs of party, whether by menaces of dismissal from office, by forced levies, or by the distribution of promises and moneys" as "incompatible with the spirit of our constitutions" and "subversive of popular liberty." The nominees were generally men who had long been identified with the Broderick wing of the party, and the new state committee was similarly drawn from the Free Soil faction. By the time adjournment came, the essentials had been accomplished and the new organization launched.[44]

Party slate-making was not complete, for the Republican convention met a week after the rival Democratic organizations disbanded.

[42] Davis, *Political Conventions,* pp. 88–89. James H. Hardy, President of the Convention, was subsequently impeached and removed from the bench for disloyalty; see *Official Report of the Proceedings, Testimony, and Argument in the Trial of James H. Hardy* (Sacramento, 1862), passim.

[43] *Alta California,* Aug. 6, 1858; Davis, *Political Conventions,* pp. 91–92.

[44] Davis, *Political Conventions,* p. 92; *Alta California,* Aug. 6, 1858.

The first day was spent in the opening formalities and maneuvering by Broderick supporters to influence the convention; the objective was an endorsement of Broderick and McKibben, a condemnation of the administration, and an endorsement of the slate chosen by the anti-Lecompton Democrats. The resolutions committee included a number of delegates who were committed to this approach. Edward D. Baker and F. P. Tracy led the battle within the convention in behalf of the anti-Lecompton program, but they were vigorously opposed by a group that demanded the charting of an independent course by Republicans.[45]

As the first day came to a close, it seemed as though Baker, Tracy, and Broderick were to be defeated. When the delegates assembled on the following day, however, it became apparent that the Free Soil Democrats had picked up considerable support. A decision was finally made to endorse one of the Free Soil Democrats, John Currey, for justice of the supreme court but reserve to the state committee the right to make nominations to the congressional seats. Sixty-two votes were cast against this proposal—an indication that a sizable bloc of the delegates did not approve of fusion with the nominal enemy.[46]

The community of political principle of the two organizations was clearly seen in their platforms. The Republicans readopted their platform of 1856 and supplemented it with resolutions taken from the anti-Lecompton platform. In one instance not a word was changed, but in others the language—though not the content—was altered. To cap Broderick's triumph, the Republicans gave him a resounding vote of confidence in a statement that described him as a senator who "evinces a regard for the interests of free labor and free men equally becoming the state which he represents and the station he occupies." Broderick and Baker had good reason to be pleased with their handiwork.[47]

Once the slates were completed, the campaign gathered steam. From the first it was apparent that Broderick's fledgling party faced an uphill battle. Starting from scratch, Free Soil Democrats had to organize in the outlying counties as well as in the major centers of population. Throughout the state, they faced a well-organized machine that

[45] *Alta California,* Aug. 6, 1858.
[46] Davis, *Political Conventions,* pp. 93–94; *Alta California,* Aug. 7, 1858.
[47] Davis, *Political Conventions,* p. 94; *Alta California,* Aug. 7, 1858.

mobilized hundreds of federal employees. In San Francisco, Broderick managed to control the regular machinery of the party and forced the Lecompton Democrats to organize afresh, but in many places it was Broderick's group that was compelled to organize independently.[48]

At first blush, the results of the 1858 election were discouraging to Broderick and his followers. Lecompton Democrats generally outpolled their Democratic rivals, the margin in one case being eight thousand. Significantly, the leading anti-Lecompton candidate, John Currey, bested his Democratic rival by a margin of two to one in San Francisco. Currey carried Sacramento as well by a substantial margin. In the hinterland, however, the Free Soil Democrats ran poorly. In some of the more isolated counties, Currey received but a handful of votes; in Merced County, for example, Currey received nine votes to his opponent's 236, and in Santa Barbara County but a half-dozen voted for Currey.[49]

The results reflected the superior organization of the Lecompton Democrats, but a number of other factors were involved. The tardiness of the anti-Lecompton Democrats in launching their organization cost them ground which they were never able to regain. The poor showing was due in part to the reluctance of the Douglas following in the Democracy to break with the regular organization. Apparently Douglas' supporters in California shared the Little Giant's fond hopes that a reconciliation of the contending factions of the Democracy would produce not only reelection in Illinois but also a presidential nomination at the next national convention. Broderick had counted on a swing of Douglas advocates into the anti-Lecompton ranks, but it never came. On the contrary, Douglas spokesmen were critical of Broderick for splitting the California Democracy. The defeat also reflected the skillful manner in which Lecompton Democrats concealed the differences that divided the party. Throughout the campaign Lecompton Democratic orators championed popular sovereignty. Vociferously they thundered the validity of this principle. Vehemently they maintained that the English Bill settled the Kansas question and restored harmony to the party. Douglas' statement, "There ought not to be any issue upon Kansas, among Democrats," was featured in their campaign rhetoric. It was an effective approach,

[48] *Alta California,* Aug. 25, 26, and 27, 1858.

[49] Election Returns, 1858, Vol. 1759, Archives of the Secretary of State, Sacramento; *Alta California,* Sept. 2, 3, and 4, 1858.

designed to display the affinity of Buchanan supporters and followers of Douglas.[50]

Even in defeat, however, Broderick could find some encouragement in the election results. Despite the manifold problems inherent in launching a new party, anti-Lecompton Democrats had come within eight thousand votes of victory. A shift of about five percent of the totals would have given them a triumph on their maiden effort. With one campaign behind them and other tests of strength in the years ahead and with a general strengthening of their organization, they had reason to look with confidence into the political future. In the light of these circumstances, they advised Douglas to turn to independent organization if he would win his battle with Abraham Lincoln for political survival.[51]

[50] Sacramento *Union,* Sept. 6, 1858; *Alta California,* Aug. 6, 1858; James A. McDougall to Douglas, Sept. 5, 1858, and L. B. Mizner to Douglas, Nov. 19, 1858, Douglas Coll.

[51] James B. Sheridan to Douglas, Dec. 8, 1858, Douglas Coll.

CHAPTER ELEVEN

The Party Battle Escalates

In late September, Broderick turned eastward again, this time as a passenger on the overland stage. The route lay across the heartland of the Trans-Mississippi West and gave him a firsthand view of the highly publicized central route of the projected "Pacific Railroad." At best, facilities were primitive. He encountered a blizzard which left him with a frostbitten foot, and in the last part of the route the stage was upset. When he arrived in St. Louis, he was nursing an assortment of bruises, a cracked rib, and frost-touched toes. The trip to the mid-continent had consumed more than six weeks.[1]

Toward the close of November he was in New York, where he celebrated the recent triumph of the anti-Lecompton ticket in Pennsylvania with George Wilkes and John W. Forney. Forney rapturously described the election results as "the Waterloo of 1858." "In all the history of politics in Pennsylvania there had never been an overthrow so overwhelming," declared this erstwhile friend of James Buchanan. Forney's language was only a slight exaggeration, for the Pennsylvania outcome was but one of a series of disasters suffered by the Democratic party in 1858. In some respects the most significant set of by-elections in the history of American politics, they resulted in the loss of eighteen Democratic seats, which, coupled with the election of ten anti-Lecompton Democrats, meant the loss of control of the House by the Democracy. The administration had been decisively repu-

[1] *Alta California,* Sept. 30, Oct. 1, Nov. 10 and 16, Dec. 18, 1858.

diated. Buchanan put it succinctly: "We have met the enemy and we are theirs." [2]

The second session of the Thirty-fifth Congress began in December in an atmosphere of gloom and foreboding for Buchanan and his advisers. The administration had pulled out all the stops in pushing the English Bill through the first meeting of Congress. It had spent its strength and driven its opponents within the party into advanced positions of hostility from which they would be difficult to dislodge. The power, prestige, and patronage of the administration had been freely expended to secure a dubious victory. Broderick had predicted in the previous spring that the Kansas question would "destroy the Democratic party in the free states." The election results clearly established the validity of that forecast.[3]

The administration was apparently not inclined to be conciliatory. Gwin chaired the Democratic caucus which organized the Senate. Broderick was dropped from the Committee on Public Lands and Stephen A. Douglas replaced as chairman of the Committee on Territories. Broderick subsequently objected to the organization of the Senate but was overruled; the arrangements stood, and the two leading anti-Lecompton Democratic senators were disciplined.[4]

The two remained defiant. To a friend Broderick wrote, "Buchanan has broken the pledges he made previous to his election; and has sold himself body and soul to the South." Far from being cowed, Broderick was ready "to make any honorable sacrifice to thwart his [Buchanan's] design in Kansas." A few days after the beginning of the new year, the news of Douglas' reelection came over the wires. Despite the covert support of the Buchanan administration, Abraham Lincoln had been defeated by the Little Giant. Douglas' survival assured his return to the Senate and a continuation of the battle to keep the Democratic party from being captured by the proslavery figures who surrounded the President.[5]

[2] Philadelphia *Press,* Oct. 20, 1858; Broderick to George Wilkes, Dec. 8, 1858, *People* v. *McGlynn,* p. 298; Roy F. Nichols, *The Disruption of American Democracy* (New York, 1948), pp. 219–221; Allan Nevins, *The Emergence of Lincoln* (New York, 1951), I, 400–404; Buchanan to Harriet Lane, Oct. 15, 1858, in John B. Moore, ed. *The Works of James Buchanan* (Philadelphia, 1908–11), X, 229.

[3] Nichols, *Disruption,* pp. 222–224; Broderick to John A. McGlynn, Feb. 4, 1858, Broderick File, Soc. of Calif. Pioneers Lib., San Francisco.

[4] Nichols, *Disruption,* p. 225; Nevins, *The Emergence of Lincoln,* I, 425–426; *Cong. Globe,* 35th Cong., 2nd Sess., p. 45.

[5] Broderick to George Wilkes, Dec. 21, 1858, *People* v. *McGlynn,* p. 298; Philadelphia *Press,* Jan. 5, 1859.

The new year was marked by an incident that was an ominous portent of things to come. In the lobby of a hotel in New York, Broderick was accosted by two men, subsequently identified as residents of New Orleans. The two baited the junior senator. At first Broderick ignored their gibes but finally turned on them, and before bystanders intervened, he belabored them with his cane. For a short time he awaited an expected challenge to a duel, but none was ever served on him. Efforts were made, with some success, to keep the incident out of the newspapers, for Broderick felt the less publicity given it, the better. It should have put him on guard against future provocations.[6]

When the Senate reconvened after the holiday recess, Broderick pushed a number of California proposals. In spite of the outspoken opposition of Senator David Yulee of Florida, he introduced a bill which called for the immediate construction of a telegraph line to the Pacific Coast. Yulee, chairman of the Committee on the Post Office, complained of the burdens of his committee and pointed out that the proposal had been considered previously and rejected. Over his objections, the bill was sent to his committee. About the same time, Broderick proposed legislation which would authorize the establishment of additional steamship facilities to the Pacific Coast. It, too, was referred to Yulee's "overburdened" committee, where it languished despite repeated attempts by Broderick to pry it loose.[7]

The deep animosity of Gwin and Broderick was displayed frequently. The chief business of the Senate was the Pacific Railroad Bill, and the two men clashed repeatedly over it. Having recently traveled over the central route, Broderick spoke from personal experience as he ticked off the advantages of this route. It had been the chief line of travel for the overwhelming majority of immigrants who had trekked overland to the Pacific. An easy grade, plentiful supplies of stone and timber, and its direct route to the great population centers on the Pacific Coast—all indicated this was the most feasible route along which to construct the transcontinental railroad. To expedite the project, Broderick proposed that a wagon road be constructed first; later it would be improved so as to serve as a bed for the railroad. In caustic language he declared the proposal to build along the southern route to

[6] George J. Bernard Affidavit, *People* v. *McGlynn,* p. 90; Hubert H. Bancroft, *History of California,* VI (San Francisco, 1888), 22.

[7] *Cong. Globe,* 35th Cong., 2nd Sess., pp. 69, 662, 733.

a Pacific terminus at Guaymas was senseless. It would be equally logical to put the western terminus in Mexico City.[8]

Gwin still pushed the construction of several parallel lines to the Pacific—one in the North, another across the Southwest. Exact routes were to be determined by the President and the financiers of the proposed railroads. At one point Broderick chided Gwin for not exerting himself in behalf of the Pacific Railroad. It was but one of a number of allusions, laced with sarcasm, which implied that Gwin was not sincerely interested in the project. In an effort to pin him down, Broderick appealed to Gwin to specify San Francisco as the western terminus of his proposed rail lines. Gwin angrily asked Broderick if the comment was an implication that he was neglecting his senatorial responsibilities. Broderick's ironic rejoinder, "I consider that my colleague has exerted his whole strength on this bill," sharpened the barb in the original allusion but barred a further exchange of unpleasantries.[9]

When Andrew Johnson of Tennessee raised a "strict constructionist" Constitutional argument to attack a federal subsidy of the railroad, Broderick met him head-on. In a long and detailed reply he pointed out that California's mineral wealth had contributed immeasurably to the general prosperity of the United States. After reaffirming his support of Johnson's Homestead Bill, he declared that the public domain could be utilized to advance this great project. As for Johnson's Constitutional objections, Broderick asked the senator to square such arguments with his support of a proposal to give Buchanan thirty million dollars—"a corruption fund" to expend in the acquisition of Cuba. Johnson made no reply.[10]

The debate on the railroad bill clearly revealed the sectional divisions within the Senate. When Senator Sam Houston expressed support for a central route, he was bitterly attacked by Senator Alfred Iverson of Georgia, who declared Houston neglected "southern interests" to curry favor with northern politicians and to further his presidential ambitions. Iverson lauded the Texas legislature for defeating Houston's bid for reelection to the Senate. It was a bitter personal attack which elicited a detailed and emotional reply from Houston.[11]

[8] *Cong. Globe,* 35th Cong., 2nd Sess., p. 357; Philadelphia *Press,* Jan. 20, 1858.

[9] *Cong. Globe,* 35th Cong., 2nd Sess., pp. 358, 417.

[10] *Cong. Globe,* 35th Cong., 2nd Sess., pp. 586, 417.

[11] *Cong. Globe,* 35th Cong., 2nd Sess., p. 352. Nevins, *The Emergence of Lincoln,* I, 440–444, presents a detailed summary of the railroad issue in this Congress.

Houston began by declaring he had no presidential ambitions but, on the contrary, was soon to retire to private life after a long career in public service. As for his recent defeat, Houston pointed an accusing finger at the administration. It was engineered by "the federal power"; patronage had been utilized to bring his senatorial career to an end. His speech of measured phrases ended with a simple declaration of his political faith: "I make no distinction between southern rights and northern rights. . . . I would see no wrong inflicted on the North or on the South, but I am for the Union, without any 'if' in the case; and my motto is, 'it shall be preserved.' "[12] Heavy applause broke out in the gallery as his voice died away, leading the presiding officer, John C. Breckinridge, to demand order.

Houston's stirring speech pointed up his and Broderick's dilemma. Advocates of union, foes of the ultras on either side of the slavery question, basically opposed to the manner in which the proslavery advisers of Buchanan were utilizing the power of the party and the administration, they were caught in a political gristmill in which the millstones were the Democracy of Buchanan and the Republican party. Both men were targets of the proslavery wing of the Democratic party, which freely used patronage to strike at them. Houston, tempered by the struggle, was purged from the Senate, but his political career was not ended. He returned to Texas, continued the battle against the proslavery wing of the Democratic party, and won the governorship in the face of incredible odds. In a display of political courage that has seldom been equaled, Houston attended the turbulent convention called to take Texas out of the Union and defiantly cast his ballot against secession. This, however, was to be his last congressional meeting. The antislavery cause lost a towering figure when Sam Houston walked out of the Senate for the last time.[13]

The battle over the Pacific Railroad continued, and as February approached, the much amended bill neared a vote. By this time it was only a shadow of the act that had been introduced, simply providing that the President could receive proposals to undertake the construction. Broderick pointed out that Gwin's political allies were responsible for gutting the measure. The final vote was thirty-one to twenty. A few days later, Gwin moved to reconsider, but to no avail. The House took no action, even on the emasculated bill, and thus the matter was

[12] *Cong. Globe,* 35th Cong., 2nd Sess., pp. 353–355.
[13] Nichols, *Disruption,* p. 255.

laid to rest until a subsequent Congress, purged of southern influence, took action.[14]

When the Lime Point purchase came up, Broderick jumped into the debate, scenting another chance to smite his enemies. He declared that speculators were behind the purchase, demanding an outrageous $200,000 for property which was worth a small fraction of that amount, and he endorsed the proposal of Senator Judah Benjamin of Louisiana to use condemnation proceedings to permit purchase at a reasonable price. Gwin listened grimly and then met the allegations with finesse, proposing that the Military Affairs Committee investigate the matter. Chairman Jefferson Davis subsequently reported that no evidence of fraud by agents of the government had been uncovered. His report did not go to the heart of the matter, for Broderick's charges were directed at the purchase itself and the propriety of paying an exorbitant price when condemnation proceedings could have been utilized. However difficult it might be to establish fraud, on its face the purchase smacked of malfeasance or inefficiency. The matter rested here, Broderick's minority report receiving little attention from his fellow senators, but Gwin and the Chivalry were to hear a great deal about the Lime Point purchase in the future.[15]

Broderick struck at the Chivalry again when appropriations for the Indian service in California were under consideration. The junior senator declared that much of the money appropriated found its way into the pockets of Indian agents. Gwin demanded particulars in the form of names, dates, and places, which Broderick failed to produce, though he did point out that Indian agents frequently put aside their duties to participate in politics. They were always out in force at conventions, Broderick declared, and went on to explain wryly that Indians were quite scarce at California political conventions.[16]

Broderick struck again at the Chivalry's "federal power" during a debate on postal appropriations. He pointed out that official statistics revealed that the salaries paid to postal employees in California were greater than those paid for similar services in twenty-three states of the Union. Postal agents in California were paid five thousand dollars annually, although their counterparts in eastern states received six-

[14] Nichols, *Disruption*, pp. 231–232; *Cong. Globe*, 35th Cong., 2nd Sess., p. 634.

[15] *Cong. Globe*, 35th Cong., 2nd Sess., pp. 577, 1240; Broderick's minority report was printed as Report Committee, No. 389, 35th Cong., 2nd Sess., MS copy in National Archives.

[16] *Cong. Globe*, 35th Cong., 2nd Sess., p. 697.

teen hundred dollars. Even clerks were paid as much as twice the salary received by clerks in other parts of the country. The Senate listened in amazement. It was almost incredible to find a senator advocating retrenchment and curtailment of salaries paid to federal appointees in his own state. Those who were aware of the manner in which the Chivalry had utilized patronage to strike at Broderick understood his motivation.[17]

Broderick brought the keen ax of economy into use again when Gwin spoke in support of an appropriation for further survey of the public domain in California. Broderick asserted that the government "has already expended over a million dollars for surveying the public lands in California, and I believe the Government has received $6,000 from the sale of public lands." Defiantly he added, "While I hold a seat upon this floor, I shall never encourage any legislation of that kind."[18]

Before the debates on federal appropriations came to an end, the ranks of Broderick's enemies had been swollen. Employees of the federal establishment, serving at the pleasure of their sponsors and drawn almost exclusively from the ranks of the Chivalry and its allies in the Democratic party, had additional reason to look with hostility on the junior senator from California. Broderick was making few friends and many enemies by these efforts. That he was somewhat uncertain he was correct was apparent from his comment, "If I have made a mistake here . . . I will try to correct it when I come here next winter, if I should live so long, and not resign in the mean time." Nevertheless, he persisted and paid the price in the opposition of a solid phalanx of federal appointees during the election of 1859.[19]

When the subject of overland stage routes arose, Broderick renewed his advocacy of the central route. He criticized the existing "horseshoe routes" which meandered through the Southwest on the way to the Pacific, charging they were nine hundred miles longer than necessary. The fact that he spoke from personal experience, having traveled over the route, must have carried some weight with his colleagues. He

[17] *Cong. Globe,* 35th Cong., 2nd Sess., pp. 1309–18, 1458–59, 1520.

[18] *Cong. Globe,* 35th Cong., 2nd Sess., p. 1580.

[19] *Cong. Globe,* 35th Cong. 2nd Sess., pp. 1318; James Johnson to Stephen A. Douglas, Jan. 18, 1859, C. S. Whitney to Douglas, Feb. 18, 1859, and Albert L. Collins to Douglas, Feb. 18, 1859, Douglas Coll., Univ. of Chicago; Henry W. Halleck to Pablo de la Guerra, Oct. 16, 1860, De la Guerra Coll., Santa Barbara Mission Archives.

spoke from personal experience again when an appropriation to secure the release of the children who had survived the Mountain Meadows massacre was under consideration. The children were in Salt Lake City, and only months before, Broderick had met with leaders of the church and had been assured they would be turned over to any responsible party who would see that they were reunited with their relatives. The modest sum was eventually appropriated in spite of Broderick's objections that it was unnecessary. Gwin expressed his horror of the incident. His approach was in sharp contrast to that of Broderick, who carefully avoided anything that smacked of "Mormon-baiting." [20]

Jefferson Davis, Stephen A. Douglas, and the two California senators participated in a general debate on the meaning and significance of the Dred Scott decision. Broderick took advantage of the debate to point out inconsistencies in Gwin's record on the slavery question. In effect, Broderick accused Gwin of being a friend of the peculiar institution when it was politically advantageous but sometimes being lured by political opportunism into the antislavery camp. The exchanges of the two men became heated and quite personal before a colleague prudently interrupted. The debate ended on an indecisive note, but there was no mistaking the bitter animosity of the two men.[21]

Congress adjourned in early March, and the two senators turned to another battleground—California. There things had gone badly for Broderick in the first months of the year. The Chivalry had utilized patronage to heal some of its wounds as well as to divide the enemy camp. Weller, Gwin, Washington, Latham, and company had become a going concern. Broderick's allies were being eliminated—John Bigler through appointment to a diplomatic post and Charles Hempstead by an appointment as superintendent of the mint in San Francisco. When he assumed his new position, the once powerful subaltern of the Broderick-Bigler wing of the party saw the political arena of California in a much different way. Soon he was preoccupied with the construction of a personal political organization—no longer was he a part of the Broderick-led faction of the Democracy.[22]

When the legislature met, Broderick members were put on notice

[20] *Cong. Globe,* 35th Cong., 2nd Sess., pp. 1500–05, 1400–04.

[21] *Cong. Globe,* 35th Cong., 2nd Sess., pp. 1259–64.

[22] Albert L. Collins to Douglas, Jan. 3, 1859, Douglas Coll.; *National Intelligencer,* Jan. 18, 1859; San Francisco *Herald,* Jan. 4, 1859; C. H. Hempstead to William Bigler, June 4, 1859, Bigler Coll., Pennsylvania Hist. Soc.

that rejoining the regular party organization would be difficult. Excluded from the Democratic caucus, they promptly went ahead with a caucus of their own. However firm their antislavery convictions, they represented a small group in the legislature. Their numerical weakness was revealed when resolutions were passed censuring Broderick for his failure to vote for the admission of Kansas under the Lecompton constitution and demanding his resignation. The previous legislature had instructed him to take this position, and his defiance left him no honorable course but resignation, declared spokesmen for the Chivalry. Apparently fearful of an extended debate, William Holden utilized a parliamentary trick to avoid it. The vote in the state Senate was twenty-three to nine in favor of the resolutions: the two-to-one edge of the Chivalry was clearly seen.[23]

In a sense the resolutions were "toothless," for there was no way that Broderick could be compelled to resign. However, they were quite useful as a means of emphasizing Broderick's alienation from a large part of the Democracy. But bringing attention to Broderick's failure to vote for the admission of Kansas under the Lecompton constitution was a weapon of two edges. Humphrey Griffith used one of the edges to strike at the Chivalry the next day. In a speech of "scathing, withering sarcasm and invective," he pointed out the inconsistencies in the position taken by those who supported the resolutions. None of them had dared to support the Lecompton constitution in the previous election, but here they were by implication endorsing it. He challenged them to go before the electorate in the upcoming campaign and take that position. A large part of his speech was a tribute to the principled behavior of Broderick and the manner in which he advocated his views regardless of political consequences. The president of the state Senate labored to repress the applause from the galleries that followed Griffith's speech.[24]

The real significance of the resolutions was their measure of the gulf that yawned between the wings of the Democracy. The chief policy makers of the party on the national as well as the state level would brook no interference with the manner in which they used their power in behalf of slavery. Broderick personified the opposition. He was

[23] *Alta California,* Jan. 19 and 22, 1859.

[24] The full text of the resolutions is in *Statutes of the State of California Passed at the Tenth Session of the Legislature* (Sacramento, 1859), No. VI. See also *Alta California,* Jan. 23, 1859.

beyond the pale, representative of the evil antislavery forces that must be eliminated from the party. The fate of Benton and Houston was to be shared by the plebeian politician of California—political oblivion was to be his lot. The Chivalry was to learn that the elimination of Broderick was an imposing task.

CHAPTER TWELVE

The Final Campaign

Broderick set out for California soon after the adjournment of Congress. On the eve of his departure, friends urged him to vacation in Europe rather than return to the Pacific Coast, where another arduous campaign was in the offing. He declined abruptly, explaining: "I am determined that my friends should succeed in the next state election in California, not on account of its being any political service to me in the future (for I am sick and disgusted with politics) but for the purpose of showing my enemies that I have not lost any of my energy and strength." It was a statement typical of this man who had battled his way to political eminence.[1]

While Broderick would not concede the field to the Chivalry, he was well aware of pressing personal and political problems that demanded his attention. His financial situation necessitated heavy borrowing. The discouraging defeat of the previous year was still fresh in his memory, and the enormous task of organization had to be tackled if the anti-Lecompton Democratic party were to be transformed into an effective political organization. The margin of defeat in 1858 had been small but significant, since it was accomplished despite the unified efforts of the anti-Lecompton Democrats and Republicans. Since the 1858 campaign, the Lecompton organization had strengthened itself through the judicious use of patronage. The once bleeding wounds produced by the Kansas question had been partially healed—the Lecompton issue was no longer the burning question that had scrambled political loyalties and made it possible for a new party to emerge.[2]

[1] Broderick to George Wilkes, Feb. 13, 1859, *People* v. *McGlynn.*

[2] Broderick to J. C. McCabe, Feb. 19, 1859, *People* v. *McGlynn;* James Johnson to Stephen A. Douglas, Jan. 18, 1859, George Hupp to Douglas, Feb. 18, 1859, Albert

The picture was not completely dark, however. The bulk of the daily press was either uncommitted or inclined to the anti-Lecompton point of view. This was offset to some extent by the weekly press, which was largely Lecompton-Democratic in orientation, although a sizable number of anti-Lecompton newspapers published weekly editions in the mountain towns and the inland agricultural settlements. The greatest single political asset in the state was the following of Stephen A. Douglas. Both camps recognized the magnitude of the Douglas influence, and newspapers of either persuasion usually alluded to him with respect. Each faction claimed Douglas, realizing that the distribution of Douglas-minded voters on election day would go far in determining success or failure. In the spring of 1859, Broderick had reason to believe that his party could capture the bulk of the following of the Little Giant.[3]

The role that the young Republican party would play in the forthcoming campaign was as yet undecided, but it too was likely to be significant. The year before, Republicans and anti-Lecompton Democrats had joined hands, but there were few assurances that they would do so again. Republican policy makers, looking ahead to the presidential election of 1860, were eager to broaden and strengthen their party. Merger, fusion, and unity might sound attractive to the uninitiated, but sophisticated politicians realized that a party in its formative years must campaign to develop political know-how, finesse, and organizational strength and muscle. Republican leaders, speaking for the political party of the future, declared the anti-Lecompton Democrats represented an ephemeral organization that would not survive the coming election.[4]

A leading Republican newspaper in San Francisco, whose editor admired Broderick but detested the anti-Lecompton Democratic party, put the matter succinctly. Broderick's party was "the great obstacle" in making California a firm, reliable Republican state. The two organizations competed for membership, and success for the anti-Lecomptonites would put them in a position to "defeat the Republican ticket next year." Republicans, therefore, should seek "to

---

L. Collins to Douglas, Feb. 18, 1859, and C. S. Whitney to Douglas, Feb. 18, 1859, Douglas Coll., Univ. of Chicago; Philadelphia *Press,* Jan. 5, 1859.

[3] Horace Greeley, *An Overland Journey from New York to San Francisco, in the Summer of 1859* (New York, 1860), pp. 126–128.

[4] Sacramento *Union,* July 15, 1859.

crush out all third parties and have a direct and distinct issue of free labor and white men on one side, and slave labor and niggers on the other." This position, taken early, was maintained throughout the campaign.[5]

Broderick was apparently convinced that his group would not only survive but grow and would one day control the party of Old Hickory. The immediate problem was the strengthening of the anti-Lecompton organization. Accordingly, soon after his April arrival in San Francisco, he began planning for the campaign. After a round of conferences in the city, he hurried off to Sacramento, where he huddled with lawmakers of anti-Lecompton persuasion. A great deal of work had to be done in the days and weeks that lay immediately ahead.

Organizational problems were numerous and pressing. In 1858 a lack of organization had resulted in a complete absence of anti-Lecompton votes in the final tally lists of some counties. In some cases the fledgling party did not run candidates on the county level, and in others no party workers were present at the polls to furnish voters with an anti-Lecompton ticket. These errors were not to be repeated. Candidates were to carry the banner in every county; and wherever political gatherings could be mustered, they were to hear the political gospel as preached by anti-Lecompton spokesmen. No office, however minor, was to be overlooked, and political workers were to be part of the scene in every polling place. No potential anti-Lecompton voter was to lose a chance to ballot because he lacked an appropriate ticket. To carry the word throughout the state, a series of mass meetings was planned, some scheduled before the campaign began officially. Issues were to be explored and the record of the administration examined. Orators were to air their persuasive rhetoric under favorable circumstances. In short, Broderick and his associates planned one of the most intensive campaigns that California had ever seen.[6]

The junior senator himself would be one of the major orators of the coming campaign and canvass the state in an unprecedented stump-speaking tour that would take him into every significant center of population. The news of Broderick's intention was greeted with scorn, and it was predicted that the voters would react to his oratory by voting for his enemies. Disparaging comments on his speaking ability

[5] San Francisco *Daily Times,* July 1 and Aug. 1, 1859.

[6] Charles E. DeLong Diary, Apr. 18 and 20, 1859, MS in Calif. State Lib., Sacramento.

did not dissuade him. Before long, it became apparent that he was an effective stump campaigner.[7]

To cap the work of preparation, anti-Lecompton Democrats founded a newspaper to act as their official organ. It appeared for the first time in early May under the masthead San Francisco *News,* and it became an effective publication whose value was to be demonstrated repeatedly. Among the advertisers in the Broderick organ were William T. Coleman, president of the 1856 San Francisco Committee of Vigilance, and Hubert H. Bancroft, then a storekeeper but subsequently the historian of California.[8]

The first two preliminary meetings of the dissident Democratic organization took place in May; both indicated considerable public support. In the first gathering, staged in San Francisco, speakers attacked the administration for its handling of the Pacific Railroad project, the Kansas question, and the Lime Point purchase. Each of these matters was to be examined repeatedly during the campaign. At the second gathering apparently a coalition was in the process of birth, for representatives of the Republican as well as the Miners and Settlers party appeared on the platform. Leaders of the regular Democratic organization expressed alarm. To add to their concern was the size and enthusiasm of the audience that assembled in what had once been a stronghold of the Lecompton Democrats.[9]

Lecompton Democrats were themselves divided, despite the purification of the party that had taken place with the withdrawal of Broderick's followers. "A large body of conservative and intelligent Democrats" marshaled by Charles Hempstead and John Nugent, editor of the San Francisco *Herald,* contested with Gwin, Washington, Latham, and Weller for position within the party. Some of the "conservative and intelligent Democrats" were supporters of Douglas, and their presence in the Lecompton organization reflected Broderick's failure to attract them to his banner.[10]

[7] San Francisco *Daily Evening Bulletin,* July 12, 1859; *Alta California,* July 27, 1859.

[8] The first number of the San Francisco *News* is described and its editorial staff listed in the *Alta California,* May 19, 1859. A file of the *News,* which ceased publication shortly after the close of the campaign, is in the State Library, Sacramento. Its editorial policy is described in detail in its issues of May 17 and 18, 1859. Advertisements of Coleman and Bancroft appeared in the issues of Sept. 2 and 5, 1859.

[9] *Alta California,* May 12 and 16, 1859; San Francisco *News,* May 17, 1859.

[10] C. H. Hempstead to William Bigler, May 25, 1859, Bigler Coll., Pennsylvania Hist. Soc.; *Alta California,* May 22 and June 6, 1859.

The coalition which Broderick was trying to put together was tested on the first day of the Republican state convention. The strategy of the anti-Lecompton Democrats was to get the two parties to agree on a single slate of candidates. Edward D. Baker, orator and intimate friend of Abraham Lincoln and Broderick, presented the case for "fusion." The prolonged debate that followed generated considerable heat and divided the convention into antagonistic groups. Before the vote was taken, it was apparent that "fusion" was a most unpopular course of action to many of the delegates. Charles Crocker led the opposition to "fusion," emphasizing the view of many Republicans that their party was the party of the future, while the "Antis" were an ephemeral organization. Perhaps the decisive factor in defeating "fusion" was the manner in which it was presented. In effect, Republicans in convention were invited to adjourn until the "Antis" had selected a ticket and then reassemble and endorse the nominees selected by Broderick and his associates. All of Baker's oratorical gifts could not make this palatable to the Republican delegates, who eventually nominated a complete slate of candidates. The platform adopted clearly revealed the community of principle and interest that bound Republicans and anti-Lecompton Democrats. While it did not endorse Broderick by name (as it had in 1858), its eight resolutions endorsed the important political stands he had taken in recent years. Broderick could look with warm approval on every phrase. The fact that the two groups shared a political outlook but could not agree on a slate was an ominous portent. In effect, the two political groups in division enhanced the prospects of the Lecompton opposition.[11]

A week after the Republicans disbanded, delegates of the dissident Democratic party gathered in Sacramento. In mid-April they had decided to hold their convention a week in advance of the Chivalry Democratic organization so that they might capture the initiative and establish the basic framework of issues within which the campaign was to be fought. Delegates came from all but six of the counties—a decided improvement over the previous year, when fourteen counties went unrepresented. Evidently the organizational work that had been outlined in April was bearing fruit.[12]

[11] Winfield J. Davis, *History of Political Conventions in California, 1849–1892* (Sacramento, 1893), p. 97; *Alta California,* June 10, 1859.

[12] *Alta California,* June 10, 1859; Davis, *Political Conventions,* p. 99. Baker became the nominee for a congressional seat in spite of his openly expressed desire for fusion; see *Alta California,* June 9 and 10, 1859.

This gathering was not the harmonious group dominated by the junior senator and called together—as spokesmen of the Chivalry declared—to rubber-stamp the plans that Broderick and his advisers had made. On the contrary, it was apparent from the beginning that while the delegates shared a common antipathy to the extension of slavery, they were divided by questions of principle, strategy, tactics, and ambition. The anti-Lecomptonites included the naïve as well as the opportunistic. It was, in short, a difficult gathering for Broderick to direct; his failures were to be seen in the work of the convention.[13]

The task of drawing up an acceptable platform proceeded quietly for a time, the delegates finding agreeable formulations to condemn the administration for its gross extravagance, "its outrages upon the rights of the people of Kansas," and its corruption and mismanagement. A proposal to commit the convention to a repudiation of the Dred Scott decision was rejected; evidently the delegates were not ready to challenge the Supreme Court openly. Everything seemed to be going well, the delegates displaying their animosity to the administration and their enthusiasm for Free Soil principles, when a series of resolutions endorsing Broderick and condemning his enemies was introduced.[14]

The lively debate that followed was sparked, in part, by the manner in which the framers of the resolutions set about their work. The statements began by praising Broderick, champion of "the rights of man" and fearless fighter of corruption and fraud. At this point the resolutions left the real world of California politics and soared skyward. A mélange of philosophical sentiments finally emerged. Free press was lauded as a great bulwark of liberty. "Christian forbearance, love and charity towards each other" was commended. Justice, moderation, temperance, frugality, and virtue were acclaimed. Dozens of speakers were incited to express their views on the relative merits of as many esoteric topics, and the convention was transformed into a philosophical debating society. The resolutions were finally withdrawn, to the obvious relief of a number of delegates, and the convention turned to the more practical task of candidate selection. As a

[13] San Francisco *News,* May 17, 1859; DeLong Diary, June 10, 1859; *Alta California,* June 7, 1859.

[14] *Alta California,* May 30, 1859; *California Police Gazette,* June 25, 1859; DeLong Diary, June 10, 1859; Davis, *Political Conventions,* p. 100.

result, Broderick's role of principled opposition to the Buchanan administration was not mentioned in the platform.[15]

The work of selecting candidates produced its share of disquieting incidents. Five men vied for the gubernatorial nomination. John Currey, a reluctant contender who preferred a supreme court nomination, bested Humphrey Griffith by a vote of 137 to 71. His surprising victory was won with the backing of Broderick, who let it be known that Griffith's support of the "Bulkhead Bill" in the last session of the legislature made him unpopular in San Francisco and unacceptable as a candidate. Griffith, incensed, aired his displeasure in a bitter declaration that stated a "poisoned chalice" had been prepared for him by Broderick. The selection of a congressional ticket also produced considerable ill will when S. A. Booker, with Broderick's help, won, defeating James W. Coffroth. Like Griffith, Coffroth was not to be appeased. Bitterly disappointed, he grudgingly accepted the result in the convention but implied that he had been treated unfairly. That night, in a fashionable restaurant, he declared the Broderick delegates wore brass collars inscribed with the name of their master. One bitter comment followed another, and soon he was engaged in a near brawl with Congressman Joseph P. McKibben. The preliminaries for a duel followed soon after, and only the intervention of a local court, which placed both men under heavy bond, prevented the meeting. It was an exciting climax to a convention, but it was also a portent of much difficulty for the anti-Lecompton Democratic party.[16]

A careful assessment of the work of the convention revealed a number of disturbing things. The disaffection of Griffith and Coffroth was a serious matter, for both were significant figures of the Broderick camp and skilled political orators. Disaffection became defection in a matter of weeks, and both turned up as stump speakers for the regular Democratic organization. Their conversion to the Lecompton faith obviously reflected frustrated ambition, but this did not alter the fact that they were effective political leaders—possessed of both talents and a personal following. Lecompton Democrats were pleased with such recruits.[17]

[15] *Alta California,* June 17, 1859; Davis, *Political Conventions,* pp. 101–102.

[16] Davis, *Political Conventions,* p. 102; *Alta California,* June 17 and 18, 1859.

[17] Sacramento *Union,* June 18, 1859; *Alta California,* June 17, 1859; DeLong Diary, June 18, 1859.

Much more serious than the defection of Griffith and Coffroth was the failure of the Douglas Democrats to enter wholeheartedly into the campaign against the Lecompton Democrats. Their reluctance to join hands with Broderick in the battle reflected the hesitancy of the Little Giant, who stood in this hour of turbulence and change in the political arena, carefully searching for the safe passage that led through the stormy political milieu to the White House. Their hesitancy also reflected the long-standing animosity of Broderick and his committed Free Soil Democrats to Douglas and his followers. For years Broderick and his followers had criticized Douglas, sometimes savagely, as "a demagogue, charlatan, and northern doughface." It was also pointed out that every friend of Mr. Broderick voted against the resolution in the legislature endorsing Douglas and the principles of the Kansas bill. Now they were singing a different tune, said Douglas spokesmen. Whatever the tune, Douglas-minded Democrats resisted the lures of the anti-Lecompton Democrats. Some responded half-heartedly; a few were committed to the anti-Lecompton standard, but most remained on the sidelines, and when the ballots were counted it was obvious that a great many of them voted the Lecompton ticket.[18]

While objective conditions had thrown Free Soil Democrats into an alliance with Douglas in recent times, a number of circumstances were now pushing them apart. The most significant factor undermining the influence of common principles was the presidential ambition of Douglas. Mesmerized by his towering aspiration, Douglas found every political step of 1859 determined by his conception of how that step affected his chances at the national democratic convention scheduled for the spring of 1860. The convention and perhaps the White House were a part of his immediate future. As the moment of truth approached, Douglas became increasingly aware of the need to maintain his standing as a regular Democrat; common political principles made for unity, but the hard, cold facts of political life led Douglas to adopt a policy of watchful waiting and neutrality between the contending Democratic parties of California. His followers sensed that decision, as week after week of the campaign passed in California without a word from Douglas in support of the "popular sovereignty Democrats" of the Pacific Coast.[19]

[18] Sacramento *Union,* Aug. 13 and 15, 1859; Davis, *Political Conventions,* p. 111.

[19] L. B. Hopkins to Douglas, Mar. 3, 1859, and James Johnson to Douglas, June 27, 1859, Douglas Coll. Douglas expressed no position on the campaign in California

Lecompton Democrats gathered a week after the convention of their Democratic opponents. From the outset it was apparent that this smooth-functioning organization was in good health. Every county but Fresno sent a delegation. It was obvious, too, that a great many of the delegates were supporters of Douglas. Richard P. Hammond, close personal friend of the Little Giant, was elected to preside. The credentials committee worked with dispatch, settling a number of disputes. Its major decision struck dismay into the heart of Governor John B. Weller, who was actively seeking a second term. By a vote of two to one, pro-Weller delegates were excluded and a slate in favor of Milton S. Latham admitted. On the second day Latham, onetime congressman, Harvard graduate, Ohio-born and a longtime resident of Alabama, was given the gubernatorial nomination. In the balloting for lieutenant-governor, John C. Downey of Los Angeles competed for a time with James Johnson, an avowed supporter of Douglas. Johnson withdrew before the actual balloting, and Downey was given the second spot on the ticket. Apparently the powers of the convention looked kindly upon this future governor of California who had come to the convention as a member of a contested delegation. Once more the crucial significance of the credentials committee work was apparent.[20]

Latham delivered a lengthy acceptance speech of broad and flexible platitudes directed to all segments of Democratic opinion. The platform adopted endorsed the Cincinnati platform, the Pacific Railroad, and the Buchanan administration. The flexibility of the term "popular sovereignty" was illustrated in a long and detailed endorsement which appeared in the platform. The convention adjourned after the staff organization of the party had been placed in the hands of the Chivalry; the state committee was dominated by figures like William Van Voorhies and Calhoun Benham. The slate making was completed, and now the political battle was at hand.[21]

---

until a week after the balloting. Then he chose Milton S. Latham as an intermediary to put his detailed views before the people in the form of a lengthy letter. Latham to Douglas, Sept. 18, 1859, Douglas Coll., reports the receipt of Douglas' letter and his plans for its publication. The *Daily Evening Bulletin,* Sept. 26, 1859, printed it. In 1860, Latham campaigned for Breckinridge against Douglas. See Davis, *Political Conventions,* pp. 113, 123, 126.

[20] *Alta California,* June 24, 1859; Davis, *Political Conventions,* p. 104; James Johnson to Douglas, June 27, 1859, Douglas Coll.

[21] The text of the speech appeared in the *Alta California,* June 25, 1859; Davis, *Political Conventions,* pp. 105–106.

At the outset of the campaign the depths of Chivalry animosity to Broderick were plumbed when David W. Perley, intimate friend and associate of David S. Terry, and long identified as a member of the Chivalry, challenged Broderick. Broderick had allegedly insulted Terry in Perley's presence, and the latter took offense. One word led to another, and before the two parted they almost came to blows. A short time later, Perley sent a formal challenge. The junior senator responded in the language that had become his trademark. In sharp words he replied that Perley knew he would not accept a challenge: "If I were to accept your challenge there are probably many other gentlemen who would seek similar opportunities for hostile meetings for the purpose of accomplishing a political object." [22]

Perley responded to Broderick's refusal in a newspaper card which accused Broderick of a number of things, including a lack of courage, and there the matter rested. It was far from closed, however, for Broderick's refusal to observe a gentleman's obligations under the code duello had not been unqualified. On the contrary, he had indicated that he would respond differently to a challenge when the campaign was over. The multitude of enemies whom he had accumulated did not miss that qualification. It was an ominous beginning to a political campaign, and while some might describe Broderick's refusal as a "perfect quietus to the spirit of modern chivalry," there was no reason to look with equanimity on the immediate political future.[23]

The 1859 campaign was the most bitter political campaign in the history of California politics—a contest in which accepted standards were cast aside and the most virulent slander aired on the stump. Before it was over, new dimensions of political vituperation had been reached, the system of democratic politics seriously damaged, and the political issues buried in an avalanche of invective. In the beginning, some of the principals attempted to campaign in the customary fashion. Broderick and his followers took that tack, for they were convinced that public examination of the issues—the corruption of the Buchanan administration, the Kansas question, and the extension of slavery into the West—would enhance their chances for victory. A comparison of the speeches made by the spokesmen of the contending

[22] Broderick to Perley, June 29, 1859, in Sacramento *Union,* July 1, 1859; San Francisco *News,* July 1, 1859; James O'Meara, *Broderick and Gwin* (San Francisco, 1881), pp. 104–106; San Francisco *Daily Times,* July 1, 1859.

[23] Sacramento *Union,* July 1, 1859.

Democratic groups shows clearly that Gwin was first to resort to invective and personal assault, while Broderick, for the most part, avoided such an approach.[24]

Broderick's announcement that he would stump the state was greeted with a roar of derision by his opponents, but soon after his first speech they were forced to reconsider. He lacked the polish and finesse of an experienced orator, but, as an unfriendly newspaper pointed out, "there is undoubtedly a native strength and energy of intellect in the man which makes him a terror to his foes." The evaluation went on to describe his expert knowledge of California politics, saying that "no one was more capable of arriving at firm conclusions and expressing them." From the first he drew large audiences which responded enthusiastically to his truculent attacks on the Chivalry and the Buchanan administration.[25]

At Forest Hill, early in the campaign, the largest crowd in the history of the community turned out to hear Broderick defend his Senate record and refute the accusation that he had expressed "unmitigated contempt for workingmen and mechanics" in his reply to Hammond. Broderick denied that charge but acknowledged that he had criticized workingmen for neglecting politics and their duties as citizens. He repeated this criticism to the workingmen in his audience: "You do submit too tamely to the dictation of men who despise you in their hearts and who would aggrandize themselves on your unrequited labor." Then he went on to appeal to them to become alert, informed, and active citizens. His speech was frequently interrupted by applause, and it was obvious that this crowd responded to his rhetoric. The only criticism which might have been made was that his speech was defensive in tone.[26]

Gwin's initial speech was in sharp contrast, superior in a number of ways, for he was a polished orator and a man of distinguished bearing.

[24] To settle the question of responsibility for introducing offensive, personal, and slanderous material into the campaign, compare the speeches of Gwin and Broderick as reproduced in the Sacramento *Union,* July and August, 1859, where the most complete record of the election speeches appeared. At the time the *Union* was an independent and one of the finest newspapers in the nation; see Forrest G. Wood, "A Frontier Newspaper and the Civil War Period: The Sacramento *Union,* 1851–1865" (unpubl. M.A. thesis, Sacramento State College, 1958). For a comparison of the campaign rhetoric of Gwin and Broderick, see the San Francisco *News,* July 28, 1859, which reports the evaluation of the Sacramento *Union,* and the *Alta California,* July 27, 1859.

[25] *Daily Evening Bulletin,* July 12, 1859; DeLong Diary, July 14, 1859.

[26] Sacramento *Union,* July 12, 1859.

His speech was a carefully composed attack on Broderick's record of opposition to the Buchanan administration. It generally was concerned with the issues, but for one offensive reference to Broderick. Gwin suggested that for him to accept a challenge to debate would be a violation of the Constitution, which forbade the infliction of cruel and unusual punishment on animals. Some thought it an admirable formulation, but others thought it went beyond the bounds of good taste.[27]

A few days later Broderick repeated his invitation to Gwin to debate. Carefully avoiding the personal response that Gwin's reference might have elicited, he declared that he was interested in exploring the issues. The bulk of his speech was concerned with the Dred Scott decision and its implications. He denied that the decision had settled the status of slavery in the territories. The basic principles of the Democratic party were not to be decided by the Supreme Court, he declared. Thomas Jefferson had defied the court, and Andrew Jackson had declared that he would not allow the justices to interpret his presidential oath or the American Constitution to him. What was good enough for such great Democratic figures was good enough for the junior senator.[28]

A few days later the largest audience of the campaign turned out to greet Broderick and McKibben at Nevada—a crowd of more than twenty-five hundred that far exceeded the Lecompton audience of a few days before. For an hour and a half Broderick held the crowd spellbound, as he ticked off a detailed indictment of the Chivalry and the administration. A cry of "Give 'em hell, Dave," encouraged him. Once more he challenged Gwin to debate; once more he turned to specific charges and accusations. A few days before, James W. Denver had defended the Lime Point purchase on the grounds that it would give employment to artisans and mechanics as the fortifications on the site were built. "Would you have your Senator vote for a measure like this that would put $200,000 in the hands of speculators?" Broderick demanded. A chorus of "No's" came from the audience. He pointed out that the land was worth about five thousand dollars and the attempt to take two hundred thousand dollars from the federal treasury to pay for it was a palpable steal.[29]

[27] Sacramento *Union,* July 15 and 18, 1859.
[28] DeLong Diary, July 14, 1859; Sacramento *Union,* July 16, 1859.
[29] Sacramento *Union,* July 19, 1859, carried the full text of the speech as well as a

Then Broderick opened a political Pandora's box, the senatorial election of January 1857. The whole story had never been told, he declared, and he went on to describe, in a few sentences, what had taken place. Broderick pointed out that his preferred candidate, Joe McCorkle, could not be elected; thus his choice was either Gwin or Latham. At first he had been inclined to support Latham, but in the midst of the election it had become apparent that Latham was untrustworthy: he had been implicated in an act of duplicity involving a mutual friend and was also engaged in dispensing favors designed to split Broderick's group. Under those circumstances, Broderick declared, Gwin was the definite lesser of two evils.[30]

The speech was Broderick's best effort in the campaign to that point. That part of it, however, which mentioned the senatorial election was a major error. It consumed the bulk of his time, overshadowing and obscuring matters of greater immediate importance. It also tended to introduce extraneous issues and personalities into the campaign. However intriguing the story might be to an audience of California voters, it did little to illuminate the issues that divided the Democracy of 1859.

A few days later, Broderick made another major error in tactics. He played directly into the hands of his enemies when in the opening of his address he invited a local politician, M. Kirkpatrick, or any other defender of the Lecompton cause, to share the platform. Then he delivered what was becoming a standard campaign speech. At its conclusion Kirkpatrick, decrying his own ability and citing his lack of preparation, proceeded to speak for an hour. A good part of his speech was personal in nature—a truculent attack which compared Broderick to Thomas Hart Benton and predicted a similar descent into political oblivion for Broderick. He said that Broderick's failure to follow the instructions of the state legislature on the Kansas question was as reprehensible as Old Bullion Benton's failure to follow the instructions of the Missouri legislature. Obviously angered, Broderick declared he was flattered to be compared to Benton, who would be remembered long after his enemies had been forgotten. He went on in some detail, complaining of Kirkpatrick's use of personalities. "There was a time when I would not have permitted that language to be used

---

detailed account of the reaction of the audience; see also San Francisco *News,* July 18, 1859.

[30] Sacramento *Union,* July 19, 1859.

towards me, but that time is past, for the moment, at least," he declared in closing.[31]

To some extent Broderick undid the damage that Kirkpatrick had done, but on the whole the incident showed a regrettable lapse of judgment by the embattled senator. The mistake reflected his faith in his cause. He had violated a cardinal rule of campaigning when he turned over his audience to the opposition to exploit, a serious error which was compounded when he pitted himself against a relatively obscure spokesman of the Lecompton Democrats. An attempt had been made at the start of the meeting to disrupt it. It had failed. Those who planned the disruption now had good reason to be pleased with that failure.[32]

A few days later Broderick began to show that the opposition's invective was getting under his skin. Still unable to entice Gwin into debate, he declared that while he was not an orator, he was a match for the senior senator. Then he went on the offensive: before the campaign was over, Broderick declared, he would prove that Gwin was "dripping with corruption." Once more he pointed out that the exchange of epithets obscured and concealed the real issues that divided the Democratic party. He would prefer to deal with the great questions of the day, Broderick said, but his speech indicated that he was not above the use of personalities. However, he still clung to the course of responsible debate, expressing his criticism of the administration and the Chivalry in terms of their combined opposition to the Homestead Bill and the Morrill Act. As he had done in the Senate, he repudiated the "spread-eagle" foreign policy of the administration and its project, to be implemented by a thirty-million-dollar fund, for the acquisition of Cuba. That proposal drew his sharpest fire, for the administration pursued this course "knowing that Spain would not sell and we would have to go to war to acquire that island." [33]

As the campaign's first month came to a close, a number of observers took stock. Broderick's stump speaking was a factor of uncertain importance but obviously one that would influence the outcome. The size of audiences assembled wherever he spoke indicated that a major portion of the electorate was interested in his detailed indictment of the Chivalry and the administration. It seemed significant to some that

[31] Sacramento *Union,* July 22, 1859; San Francisco *News,* July 23, 1859.

[32] The attempt to disrupt the meeting was described by Charles A. Sumner to the editors of the Sacramento *Union,* published in its issue of Aug. 4, 1859.

[33] Sacramento *Union,* July 22 and 25, 1859.

the campaign had begun auspiciously but then descended into an exchange of slander and vituperation. The responsibility for the metamorphosis was placed on the Chivalry, for they had been the first to use such tactics. "The language they have used in reference to Broderick since the Lecompton question is indefensible" was the judgment of one observer.[34]

No change in tactics was to be detected as the campaign continued. If anything, the language of personal insult became more prominent. Gwin's speech was not only insulting but menacing: "Broderick is going through the state attacking private characters and at the same time announces he will not be responsible as in the San Francisco difficulty with Perley. What can you do with such an individual? If we club him, it will do no good; if we kill him it will only make him a martyr." [35]

A few days later Broderick spoke from the same platform from which Gwin had threatened him. Those who came to hear a response in the same coin were disappointed. Dismissing Gwin's personal attack, Broderick again declared such an approach was designed to obscure the real issues of the campaign. In forthright terms he expressed complete agreement with the Freeport doctrine of Stephen A. Douglas. When asked if he intended to support the 1860 presidential candidate of the Democracy, he replied in carefully chosen words: "only if committed to the doctrine of popular sovereignty." The following day Broderick declared that if Gwin resorted to personal violence to vindicate himself and settle his differences, he would find the junior senator prepared. Then he scornfully read an excerpt from a Lecompton newspaper which justified Gwin's language of personal attack by declaring that it was known that Broderick intended to use such language and tactics. In the same speech Broderick attacked the administration, quoting a letter which a Lecompton Democrat had written to the President. It stated that the award of a particular naval contract to a specific party in Philadelphia would assist the administration politically. Buchanan had endorsed the letter and sent it along to the Secretary of the Navy. Broderick invited his listeners to judge a President and an administration which would utilize military procurement for political purposes.[36]

A few days before this gathering, a Lecompton meeting had broken

[34] Sacramento *Union,* July 26, 1859; San Francisco *News,* Aug. 4, 1859.
[35] Sacramento *Union,* July 29, 1859.
[36] Sacramento *Union,* Aug. 1 and 2, 1859.

up in disorder. Broderick's meeting was to end on a similar note. Once more he invited supporters of the opposition to speak. One Lecompton Democrat accepted the challenge and took the opportunity to air a personal attack on Broderick. Another charged that the anti-Lecompton Democrats and the "Black Republicans" were political allies. Broderick branded the charge false, and on this unenlightened note the meeting ended.[37]

A few days later Broderick repeated his charge that his encounter with Perley had been arranged by his enemies, who, he said, "sought to engage me in a difficulty and remove me." Then he turned to a new theme, one which evidently troubled him. He declared that many laboring men in California opposed him and then went on to try to explain the basis of their hostility:

> It is true, fellow-citizens, that I did meet with bitter and unrelenting opposition from a great many mechanics and laboring men in this State, and why? The designing and crafty politicians who loaf about your county seats; who dress well; who are always cleanly shaved; who are in constant readiness to receive a treat—these fellows are always telling about "Broderick," "Broderick," "Broderick." They said I was a shoulder-striker. Well, I have never given much evidence of such a disposition or character. [Laughter]. . . . These neatly-dressed gambling politicians appeal to you, working men, in this way, and do you make a favorable response to them? Let any one of you dare to attempt to rise to any position, and you will be met with the same style of attack.[38]

By the close of the month Broderick was in the far northern part of the state, still maintaining the exhausting schedule he had set in the first week of the campaign. In Red Bluff a large and friendly audience heard what had become his standard campaign speech. Once again he dismissed the use of personal vituperation, and once more he declared that he would respond to Gwin's menace of personal combat. For the third time in the campaign he invited the opposition to come forth with a speaker. This time E. J. Lewis, an assemblyman, responded. For more than an hour he monopolized the attention of the crowd. Much of what he had to say was personal and caustic. Broderick responded in kind. As the senator was leaving the stand, Lewis made a sneering allusion to the "foreman of the red rovers"—a reference to

[37] Sacramento *Union,* Aug. 1 and 2, 1859; San Francisco *News,* Aug. 5, 1859.
[38] San Francisco *News,* Aug. 5, 1859; Sacramento *Union,* Aug. 3 and 4, 1859; *Wilkes' Spirit of the Times,* Oct. 22, 1859.

Broderick's career as a volunteer fireman. Broderick's response was heated and personal, and the meeting disbanded on this sorry note of charge and countercharge.[39]

As Broderick turned south for the final weeks of the campaign, a friendly newspaper warned him that he was falling into a trap set by his enemies. The aspersions on Broderick's courage and character were designed to entice him to personal combat. This was the objective of the Lecompton chorus of defamation. Broderick was assured that there was no need for him to establish his courage "so far as the people are concerned." The item was read by a substantial part of the California citizenry, and it must have come to the attention of the senator himself. Apparently the warning had little influence, for he continued to meet threat with unvarnished defiance.[40]

In late August, as the campaign neared its close, Broderick appeared before the largest gathering in the history of Sacramento. The hesitation that had marked his earlier speeches was gone, and he spoke to the concourse in a clear and sonorous voice. The opening sentence set the tone of the address: "I cease to be on the defensive. . . . it is my turn to be public accuser, to bring forth proof from living and dead and obtain convictions from the great jury—the half million people of this state." His vehement declaration, "I come tonight to arraign before you two great criminals, Milton S. Latham and William M. Gwin," was followed by a burst of applause. When the crowd quieted, Broderick began a detailed account of the senatorial election of 1857.[41]

The dramatic and intriguing story that followed had never before been told in such detail. The manner in which Broderick had chosen to support Gwin instead of Latham for the second Senate seat was reviewed. Then Broderick described the letter which Gwin had written, explicitly renouncing all claims to federal patronage to Broderick, "provided I am elected." Broderick said the letter had been given to W. I. Ferguson, one of his associates; and then in a few but powerful words he declared the letter had led to Ferguson's death.[42]

[39] Sacramento *Union,* Aug. 6, 1859; San Francisco *News,* Aug. 5, 1859.

[40] Sacramento *Union,* Aug. 6 and 8, 1859; newspaper clipping, "Correspondent of the New York *Herald,*" n.d., ca. Aug. 1, 1859, in Henry H. Haight Scrapbook, I, 124, Soc. of Calif. Pioneers Lib., San Francisco; John McDougal Affidavit, *People* v. *McGlynn,* p. 277.

[41] Sacramento *Union,* Aug. 10 and 11, 1859; *Alta California,* Aug. 11, 1859.

[42] Sacramento *Union,* Aug. 11, 1859; San Francisco *News,* Aug. 11, 1859.

The crowd stood in hushed silence to hear the details of this sensational story. Ferguson, onetime associate of Lincoln when both were young and aspiring lawyers, had evolved politically from Whig to anti-Lecompton Democrat. A former state senator from Sacramento, Ferguson had died of a mortal wound inflicted on him by William M. Gwin's political aide, George Pen Johnston, in a duel in the summer of 1858. The fact that the wound was inflicted on the field of honor and that Ferguson refused to submit to surgery, which might have saved his life, were mitigating circumstances in Johnston's trial.[43]

Broderick charged that the duel and the events that followed it represented a desperate effort by Gwin to obtain the letter and suppress its contents. Shortly after Ferguson's death, his desk was rifled, but the letter had not been obtained. Broderick produced the letter and proceeded to read it, commenting as he finished, "Let Dr. Gwin or any of his set deny its authenticity and I will prove that he wrote it, letter for letter, comma for comma." He paused for a moment as though considering whether he should continue, and then closed by saying he would comment on it further after Gwin had a chance to say something about it.

Other speakers followed Broderick that night. Congressman Joseph McKibben and John Conness both stressed the concern which the administration displayed for slavery and the equal concern that Scott and Gwin displayed for the interests of the Pacific Mail Steamship Company. The Lime Point "swindle" was examined again, and McKibben invited the audience to consider the assertion that the site was extremely valuable for "suburban residences or sites for warehouses." This justification was almost ludicrous, and the congressman invited his listeners to judge the integrity and intelligence of those who used such an argument.[44]

Broderick's speech was the most dramatic but probably the least effective of the three addresses. The largest crowd of the campaign had turned out to hear him. However intriguing the detailed story of

[43] A detailed account of the Ferguson-Johnston duel appears in Winfield J. Davis, "Notes on the History of California," p. 352, MS in Huntington Lib.; cf. San Francisco *Examiner,* Mar. 5, 1884. The *Examiner* was edited by Johnston, Benjamin F. Washington, and Charles Weller, stalwart members of the Chivalry during the 1850's. Johnston was described as "a Democrat of the Southern school" and "an intimate of William Gwin."

[44] Sacramento *Union,* Aug. 11, 1859.

the senatorial election, it did little to illuminate the issues. On the contrary, Broderick helped to obscure them by bringing this election of a bygone year to the center of the stage. In that respect the speech was an ineffective effort that wasted a major opportunity to inform and educate the citizenry. Had one accepted Broderick's version at face value, it would have added little to his understanding of the political differences that had split the Democratic party of California.

Broderick compounded this error in some of his later campaign speeches. In one he spoke to a sympathetic audience which greeted his first reference to Gwin with a shouted admonition to forget "Old Gwin." It was a friendly remark which should have warned Broderick that he was beating a dead horse, but he was not to be dissuaded and spent the bulk of his time on the author of the "scarlet letter." He struck more responsive chords when he invited his listeners to contemplate the possibility that the administration would reopen the slave trade and also open the West to slavery. "Can you support an administration that would bring slave labor into the West to compete with free labor?" he asked. The response was a booming chorus of "No's." [45]

In his final speech of the campaign, Broderick avoided the "scarlet letter" as well as the "archvillains" Gwin and Latham. Realizing that this was his last opportunity, he made a determined effort to delineate the issues that divided the Democracy of California into warring camps. The basic difference, he declared, was the attitude each took toward the issue of slavery. The Lecompton Democrats and the administration would protect it and extend it. "The fiat of the administration has already gone forth in favor . . . of intervention to foist slavery on the Territories. This is the real issue. You fellow citizens who are laborers and have white faces, must have black competitors." [46]

This was the last major effort that Broderick made to sway the California voter. He had carried out the pledge he had made at the beginning of the campaign that he would stump the state. Other stump speakers were active. Gwin, Latham, and Weller were conducting a campaign of their own, exploiting every facet of the political picture to their advantage. They stressed the lack of principle that motivated the anti-Lecompton Democrats; the issue between the two wings of the party was "patronage and nothing else." They frequently decried the

[45] Sacramento *Union,* Aug. 18, 1859; San Francisco *News,* Aug. 19, 1859.
[46] Sacramento *Union,* Aug. 31, 1859.

supposed sympathy of Douglas for the anti-Lecompton Democrats, declaring that Senator Douglas had no sympathy for anyone who placed himself outside of the Democratic organization and who would finally fall into the Republican ranks. Republican Leland Stanford joined Gwin in stressing the ephemeral nature of the anti-Lecompton organization. In almost identical language they predicted that the election of 1860 in California would be contested by a single Democratic party and a Republican party. Gwin warned Douglas supporters that anti-Lecompton delegates would not be admitted to the forthcoming Charleston convention, "if they dare send delegates." [47]

As the campaign turned into the final stretch, efforts to effect a fusion of the Republican and anti-Lecompton Democratic tickets continued. Horace Greeley, editor of the New York *Tribune* and the most prominent tourist in California, urged fusion on the Republicans, but one Republican leader objected to the "acceptance of an invitation for us to commit suicide this year with the promise of a glorious resurrection next." In a real sense the outcome of the election of 1859 was being decided by the election still a year away. Douglas strategists had their eyes firmly fixed on the forthcoming Charleston convention and were unwilling to do anything to endanger the Little Giant's prospects. A Republican leader demonstrated this concern with the future by writing, "This year they [the anti-Lecompton Democrats] occupy middle ground, next year they will be submerged in the great Republican tidal wave of 1860." [48]

Despite all the attempts made to prevent fusion, a joint ticket of sorts finally emerged when a number of anti-Lecompton and Republican candidates resigned on the eve of election. Four days before the actual balloting a joint ticket emerged on the congressional level,

[47] Thomas C. Browne to Douglas, Sept. 19, 1859, Douglas Coll.; Sacramento *Union,* Aug. 13 and 15, 1859. Gwin and Stanford stressed the ephemeral nature of the anti-Lecompton party; see the Sacramento *Union,* Aug. 15, 1859, for Gwin's views and the issue of July 15, 1859, for Stanford's opinion. William F. Thompson, "The Political Career of Milton Slocum Latham of California" (unpubl. M.A. thesis, Stanford Univ., 1952) is a sympathetic account of Latham's political career.

[48] Greeley was welcomed to the city of San Francisco by such Broderick intimates as John A. McGlynn and John White, editor of the San Francisco *News;* see its issue of Aug. 7, 1859. His views on the need for a joint election effort by Republicans and anti-Lecompton Democrats is set forth in a statement published in the San Francisco *Times,* Aug. 20, 1859, and the *Alta California,* Aug. 22, 1859. C. Washburne to Cornelius Cole, telegram, Aug. 25, 1859, Cole Coll., Univ. of Calif., Los Angeles, urges "fusion" on the Republican party. Opposition to this move is expressed by S. D. Parker to Cole, Aug. 20, 1859, Cole Coll. See also *Alta California,* Sept. 4, 1859.

where Baker and McKibben became the nominees of a united ticket through the resignation of a Republican and an anti-Lecompton candidate. Such belated unity was of doubtful value, however. In four short days the information had to be distributed throughout the state and new ballots prepared by the respective parties. In such instances, fusion was likely to produce confusion.[49]

The election produced the largest vote in California's history, as a little more than one hundred thousand voters trooped to the polls. From the first it was apparent that the Lecompton Democrats had won, but it was not until the returns from the more isolated sections of the state were counted that the magnitude of the victory was revealed. In 1858 the margin of victory was eight thousand, but in 1859 it swelled until the Lecompton Democratic majority reached twenty thousand. In 1859 Broderick and his associates carried two counties—one by a margin of two votes—whereas in 1858 they had carried eleven. In San Diego only one hardheaded voter cast a ballot for the anti-Lecompton Democrats. In the major centers of population, such as San Francisco, Sacramento, Marysville, and Placerville, the anti-Lecompton Democrats made a strong showing, but in the "remote little places like Fresno, Tulare, and San Bernardino, etc., the Lecomptonites have majorities of fifty to one or more." The lack of organization of Broderick's wing of the Democracy and the Lecomptonites' monopoly of both federal and state patronage were reflected in these figures.[50]

The results rather clearly indicated that the Broderick organization failed to enlist the Douglas following beneath their standard of popular sovereignty. The bulk of the pro-Douglas group stayed with the Lecompton Democratic organization, accurately reflecting the choice

[49] Opposition to fusion was widespread and continued after a joint ticket was partially accomplished. See Leland Stanford to William P. Jones, Aug. 13, 1859, quoted in George T. Clark, *Leland Stanford, War Governor of California* (Stanford, Calif., 1931), pp. 89–90. E. W. Read to Cornelius Cole, Sept. 11, 1859, Cole Coll., expresses similar sentiments. Henry H. Haight, Chairman, Republican State Central Committee, to Republicans of California, in Sacramento *Union,* Aug. 30, 1859, apparently closed the door on fusion, but a partial joint ticket was subsequently worked out with the withdrawal of some of the competing Republican and anti-Lecompton candidates. See *Alta California,* Sept. 5, 1859; San Francisco *News,* Sept. 6, 1859; Davis, *Political Conventions,* p. 107.

[50] *Alta California,* Sept. 9, 10, and 11, carried the returns as they became available. Davis, *Political Conventions,* pp. 108–109, summarizes the statewide totals. Election Returns, 1859, Vol. 1759, Archives of the Secretary of State, Sacramento, contains the county by county breakdown. The reaction of the Broderick newspaper, the San Francisco *News,* appears in its issues of Sept. 9 and 10, 1859.

that Douglas had made. While Douglas did not direct his supporters to stay with the Lecomptonites, his failure to come to the aid of the anti-Lecompton Democrats, champions of popular sovereignty, was a clear indication of his appraisal of the political situation in California. Although he carefully refrained from an alliance with either group, he issued a long letter on the political issues of the campaign one week after the voting had taken place. Milton S. Latham was Douglas' agent, making the necessary arrangements to see that it was given wide circulation through the press. Latham had campaigned tirelessly as the Lecompton candidate for governor. His principal objective was to convince Douglas Democrats to stay with the Lecomptonites. As a Douglas correspondent pointed out in a letter to the Little Giant, "He stole some of your popularity with the masses by telling them he was sound on the 'Douglas' question, winking at them with the left eye and at Buchanan's friends with the right." A year later Douglas found his professed friend and supporter Latham campaigning as tirelessly for his presidential opponent, John C. Breckinridge.[51]

The failure of the Republicans and the anti-Lecompton Democrats to join hands played a role in determining the outcome. Last-minute fusion produced confusion; one of the withdrawn candidates, S. A. Booker, received almost three thousand votes. Greeley's effort to bring about a unified ticket was more than offset by the efforts of Republicans like Leland Stanford and F. P. Pixley. Broderick's vehement denial that he was in league with the "Black Republicans" did little to bring about the unity of action that was essential.[52]

In some respects the loss was Broderick's personal responsibility. In the beginning he had indicated that the examination and discussion of the issues would produce a victory for the anti-Lecompton Democrats; however, in the course of the campaign he responded to the barrage of personal invective that was thrown at him. It was intended to conceal the issues, he said, and then he proceeded to allow it to divert him.

[51] Douglas' letter was published in the San Francisco *Daily Evening Bulletin,* Sept. 26, 1859. Latham to Douglas, Sept. 18, 1859, Douglas Coll.; Robert W. Johannsen, ed. *The Letters of Stephen A. Douglas* (Urbana, Ill., 1961), p. 453; James Johnston to Douglas, Sept. 19, 1859, David D. Colton to Douglas, Oct. 4, 1859, C. S. Whitney to Douglas, Sept. 12, 1859, Douglas Coll. Douglas' correspondents reported in detail Latham's appeal to Douglas-minded Democrats and forthright supporters of the Buchanan administration.

[52] Election Returns, 1859, Vol. 1759, Archives of the Secretary of State, Sacramento. San Francisco *News,* Aug. 31, 1859, Sacramento *Union,* Aug. 20, 1859, and *Alta California,* Aug. 23, 1859, reported in detail the opposition of Pixley. Each editor commented on the transformation of Pixley from a firm supporter to an adamant antagonist of Broderick.

While he never responded in kind, he devoted a major part of many of his campaign speeches to attacks on the personal integrity of Gwin and Latham. Both men were apparently vulnerable, and in one speech after another Broderick thundered the tale of perfidy and dishonor in the senatorial election of 1857. Establishing the lack of principle of Gwin and Latham as they vied for one of the major prizes of the American political scene did little, however, to illuminate the differences between the two wings of the party.

Broderick's failure to build a viable political party that could not only battle but win in 1859 was, in the final analysis, but one aspect of the "epoch's tragedy." He had challenged the most formidable array of political power in the United States. In this period when professional politicians staffed and ran state and local committees, held caucuses, controlled conventions, and parceled out honors, the political machinery was controlled by those who dispensed patronage. In California, patronage on the state and federal level had been distributed over a decade to produce a phalanx of officeholders who united behind the regular organization in 1859. The postmasters, who numbered in the scores, employees in the customs service, appointees in the mint, the Indian service, and the land office—all held office at the discretion and pleasure of the appointing officials. The influence of such appointees was significant in all of the states; in California it was almost decisive. A reporter in San Francisco compiled a revealing list of the principal federal officers in California to illustrate the influence of the Chivalry. Among the names mentioned were Benjamin F. Washington, collector of San Francisco, from Virginia; Richard Roman, appraiser-general, from Texas; W. B. Dameron, surveyor of San Francisco, from Mississippi; James Y. McDuffie, Indian agent, from Georgia; Austin E. Smith, Navy agent, from Virginia; John T. Eaton, Indian agent, from Georgia; Charles Hempstead, superintendent of the mint, from Missouri. James W. Mandeville, surveyor-general, from New York, was the lone Yankee in this collection of Southerners. The report went on to point out that these officers appointed hundreds of subordinates and constituted an army of political workers which was mobilized at important times to win political battles for their commanders. The victory they won in 1859 demonstrated their effectiveness.[53]

[53] George Fort Milton, *The Eve of Conflict* (Boston, 1934), p. 402, describes the control of patronage as the power to control the machinery of politics, thereby

Postelection analyses emphasized the importance of the federal power and the failure of the anti-Lecompton Democrats to "force their adversaries to make and contest the real issue." The Lecompton Democrats "unblushingly proclaimed that the only difference between you [Douglas] and Mr. Buchanan was a personal one, that the political one was a past issue and that you were as much an Administration man as any of them," reported a Douglas lieutenant. Another observer declared Broderick's error lay in neglecting the issues and seeking a "personal endorsement." A leading Republican pointed out that an attempt had been made "to reprove Democracy with Democracy" and it had failed.[54]

However severe the defeat might appear at first blush, the perceptive observer could see features in the election results that promised well for the future. California was the lone exception to the general election picture of 1859, and even here the margin was but twenty thousand out of a hundred thousand votes. A shift of a little more than ten percent of the totals would change the result. An essential first step was the creation of a unified opposition to the Lecompton Democrats. Since the Lecompton organization was based on federal patronage, a new national administration would fundamentally change the situation.[55]

---

preventing "the registration, against the will of the controlling group, of any other than the most deep-seated and persistent public demand," calling it "the epoch's tragedy." Edmund Randolph described and analyzed the "federal power" in California politics in a speech published in the Sacramento *Union,* Aug. 31, 1859. Edward D. Baker went over the same ground in a speech reported in the San Francisco *News,* Aug. 25, 1859. The Chivalry monopoly of federal patronage is described in the San Francisco *News,* Aug. 18, 1859. For further details on the extent of patronage and its influence on political affairs in California, see the Philadelphia *Press,* Oct. 10, 1859, and the issues of the San Francisco *News* of May 26 and 27, June 8 and 24, 1859. The issue of June 24, 1859, included a detailed list of Chivalry members who held federal appointments; the issue of June 8, 1859, contains a list of hundreds of postmasters who held office at the pleasure of the Chivalry. See also Henry W. Halleck to Pablo de la Guerra, Oct. 18, 1860, De la Guerra Coll., Santa Barbara Mission Archives; Albert L. Collins to Douglas, Feb. 18, 1859, Douglas Coll. A partial and impressive list of patronage appointments in California available to the President appears in Roy P. Basler, ed. *The Collected Works of Abraham Lincoln* (New Brunswick, 1953), IV, 304–306.

[54] Charles E. DeLong to Douglas, Oct. 3, 1859, and James Johnson to Douglas, Sept. [?], 1859, Douglas Coll.; Cornelius Cole to Edwin Morgan, Sept. 30, 1859, and Cole to William H. Seward, Sept. 20, 1859, Cole Coll.

[55] See Roy F. Nichols, *The Disruption of American Democracy* (New York, 1948), pp. 243–267, for a searching description and analysis of the elections of 1859. Frederick W. Seward, *Seward at Washington as Senator and Secretary of State: A Memoir* (New York, 1891), p. 493, describes the state elections of 1859 and their implications.

The unity that was essential was not to be easily achieved. Douglas supporters peered into the future in an effort to chart a course that would lead to a victory in Charleston and eventuate in the White House. They shied away from the independent organization, but anti-Lecompton Democrats, in spite of the defeat of 1859, were inclined to preserve and strengthen their new party. In some ways anti-Lecompton Democrats had limited options, for by this time the policy makers of the Lecompton organization had shut the doors against dissident Democrats who swallowed their pride and sought reentry into their ancestral political home.[56]

Douglas was advised to court the independent organization, for the Lecompton Democrats were not to be trusted. They "hate you most bitterly whilst at times they profess to admire you," was the settled judgment of one observer. Richard P. Hammond, stalwart of the Chivalry camp, saw the situation in a different light. Professing his admiration for the senator from Illinois, Hammond saw the problem of building a unified Democratic movement as a practical political problem. The anti-Lecomptonites should simply rejoin the regular organization, he declared, so that they might again become an influential factor in the united party.[57]

The realm of political speculation was dominated for months by the forthcoming election of 1860. Much of the planning for the political future was based upon what had taken place in the campaign of 1859, but before California voters went to the polls again, a new set of factors and circumstances was shaping the political milieu. The new political panorama did not include Broderick, however, for long before it took shape, the most effective leader of the antislavery wing of the California Democracy was but a memory.

[56] Alfred Reddington to Douglas, Oct. 14, 1859, as state chairman of the anti-Lecompton Democratic party expressed vehemently the need for an independent organization; Charles E. DeLong to Douglas, Oct. 3, 1859, agreed; both in Douglas Coll.

[57] Richard P. Hammond to Douglas, Oct. 2, 1859, and Charles E. DeLong to Douglas, Oct. 3, 1859, Douglas Coll.

CHAPTER THIRTEEN

The Field of "Honor"

The campaign of 1859 was the most bitterly fought in the history of California. It began on a respectable level but rapidly descended into a contest characterized by slander and invective. Violence and the threat of violence were themes which lay half-hidden in the rhetoric of stump speakers. It was freely predicted that the "code duello" would be the final arbiter of the differences between Broderick and his opponents. Gwin, Latham, Broderick, and others were expected to meet on the field of honor after the balloting and there vindicate themselves. Although Broderick spurned a challenge to personal combat at the beginning of the campaign, he indicated repeatedly that he was "responsible" for what he said on the stump. If his enemies desired, they might pursue the matter and elicit a different response to a challenge. As the campaign proceeded through the long, hot summer of 1859, it escalated in violence. Broderick was the principal target of the opposition. His refusal to fight Perley was ascribed to cowardliness, and he was attacked with every verbal weapon that the opposition could muster. Apparently convinced that these tactics were designed to obscure the issues, Broderick was inclined to refuse to engage in personalities, but as the assault mounted in magnitude and malignity, his attitude changed. His speeches reflected a new stance and were marked with trenchant comments on the honesty and integrity of Gwin and Latham.[1]

[1] Broderick to D. W. Perley, June 29, 1859, in Sacramento *Union,* July 1, 1859; San Francisco *News,* Aug. 4 and 5, 1859. In late August, Broderick acknowledged the effectiveness of the Lecompton tactics, declaring, "For the last ten days my attention has been diverted from the issues involved in the campaign, in replying to Mr. Gwin, Milton S. Latham and Governor Weller"; see San Francisco *News,* Aug. 20, 1859; Sacramento *Union,* Aug. 6, 1859.

Broderick was warned by one of the principal newspapers of northern California that he was falling into a snare. In clear and explicit terms he was warned that the "imputations upon his personal courage and honor," the Perley affair, and the campaign of slander directed at him were all designed to force him into a "personal encounter." It would be difficult to find in American political history "so premeditated and daring a scheme of outrage against the laws and violence against an opponent," wrote the editor of the Sacramento *Union*.[2]

Aware of the hazards of the field of honor, veteran of one duel that almost cost him his life, and sensitive to the subtle meanings of the language and behavior of his opponents, Broderick had good reason to be cautious. But he apparently was not inclined to back away from a personal collision. Even when asserting that there were many people who "would seek similar opportunities for hostile meetings, for the purpose of accomplishing a political object," Broderick indicated that he could be provoked into the acceptance of a challenge.[3]

The challenge came soon after the polls closed. Broderick's opponent was neither Gwin nor Latham but a tall, truculent, onetime Texan, then serving as chief justice of the California Supreme Court. A stalwart of the Chivalry, David S. Terry was one of the most colorful figures to wear the ermine of a justice.[4] Elected in 1855 as a Know-Nothing, he had become embroiled in the battle between the Vigilance Committee of 1856 and its opposition. In the course of that struggle, a clash had taken place when a member of the committee attempted to arrest a man in Terry's presence. Terry intervened and, in the struggle, inflicted a near fatal wound on the vigilante with his favorite weapon, a Bowie knife. Incarcerated by the committee, Terry's fate hung in the balance while the wounded man fought for his life. The chief justice was eventually released; his escape from summary justice by the committee reflected his exalted position as well as the fact that he had powerful friends within the committee. In July 1859 he competed unsuccessfully for a nomination as a Lecompton Democrat to a second term on the court. Out of that effort came the first of a series of events that led to his fateful meeting with Broderick.

Invited to address the Lecompton convention, Terry made a bitter

[2] Aug. 13, 1859.

[3] Broderick to Perley, June 29, 1859, in Sacramento *Union,* July 1, 1859.

[4] The best and most recent biography is A. Russell Buchanan, *David S. Terry of California: Dueling Judge* (San Marino, 1956).

and partisan speech. In searing words he invited his listeners to consider their opponents "a miserable remnant of a faction, sailing under false colors." The anti-Lecompton Democrats, charged Terry, had no principles or program. "They are . . . the personal chattels of a single individual, whom they are ashamed of. They belong, heart and soul, body and breeches, to David C. Broderick." Terry went on to attack them for claiming the support of Stephen A. Douglas. "It is well known to them as to us—that the gallant Senator from Illinois . . . has no affiliation with them, no feeling in common with them." He closed with a charge that struck a responsive chord in the minds of the delegates. "Perhaps they do sail under the flag of Douglas," said Terry, "but it is the banner of the black Douglass whose name is Frederick, not Stephen." Frederick Douglass was the ex-slave and editor who was a national figure in the abolitionist movement. Prolonged applause followed, which might have been some consolation when Terry was passed over for W. W. Cope by the convention.[5]

The address was typical of hundreds of those delivered during the fifties, as speakers of Chivalric background labeled the opposition with the abolitionist tag. By the late fifties, the term had become freighted with connotations and conjured up in the minds of those who heard it an image of an irrational and obsessed man who would resort to any means to effect the emancipation of the oppressed slaves of America. Politicians found the tag effective when attached to opponents. It was a useful device to avoid the serious discussion of issues and program, and it was especially effective when the target was known for his antislavery convictions. Broderick was quite vulnerable to this form of attack.

Broderick commented on Terry's speech the next day; to a group of friends in a San Francisco hotel, he pointed out that he had supported Terry during the time of his incarceration by the Vigilance Committee. Although Terry's own friends deserted him in his hour of need, Broderick had spent money lavishly to sustain a newspaper which defended him and advocated his release. "I once considered him," Broderick declared, "the only honest man on the Supreme bench but I take it all back." Perley, former law partner and close friend of Terry, overheard Broderick's words and threatened to report them to the justice. The senator invited him to do just that. One word led to

[5] James O'Meara, *Broderick and Gwin* (San Francisco, 1881), p. 226; Buchanan, *David S. Terry,* pp. 93–94.

another, and before Perley left, he was incensed not only at what Broderick said about his friend but on his own account. His challenge was subsequently spurned by Broderick, and there the matter rested until Terry reopened it.[6]

The election results were still coming in when Terry initiated the "hostile correspondence" that culminated in his meeting with Broderick. His first note to the junior senator demanded a retraction, at the "earliest opportunity," of the remarks which Broderick had made about him. Broderick guardedly replied that he would like Terry to be specific, and this elicited from Terry: "The offensive remarks to which I alluded are: 'I have heretofore considered and spoken of him (myself) as the only honest man on the Supreme Bench; but I now take it all back.'" Terry went on to point out that Broderick could best remember the exact words and closed with: "What I require is, the retraction of any words which were used, calculated to reflect on my character as an officer or a gentleman."[7]

This epistle did not shut the door to a satisfactory settlement without resort to the code duello. It was entirely proper for them to approach this matter carefully, exploring every nuance of language used, before committing themselves. When Broderick received the second message, he requested of Terry's intermediary time in which to consider and compose a reply. Terry's second responded that "there was no disposition on our part to hurry him in the least except on account of others than the parties immediately concerned." Calhoun Benham, who used this phrase, reported it to Terry with an explanation that "he would readily divine what I meant." There can be little doubt that Broderick understood these cryptic words, which throbbed with meaning. They suggested that Broderick had a number of opponents to duel, of whom Terry was but the first. The door to a peaceful settlement was partially shut by Benham when he hurried Broderick's reply.[8]

Broderick's response still left the door open. He stated that his remarks "were occasioned by certain offensive allusions of yours concerning me, made in the Convention at Sacramento." They may have

[6] O'Meara, *Broderick and Gwin,* pp. 226–227; A. A. Selover Statement, MS in Bancroft Lib.; San Francisco *News,* July 1, 1859.

[7] Terry to Broderick, Sept. 8, 1859, Broderick to Terry, Sept. 9, 1859, Terry to Broderick, Sept. 9, 1859, all in Terry-Broderick Correspondence, Soc. of Calif. Pioneers Lib., San Francisco.

[8] Benham to Terry, Sept. 9, 1859, Terry-Broderick Correspondence.

been heated and unguarded, implied Broderick by linking his remarks to those spoken earlier by Terry. As far as his memory served him, Broderick continued, he had said something about supporting and defending Terry during his incarceration by the Vigilance Committee when "he paid two hundred dollars a week to support a newspaper" in Terry's defense. He had also stated "heretofore that I considered him (Judge Terry) the only honest man on the Supreme Bench—but I take it all back." The message closed, "You are the proper judge as to whether this language affords good ground for offense." On the whole, the reply was equivocal and still provided for a further exploration of the views of the two men. The burden for taking the matter further was now placed on Terry.[9]

Terry, experienced in the subtleties of language, had good reason to ponder the reply and consider carefully his next step. Should Broderick's withdrawal of an endorsement of Terry be considered the kind of serious provocation that demanded satisfaction under the code? In the final analysis, Broderick had not directly attacked the honor or integrity of the judge. How long the matter was considered and what led to the final decision is unknown. After consultation with his seconds, Terry drew up a peremptory challenge that precluded further exchanges on the meaning and significance of Broderick's remarks. The chief justice of the California Supreme Court demanded that the senator render the "satisfaction usual among gentlemen." [10]

The challenge was brought to Broderick after midnight. The hour was noted by Broderick in his curt response: "Your note of the above date has been received at one o'clock A.M., September 10th. In response to the same, I will refer you to my friend, Hon. J. C. McKibben, who will make the necessary arrangements." The details of time, place, weapons, and procedures were to be left to McKibben and David D. Colton, acting for Broderick, and Calhoun Benham and Thomas Hayes, seconds for Terry. Broderick, the challenged party, was entitled to name the weapons and the terms of combat. The arrangements, which differed from the usual in only two respects, were made. The word to fire was to be followed by a count of one, two; no further firing was to take place after the second count. The meeting

[9] Broderick to Terry, Sept. 9, 1859, Terry-Broderick Correspondence.

[10] Terry to Broderick, Sept. 9, 1859, Terry-Broderick Correspondence; S. H. Brooks statement in San Francisco *Examiner,* Aug. 18, 1889, p. 9, col. 3.

was to take place on a farm near Lake Laguna in San Mateo County.[11]

Terry's seconds objected to the place of meeting as well as the unusual mode of firing, but McKibben and Colton defended the latter on humanitarian grounds and refused to consider any change. Terry's seconds persisted, asking "whether or not said article is insisted upon as a *sine qua non* to their meeting. . . ." They demanded that Broderick be consulted and that he give a "categorical answer in writing." Colton and McKibben refused to discuss the matter with Broderick, for it gave him no advantage and did not handicap Terry. They intimated that Terry could decline the terms proposed. In insisting on the proposed mode of firing, McKibben and Colton were being less than candid. Broderick was a crack shot with a pistol, having perfected his ability at "hip-shooting" at a gallery in San Francisco after long hours of practice. Limiting the time of firing apparently was a deliberate attempt to take advantage of his ability to shoot accurately and rapidly.[12]

Benham and Hayes reluctantly agreed to the terms, and final arrangements were completed on September 10. The two men were given the balance of that day and the next to make any final preparations. Attempts were made to avert the duel but to no avail. A. P. Crittenden, Edmund Randolph, and David Maloney made such efforts but were prevented from seeing Broderick by one of his associates, Andrew Jackson Butler. Butler is reported to have said, "These Chivs have got to learn that there is one man they can't back down. The fight has got to come and this is the best time for it." These words may have reflected Broderick's view of the inevitability of a clash. If there were other representatives of the Chivalry who thirsted to challenge him, a postponement or avoidance would settle nothing. The best course might very well be a showdown now, which would teach his adversaries prudence.[13]

The news of the clash went out from San Francisco in ever-widening

[11] Broderick to Terry, Sept. 10, 1859, Terry-Broderick Correspondence; O'Meara, *Broderick and Gwin,* p. 238. The "Articles" or arrangements for the duel are in the Terry-Broderick Correspondence, Soc. of Calif. Pioneers Lib.

[12] John Daggett Statement, "Broderick Resolutions, 10th Session—1859," Bancroft Lib.; Buchanan, *David S. Terry,* p. 102; George R. Brown, ed. *Reminiscences of Senator William M. Stewart of Nevada* (New York, 1908), pp. 119–120; A. E. Wagstaff, *Life of David S. Terry* (San Francisco, 1892), p. 194.

[13] O'Meara, *Broderick and Gwin,* pp. 235–236; Hubert H. Bancroft, *History of California,* VI (San Francisco, 1888), 731–732; Ben C. Truman, *The Field of Honor* (New York, 1884), pp. 396–397; Wagstaff, p. 194.

circles until it reached James Buchanan in Washington. In fact, Terry was identified as Broderick's opponent in a note John Nugent sent to the President before Terry's peremptory challenge was written. The editor of the *Herald* reported the Lecompton victory and closed with the terse announcement: "Judge Terry of the Supreme Court has commenced a hostile correspondence with Mr. Broderick. It will in all probability result in a fight. Broderick and Gwin will *not* fight." Written before the identity of Broderick's opponent was publicly known, this curious note was sent off with the eastward bound Overland Mail.[14]

Until the last moment, a substantial body of opinion felt that the duel would be averted. Newspapers speculated on the possibility, and one journalist flatly predicted, "The whole matter will be amicably settled by friends satisfactorily to the parties." All such efforts were doomed to failure, although an unexpected delay occurred when the two principals were arrested upon their appearance on the dueling site in the early morning of September 12. Arrested on a warrant obtained from the court of Justice W. B. Maxon of San Mateo, the two men were taken to San Francisco. Mark Brumagin, who instituted the proceedings, was a supporter of Broderick; Justice Maxon was an anti-Lecompton Democrat; evidently some of the senator's friends were quite interested in preventing the duel.[15]

Haled before Judge H. B. Coon, the two men were set free by the court, which held that no offense against the laws had been committed. The bench explained that while dueling was illegal, an attempt to engage in a duel was not, and therefore the justice and the senator were beyond the reach of the court. Coon's ruling was soundly criticized; and Broderick's counsel, Edward D. Baker, shared the disappointment of the senator's friends. It was "evidently the design of Broderick's friends to have him held to bail, that it [the duel] might not take place and it was Broderick's secret wish and when the Judge declined to hold him to bail, he was very disappointed," commented a contemporary. In view of the manner in which a Sacramento court a few months before had prevented a duel by placing the prospective duelists under heavy bond, Coon's ruling was illogical. There is much

[14] Nugent to Buchanan, Sept. 9, 1859, Buchanan Papers, Pennsylvania Hist. Soc.

[15] Wagstaff, p. 194; A. A. Selover Statement, MS in Bancroft Lib.; *Alta California,* Sept. 12, 1859. Maxon is identified as an anti-Lecompton Democratic candidate for the legislature in San Francisco *News,* Sept. 4, 1859.

justification for a contemporary's charge that "Judge Coon is responsible, in my judgment, for that duel." [16]

The two antagonists left the courtroom accompanied by their friends, to meet next on the field of honor. Broderick spent the night with Edward D. Baker at the home of Leonidas Haskell near Black Point. The seconds for each principal made new arrangements. On September 13, an hour or so before dawn, Broderick and Terry made their respective ways to the site. The time and place of the meeting was an ill-kept secret, for close to eighty spectators were on hand to witness this historic encounter between a United States senator and a justice of the California Supreme Court. The day dawned bright and clear, a sparkling sun beaming down on the scene through a sky lightly studded with wisps of clouds.[17]

Any advantage that Broderick might have had as a result of the terms of the duel was more than offset by his physical condition. He had just emerged from an exhausting campaign in which his health had been a problem. The magnitude of the defeat that he and his followers had suffered was being brought home to him with every fresh dispatch that reached San Francisco from the hinterland. Physically and psychologically he was poorly prepared for a combat that might cost him his life. The night before he had lain on the floor until the early hours of the morning drinking coffee and conversing with Baker. No record of what they discussed survived, but one witness declared Broderick "was fey—all night," that is, a man who was deeply disturbed.[18]

The general behavior of the two parties was in sharp contrast when they met in the early morning sunlight. Terry's seconds were calm, collected, and assured as they went about their business. Broderick's seconds revealed their uncertainty and inexperience: Leonidas Haskell partially removed Broderick's cravat and then walked away for a moment wringing his hands before he returned and finished the task.

[16] *Alta California,* Sept. 13, 1859. *California Police Gazette,* July 9, 1859, includes a biographical sketch of Coon. See Annis Merrill, "Statement of Early Recollections on Early Days in San Francisco," pp. 7–8, MS in Bancroft Lib. Sacramento *Union,* June 18, 1859, describes the action of the court in Sacramento; cf. *Alta California,* June 17 and 18, 1859; DeLong Diary, June 18, 1859, MS in Calif. State Lib., Sacramento.

[17] Buchanan, *David S. Terry,* pp. 103–104; Carroll D. Hall, *The Terry-Broderick Duel* (San Francisco, 1939), pp. 28 ff.; Truman, pp. 406–410.

[18] John White Affidavit, in *People* v. *McGlynn,* p. 265; Leonidas Haskell Statement, MS in the possession of Broderick Haskell, Redding, Calif.

The senator himself was apparently composed, his eyes traveling over the crowd, now and then making an almost imperceptible sign of recognition.

A toss of a coin was used to determine position and the weapons to be used. Two sets of pistols were on hand, one the property of a gunsmith, Andrew J. Taylor, the other provided by the Terry party. Terry won the toss for weapons, whereupon his pistols were produced and loaded. They were of Belgian make, eight-inch barrels which used Derringer-size balls and had hair triggers. They were the property of a friend of Terry; he had not only seen them before this meeting but had practiced with them.

When the pistols were chosen, the gunsmith loaded Broderick's and declared the trigger was set too finely. The gun could be set off by a jerk or jar, he declared, but his objections went unheeded. Broderick displayed signs of nervous tension for the first time when he examined the gun. He looked it over carefully, his hand changing position repeatedly, as if he were having trouble getting the feel of the weapon. The seconds stepped away from the principals, who faced one another at an ominous distance of twenty paces. Jack Hays, sometime sheriff of San Francisco, stalwart of the Chivalry and Texas Ranger, lingered for a moment for a last word with Terry.[19]

At quarter past seven, Colton queried, "Gentlemen, are you ready?" Terry answered in the affirmative, but Broderick hesitated, his hand still seeking an appropriate hold on the handle of the weapon. Finally with a nod he indicated he was ready. Both men shot between the words "fire" and "two." Broderick's bullet spent itself in the ground about nine feet in front of him, the weapon firing as he raised it. From ten paces away, a distinct second or so later, Terry's bullet sped on its way. It struck Broderick in the right chest, staggering him. Ploughing through the chest cavity, the ball fractured the sternum and perforated the left lung before it came to rest near his left armpit. Broderick stood erect for a moment, tried to brace himself, and then fell prone on the grass. For a second, as the shots echoed in the distance, there was quiet. Then a shouted, half-strangled cry came

[19] O'Meara, *Broderick and Gwin,* p. 243; George E. Barnes statement, San Francisco *Bulletin,* Nov. 2, 1895, p. 13, col. 4; Barnes was an eyewitness. San Francisco *Steamer Times,* Sept. 20, 1859, printed much of the testimony, including that of Bernard Lagoarde, gunsmith, at the official inquest into the death of Broderick. Wagstaff, p. 193, reports that Terry had practiced with the pistols.

from the crowd, "That's murder, by God!" A general melee between the friends of the two duelists seemed imminent.[20]

Restraining hands and admonishing voices dealt with the emotional Broderick partisans. Surgeons hurried forward to stem the crimson flow that poured out of the wound, while Terry stood erect, still in the classic stance of the duelist. It was soon obvious that a second firing was out of the question, for any further "satisfaction customary among gentlemen" was not to be obtained from Broderick. A wagon was brought and the senator tenderly lifted and placed on a mattress within it. The party set off for the Haskell home, retracing the route that it had followed to the dueling site a few hours before. En route Broderick was told that his wound was not a serious one, but he complained of the feeling of massive weight on his chest. Upon arrival, the fallen gladiator was carried to a second-floor bedroom which overlooked the ocean. There his physicians tended him around the clock. Their reports on his condition, at first optimistic, changed slowly as his condition worsened. The city seized every scrap of information that came out of the sickroom.

Broderick's sorrowing friends gathered around his deathbed, and for three days their hopes rose and fell with his changing condition. At times he conversed in heavy whispers, his body racked with pain, in spite of the liberal use of drugs. A short time after midnight, September 16, 1869, he lapsed into unconsciousness, and at twenty minutes past nine on the following morning he died.[21]

That the duel was a by-product of the political animosities generated in the course of the proslavery and antislavery struggle within the Democratic party is beyond doubt. It was so regarded by most contemporary observers, who made earnest but generally futile efforts to look at the matter objectively. The Sacramento *Union* had warned weeks before the duel took place that Broderick's enemies intended to provoke him into accepting a challenge. The senator himself had

[20] George E. Barnes statement in San Francisco *Bulletin,* Nov. 2, 1895, p. 13, col. 4; Truman, pp. 397–398. Among the numerous accounts of the duel in addition to those cited above are: Dolores Waldorf, "Hair-Trigger Drama," San Francisco *Call-Bulletin,* Oct. 10, 1955, Sec. C, p. 58, and an account by S. H. Brooks, who was one of Terry's seconds, which appeared in the San Francisco *Post,* Dec. 16, 1882, p. 2, col. 3. There is general agreement on the arrangements and staging but much disagreement on: (1) whether Broderick was victimized by a "trick" pistol and (2) whether Terry could have held his fire when Broderick's pistol misfired.

[21] *Alta California,* Sept. 14, 15, 16, and 17, 1859.

rejected one challenge and pointed out that there were many people who sought to meet him on the field of honor to "accomplish a political object." The Philadelphia *Press,* far removed from the scene, interpreted the ominous reports of the virulent campaign as portents of an attempt to remove Broderick from the political picture of California. The *Alta California* described it as "the more virulent type of political quarrel" and predicted that similar encounters were in the offing, "all of them arising out of political differences." [22]

The first incident in the chain that led directly to the fatal meeting was a bitter and partisan address delivered in a political convention. This led directly to the first challenge, which was spurned by Broderick. The effort to force him into a personal clash on the field of honor continued throughout the campaign as one Lecompton speaker after another cast aspersions on Broderick's courage, and William Gwin, in the course of one speech, questioned an audience as to appropriate treatment of Broderick, posing alternatives of "clubbing him or killing him." Dueling was far more common in California in the fifties than is generally realized; a great many of the clashes arose out of personal differences. However, the most famous duel of California's history can never be understood except in terms of the political milieu of which it was a part. The duel which took the life of the only United States senator to die in this manner was a political affair.[23]

Whether a conspiracy to remove Broderick and accomplish a political object was part of the story is difficult to ascertain. A number of circumstances indicated to some observers that such a conspiracy existed, and years later one of Broderick's associates published an account that flatly characterized the duel as "a foul murder." It was charged that Terry was the chosen instrument of a cabal to eliminate Broderick from the political scene. The report that he met with Gwin after the duel sharpened the suspicions of some individuals; the fact that his party provided the pistols—one of which so conveniently misfired—was a telling fact which convinced many people that Broderick had been removed from the scene through "murder most foul." [24]

[22] Sacramento *Union,* Aug. 13, 1859; Philadelphia *Press,* "Letter from Occasional," Oct. 11, 1859; *Alta California,* Sept. 13, 1859.

[23] Broderick to Perley, in Sacramento *Union,* June 29, 1859; William M. Gwin speech at Shasta, Calif., in Sacramento *Union,* Aug. 1, 1859. S. H. Brooks, Terry's second, declared flatly, "It had its origin in politics." See San Francisco *Examiner,* Aug. 18, 1889, p. 9, col. 3.

[24] Cornelius Cole to W. H. Seward, Sept. 20, 1859, Cole Coll., Univ. of Calif., Los Angeles; George Ihrie to Stephen A. Douglas, Sept. 29, 1859, Douglas Coll., Univ. of

There are a number of circumstances that tend to offset such suspicions. Far from being a chosen instrument of a cabal, Terry evidently thought in terms of an avoidance of the clash until the last moment. He assured his wife in so many words that he thought the matter would be settled "without recourse to the final argument," hardly the sentiments of a man who had been selected to assassinate an opponent under the cover of a duel. That message, coupled with his failure to resign from the supreme court until the duel had been staged, seems to indicate that Terry acted as an individual in search of vindication for a slur cast on his personal reputation.[25]

The question of Terry's motivation is of more than academic importance. A careful examination of his background and career indicates that Terry was an example par excellence of the "militant South." Steeped in the traditions of plantation society, Terry personified the southern cavalier whose life was ordered by well-integrated and formulated codes of personal conduct. A unifying theme of the code of the Chivalry was the concept of personal honor; and Terry, the prototype of the Chivalry in California, was ever ready to rise in militant defense of his honor and reputation. Anyone who cast reflections on his character must pay the price in the form of an apologetic retraction or the "satisfaction usual among gentlemen." To defend personal honor and dignity through personal warfare was not only the right but the duty of the southern gentleman. Once the relationship between Terry and Broderick had degenerated into mutually antagonistic feelings and publicly expressed animosities, Terry was carried by the iron logic of events to a settlement on the field of honor.[26]

Broderick, like Terry, was a proud man who was quick to respond to a personal affront. Terry represented the Chivalry of the South—which pictured itself the aristocracy of America; Broderick was representative of the aristocracy of the poor. Born the son of an Irish

---

Chicago; Alfred Robinson to Pablo de la Guerra, Apr. 16, 1861, De la Guerra Coll., Santa Barbara Mission Archives; San Francisco *Steamer Times,* Sept. 20, 1859; John Currey, *The Terry-Broderick Duel* (Washington, D.C., 1896). Currey had been the 1859 gubernatorial candidate of Broderick. His distinguished legal career included service on the California Supreme Court, to which he was elected in 1863.

[25] David S. Terry to Cornelia Runnels Terry, Sept. 9, 1859, Terry Coll., Huntington Lib.; Wagstaff, p. 217.

[26] John Hope Franklin, *The Militant South: 1800–1861* (Cambridge, Mass., 1956), pp. 36–48, presents a perceptive analysis of the propensity of representatives of the Chivalry to engage in personal warfare; cf. W. J. Cash, *The Mind of the South* (New York, 1960), pp. 73–76.

stonecutter, he had risen to the heights of political power. Convinced that he was the intellectual and social equal of the representatives of any group in American society, he was quick to react to aspersions on himself or the immigrant or working-class groups with whom he identified. On at least a half-dozen occasions, he had been involved in incidents of "personal warfare" in defense of his reputation. In clashes with guns, knives, and fists, he had indicated that he would not back away from a fight. Like his hero, Andrew Jackson, he was a man of firm opinions who stood ready to defend them by intellectual as well as physical means. His speeches were filled with stark nouns and adjectives, and when a subject of importance was involved, he called a spade by its proper name and did not shrink from the physical.[27]

The events which culminated in his duel with Terry, however, indicated rather clearly that he was not anxious to resort to the "final argument." On the contrary, Broderick, as well as his friends, tried to avoid the duel. As a California politician he was in a most difficult position, for his avoidance could not simply take the form of a refusal to meet Terry. A straightforward declination would lend credence to the charge that had been made repeatedly during the campaign, that he was devoid of courage. At the time, dueling was illegal but was tolerated by a large segment of the public, which accepted it as a part of the world of politics. While he hesitated, anxious to find an acceptable way out of the impasse, Terry's second, Calhoun Benham, forced him to make a decision. The precipitous haste of Benham in delivering a peremptory challenge in the middle of the night was significant. His statement, when Broderick complained of the haste, that "there was no disposition . . . to hurry him . . . except on account of others than the parties immediately concerned" was a further indication to Broderick that it was to be difficult, if not impossible, to avoid the

[27] Broderick had been involved in a number of personal encounters, including a duel in 1852. See Truman, pp. 486–489, for an account of the Smith-Broderick duel in 1852; *Alta California,* Feb. 25, 1852, for an account of Broderick's battle with a representative of the Chivalry which left him with lasting scars. The latter incident is described in O'Meara, *Broderick and Gwin,* p. 31, and in Antonio María de la Guerra to Pablo de la Guerra, Feb. 25, 1852, De la Guerra Coll. A year before, Broderick was involved in an incident in which he faced down his armed opponent; see *Alta California,* Jan. 11, 1851, for a detailed account; cf. O'Meara, *Broderick and Gwin,* p. 28, and Jeremiah Lynch, *The Life of David C. Broderick* (New York, 1911), p. 53. George J. Bernard Affidavit, in *People* v. *McGlynn,* p. 90, describes Broderick's encounter with two "Southern gentlemen" in a hotel in New York in January 1859; cf. Bancroft, *History of California,* VI, 722. The San Francisco *Steamer Times,* Sept. 20, 1859, published an analysis of Broderick's personality, which explained how he acquired a host of strong friends as well as many relentless and malignant enemies.

confrontation without seriously undermining his position.[28] The circumstances of the duel were manifestly unfair to Broderick, but he and his seconds waived any consideration of those circumstances when they agreed to meet Terry on that fateful day in September. On the other hand, the hair trigger of the gun which effectively disarmed Broderick was the focus of much attention and comment. The official armorer testified under oath that he had not only ascertained the defective nature of Broderick's pistol but brought it to the attention of his seconds. However, Colton and McKibben subsequently issued a joint statement that they were unaware of any difference in the pistols at the time of the duel.[29]

The hair trigger was obviously of decisive importance. It was precisely the kind of weapon that handicapped Broderick. That he found it difficult to fire with a light-triggered weapon was known to a great many people in San Francisco. Apparently the difficulty grew out of Broderick's experience in his duel with Caleb C. Smith in 1852, when his gun jammed on the first shot. While he struggled desperately to free the jammed weapon, his opponent fired away. One of his final shots struck Broderick's watch pocket in his vest, shattering the timepiece and inflicting minor flesh wounds. That brief moment of terror which he experienced as he huddled over a jammed revolver while the bullets of his antagonist whistled about him left a lasting impression. It may explain, in part, his preoccupation with the pistol presented to him prior to his duel with Terry.[30]

It may also explain Broderick's difficulty with light-triggered weapons. Following his duel with Smith, Broderick practiced in a gallery in San Francisco until he became a skilled marksman. In firing he frequently displayed an idiosyncrasy which caught the attention of a gunsmith as well as a friend who practiced with him. Whenever the weapon had a light trigger, Broderick would misfire. When the guns were heavy-action revolvers, however, Broderick had no such problem. The trouble probably grew out of his duel with Smith. The lasting impression of terror that he experienced as he tried to free his jammed revolver apparently impelled him to pull a trigger forcefully there-

[28] *Harper's Weekly,* Oct. 22, 1859; James M. McDonald, "Recollections of Early Days in San Francisco," typescript in Bancroft Lib.; Calhoun Benham to Terry, Sept. 9, 1859, Terry-Broderick Correspondence.

[29] *Alta California,* Sept. 14, 1859; *Daily Evening Bulletin,* Sept. 17, 1859; San Francisco *Steamer Times,* Sept. 20, 1859.

[30] Truman, pp. 486–498; cf. New York *Times,* Apr. 17, 1852.

after. With a heavy-action revolver, a quick, firm pull did not impair accuracy; but when the trigger was light, the heavy hand led to exactly the kind of difficulty Broderick experienced in Taylor's gallery and on the field of personal combat with Terry.[31]

Broderick's seconds deliberately arranged for an abbreviated firing time so that they might display Broderick's skill at hip-shooting to best advantage. But any advantage to be derived from the mode of firing was more than offset when Broderick lost the toss for the choice of weapons. The toss, as subsequent events showed, was not for weapons, but for his life.

Had the duel been fought under the usual circumstances, there would have been considerable criticism of Terry and his friends. Public opinion, or at least a substantial part of it, would have looked askance at the manner in which the game had been stalked and the manner in which the most effective leader of the antislavery Democracy had been eliminated from the political arena. But this duel was surrounded with peculiar circumstances which tended to heighten and sharpen the criticism directed at the Chivalry and Terry—its champion. A large part of the populace simply refused to accept the idea that Broderick had died in a typical affair of honor.[32]

[31] Brown, *Reminiscences of William M. Stewart,* pp. 119–120, describes the practicing that went into the mastery of hip-shooting by Broderick and his difficulty with light-triggered weapons; Truman, pp. 396–398; George E. Barnes statement in San Francisco *Bulletin,* Nov. 2, 1895, p. 13, col. 4.

[32] *Harper's Weekly,* Oct. 22, 1859; *Frank Leslie's Illustrated Newspaper,* Oct. 29, 1859; Philadelphia *Press,* Oct. 11, 1859; *Wilkes' Spirit of the Times,* Oct. 22, 1859; San Francisco *Bulletin,* Sept. 17, 1859; *Northern Californian,* Sept. 28 and Oct. 5, 1859; San Francisco *Steamer Times,* Sept. 20, 1859; newspaper clipping probably from the *Pacific* (ca. September 1859), in Benjamin Hayes Scrapbooks, XVII, 100, Bancroft Lib.; *Alta California,* Sept. 24, 1859; Bancroft, *History of California,* VI, 733–738. See also Howard K. Beale, ed. *The Diary of Edward Bates, 1859–1866* (Washington, D.C., 1933), p. 49; the entry dated Oct. 12, 1859, clearly reveals the assessment of the nature of the duel by a Republican presidential hopeful.

CHAPTER FOURTEEN

Epilogue

Broderick's body was taken to the Union Hotel in San Francisco, which had been the scene of the funeral of his friend William I. Ferguson the year before. Ferguson, too, was a victim of the "code duello," killed in a savage duel with a prominent "Chiv," George Pen Johnston. The coffin of Broderick was placed on a bier surrounded by white roses, and then the doors were thrown open to the throngs who came to pay their last respects. For hours they passed before the catafalque, until thousands had joined in the tribute. In the early morning hours, when the flow of mourners slackened, a number of Negroes came to pay their last respects to their fallen champion. About the same time, Edward D. Baker put the finishing touches to a funeral oration that remains a model eulogy.

The funeral brought together the largest crowd that had ever assembled in the Golden State, an immense concourse which packed Portsmouth Square.[1] The surrounding buildings were draped in black, signs of mourning which were in sharp contrast to the bright skies that looked down as Baker began.[2] The crowd quieted as the first of his words came forth. The exalted phrases of this accomplished orator did not conceal the genuine grief under which he labored. Briefly reviewing Broderick's early life, Baker turned to a description of his political career. He pointed out that it had been marked with defeat and adversity: "It would be idle for me, at this hour and in this place, to

[1] *Frank Leslie's Illustrated Newspaper,* Oct. 29, 1859, pp. 346–347, gives a detailed description of the funeral.

[2] San Francisco *Steamer Times,* Sept. 20, 1859, includes the text of the eulogy delivered by Baker.

speak of all that history with unmitigated praise: it will be idle for his enemies hereafter to deny his claim to noble virtues and high purposes."

In the course of his political career in California, said Baker, Broderick had boldly denounced "the special legislation which is the curse of a new country," and fought all efforts "to strike out the salutary provisions of the Constitution which guarded free labor." His attempt to bring about a premature election of a senator in 1854 was a "violation of the true principles of representative government, which no reason, public or private, could justify." But, Baker continued, "if ambition, 'the last infirmity of noble minds,' led him for a moment from the better path, let me remind you how nobly he regained it." Then Baker flung a question at his listeners, inviting them to compare Broderick and his enemies. "Consider his public acts—weigh his private character—and before the grave encloses him forever, judge between him and his enemies!" "Who was his superior?" asked Baker, and then answered by declaring flatly that there had never been in the history of the state "a citizen who has borne public relations more stainless in all respects than he."

On the other hand, Baker continued, Broderick was a political figure whose memory demanded a public judgment based upon an examination of his career. "What was his public crime?" questioned Baker, and then answered with a review of Broderick's election and his devotion to the doctrine of popular sovereignty till the day of his death. When Broderick discovered that President Buchanan had betrayed his party and principles in the Lecompton crisis and was bent on forcing slavery on an unwilling people, "in the high performance of his duty as a Senator, he rebuked the Administration by his voice and his vote, and stood by his principles."

Broderick threw "the whole weight of his character" into the battle. He attempted to arouse and organize the people to "an indignant sense of the iniquitous tyranny of federal power," and in the process he grew into a towering figure of courage and integrity. Regardless of how one looked at the Lecompton crisis, it was impossible, said Baker, not to admire Broderick for his principled opposition to the aggregations of power that he challenged. "Who can doubt," he questioned, that Broderick would not be "resting on a bloody bier" but "reposing in the inglorious felicitude of Presidential sunshine," had he chosen differently.

Had Broderick "surrendered his free thought, and bent in submission to the rule of the Administration," he would have been feted and he would be a respected figure of his party. As for his public crime, Broderick's own words told the tragic story, "I die because I was opposed to a corrupt administration and the extension of slavery." Others might attempt to gloss over the manner of his death, but his words and circumstances precluded the acceptance of other explanations. His death had "been long foreshadowed—it was predicted by his friends—it was threatened by his enemies: it was the consequence of intense political hatred." The people of California would not be misled, for they were too well acquainted with these facts. "His death was a political necessity" declared Baker, "poorly veiled beneath the guise of a private quarrel."

As the orator turned to an examination of dueling in general and the Terry-Broderick duel in particular, his language became that of the courtroom: "The code of honor is a delusion and a snare; it palters with the hope of a true courage and binds it at the feet of crafty and cruel skill." As for the duel which led to Broderick's death, Baker would leave it to the courts to separate fact from rumor. Only indirectly did he refer to the misfiring of Broderick's weapon: "Whatever in the code of honor . . . demands or allows a deadly combat where there is not in all things entire and certain equality, is a prostitution of the name, is an evasion of the substance, and is a shield, emblazoned with the name of Chivalry, to cover the malignity of murder."

Then returning to Broderick, Baker began his peroration. This man, he declared, inherited poverty and obscurity; he died a senator, "having written his name in the history of the great struggle for the rights of the people against the despotism of organization and the corruption of power." Throughout his career, Broderick championed free labor. "Who can appeal to the communities of the Atlantic who love free labor?" Baker questioned. "Who can speak for masses of men with a passionate love for the classes from whence he sprung? Who can defy the blandishments of power, the insolence of office, the corruption of administrations? What hopes are buried with him in the grave!" [3]

Baker's voice carried the words of measured sorrow to the furthest reaches of his vast audience. As the last echoes of his words died

[3] The quotations are taken from "Oration by Col. E. D. Baker," in Jeremiah Lynch, *The Life of David C. Broderick* (New York, 1911), pp. 245–253.

away, the preparations for the funeral procession were completed. The cortege that led through the streets to the Lone Mountain cemetery was the largest such assemblage in the history of the city. A Jesuit priest spoke a few brief words at the graveside, and then the throng slowly dispersed. A handful of mourners remained to make a more personal tribute to Broderick. A few years later a monument was erected over the grave, an imposing granite obelisk mounted on a stone foundation, paid for through public subscription and a legislative grant. On its base appeared a simple epitaph: "David C. Broderick, Mechanic: Senator: Born Washington, D.C., February 4, 1820."[4]

The political impact of Broderick's death was tremendous. No matter how skillfully the matter was written off as a personal quarrel, the public was convinced that Broderick fell on the field of honor because of his opposition to the "extension of slavery and a corrupt administration." Baker's phrase, "his death was a political necessity," was widely used to explain the circumstances that led to the duel. The Chivalry, though benefiting immediately from the elimination of its most effective opponent, was struck a blow from which it never fully recovered.[5]

California Free Soil Democrats were demoralized by their recent defeat and the death of their leader. David D. Colton, political aide to the senator, wrote to Douglas for guidance. Using Baker's phrase, "his death was a political necessity," Colton asked for advice on the future political course of anti-Lecompton Democrats. He stressed the strength of Broderick's faction in California and suggested that the anti-Lecomptonites would have gotten an additional fifteen thousand votes, had Douglas' recent statement on the political situation been published before the balloting. He closed with a blunt warning: "Do not place the least confidence in any of the present officeholders in this

[4] San Francisco *Call,* Mar. 27, 1887, p. 1, col. 3; Ann C. Hart, *Lone Mountain, the Most Revered of San Francisco's Hills* (San Francisco, 1937), p. 23. The monument was demolished when the cemetery was moved in 1948. A bust of Broderick, part of the monument, was turned over to the California Historical Society for preservation.

[5] Hubert H. Bancroft, *Retrospection, Political and Personal* (New York, 1915), pp. 198–200; *Frank Leslie's Illustrated Newspaper,* Oct. 22, 1859; A. P. Crittenden to John J. Crittenden, Sept. 18, 1859, Crittenden Papers, Library of Congress; Theodore Hittell, *History of California* (San Francisco, 1898), IV, 277; San Francisco *Steamer Times,* Sept. 20, 1859; *The Northern Californian* (San Francisco), Oct. 5, 1859; *Colonel Alexander K. McClure's Recollections of Half a Century* (Salem, Mass., 1902), p. 32; *Alta California,* Sept. 21 and 23, 1869; Etta Olive Powell, "Southern Influences in California Politics before 1864" (unpubl. M.A. thesis, Univ. of Calif., 1929).

state nor in the Lecompton State Committee, or any of these professed Douglas Democrats . . . for depend upon this . . . no man will get the support of the leading Lecompton men in this State unless he is a *Sound Pro-Slavery man*." [6]

Douglas, however, was not inclined to close the door on the possibility of uniting the two wings of the California Democracy. Still influenced by Hammond and Latham, his professed supporters, he brushed aside Colton's warning of the deep-seated proslavery animus of Lecompton politicians and urged Colton to strive for unity. Colton responded with a pledge to "effect a compromise perfectly fair and honorable to both branches of the party." [7] Broderick must have stirred uneasily in his grave.

The impact of Broderick's death was not confined to California and the Democratic party. On the contrary, the tragic duel and its outcome made a tremendous impression in the North. Republicans everywhere made resolves to avoid a similar fate. Francis Preston Blair promised associates he would "be careful with his own life in Missouri for he knew that he had been a marked man for years." James Buchanan responded heatedly to an accusation that he bore a measure of responsibility for Broderick's death. When the charge appeared in the columns of a paper edited by a former friend and supporter, Buchanan threatened legal action. The editor invited him to proceed, then cited the record of the administration's opposition to Broderick. He criticized the administration for its hostility to Douglas but declared the "page that describes that . . . is bright and clean in comparison with that which preserves for the amazement and indignation of posterity the record of the hostility and cruelty practiced upon Mr. Broderick." [8]

A few days after the news of the duel reached the East, John Brown, who had been involved in his own way in the battle against slavery, staged the raid on Harper's Ferry, October 16–18, 1859. Within hours it was reported in eastern and southern newspapers, and it dominated the nation's press for the balance of the year. The Broderick-Terry story was driven from the front pages and the attention of the American people by the reports of the raid, the investigations, the trial and execution of Brown. The curtain of historical

[6] Colton to Stephen A. Douglas, Oct. 4, 1859, Douglas Coll., Univ. of Chicago.

[7] Colton to Douglas, Dec. 5, 1859, Douglas Coll.

[8] William E. Smith, *The Francis Preston Blair Family in Politics* (New York, 1933), I, 490; Philadelphia *Press,* Oct. 10 and 15, 1859.

oblivion began to drop on the memory of David C. Broderick, but it was stayed momentarily when the nation's lawmakers paused to pay their last respects to him.[9] His appointed replacement, Henry P. Haun, initiated the proceedings in the Senate with a brief announcement. The distinguished senators who followed showed rather clearly that they were not inclined to accept Haun's and the Chivalry's explanation of the duel and Broderick's death: "having fallen in an unfortunate conflict, which was engendered by the use of unguarded expressions by the deceased, personal in their character, towards another distinguished gentleman."

Senator John J. Crittenden was the first to express his respects and regrets in a surprisingly frank and personal endorsement of the senator: "He was a man, and we shall not look upon his like again." William H. Seward, Republican of higher law fame, followed Crittenden in an equally warm tribute. The words came with ease and confidence, and there was no mistaking their import. In such phrases as "a Senator, than whom none more incorruptible ever entered these Halls," he informed the world of his admiration for Broderick. Senator Ben Wade's tribute described Broderick as "frank, outspoken, and sincere," an unusual man of courage whose "love of justice was remarkable."

Senator Robert Toombs of Georgia was in some ways the most surprising of the speakers who participated. Toombs was fully aware of the fact that Broderick was in life an uncompromising opponent of slavery. In life and death he was regarded in the South as a firebrand, but Toombs described him as "a faithful, an honest, an upright, a fearless Senator." Toombs's words were clear and unequivocal: "I found him bold, honorable, truthful, attached to the interests of his country, 'clear in his office,' and a man that I considered an honor to the American Senate."

The House paused the same day to pay its respects to Broderick. As in the Senate, John C. Burch, a Broderick opponent, began with a formal announcement of Broderick's death which was similar in tone and content to Senator Haun's statement. The most revealing sentence closed his tribute; the involuted prose displayed a reluctance on the

[9] *Cong. Globe,* 36th Cong., 1st Sess., pp. 748–755. The failure of Douglas to participate in the memorial is intriguing. George Wilkes to Douglas, Oct. 11, 1859, Douglas Coll., suggested that Douglas participate to keep Gwin from insulting the memory of Broderick by the "mockery of a eulogy."

part of the speaker to come to grips with the sentiment, but it finally emerged as a description of the manner in which Broderick enchained his associates to him.

No speaker that day had known Broderick longer or better than John B. Haskin, congressman from New York. His voice and rhetoric revealed his deepest feelings as he reviewed the highlights of his long association with Broderick that went back to boyhood days and attendance at "one of those great 'people's colleges' of the North—a free school." Haskin went on to describe Broderick's thirst for knowledge, displayed in the purchase of a library with the first money he earned. His leisure hours, Haskin declared, were marked by the mastery of grammar, and reading was one of his favorite pastimes. "I may with truth and justice say, that for energy of purpose, integrity of character, and fidelity to friends and to friendships, he had no superior," the congressman's accolade continued, with much meaning for those who knew Broderick. "He had no model among the great men of the country to follow; but if there ever was a Senator of the United States who united in his person and in his character, more of the prominent traits of the statesman and hero, Andrew Jackson, than those of any other, it was David C. Broderick."

Congressman John Hickman of Pennsylvania, who had stood with Broderick in the fight against the Lecompton constitution, echoed the sentiments of Haskin. He predicted that "the last words of a dying seer . . . may yet be trumpeted at the mouths of cannon on the field of war." His audience heard them without an open reaction. They heard as well Hickman's analysis of Broderick's character and temperament. His understanding of people, declared Hickman, was his great strength. "He had a quick perception of ruling motives, and his charity was great." That understanding of motivation brought people to Broderick's side and bound them to him with hooks of steel. Then Hickman turned to another characteristic of the fallen senator which explained his success as a political leader. "Without a tie of blood to bind him in selfishness to the world, the glory of his country and the happiness of her people gave direction to all his thoughts," Hickman declared. Broderick's devotion to the interests of free labor and his consecration to the interests of the farmer, the mechanic, and the laborer were complete. "Their loss is irreparable and I would bid them know it." Hickman's tribute closed with a statement of stark simplicity which attested the devotion of Broderick's friends: "I need not say I loved him—yea, with more than a brother's love; I shall never forget him; no, neither in calm nor storm. I would embody his spirit, if I could, in an undying frame, that the friendless and oppressed might look forward in unfailing hope."

Republicans Anson Burlingame of Maine and Isaac B. Morris of Illinois, as well as the "Incredible" Dan Sickles, also participated in the tribute. Sickles spoke in grudging admiration, for the two men, though of the same party, had differed from the time their paths crossed in the meeting places of the Democracy of New York. Without specifying, Sickles suggested that some of Broderick's admirable qualities were "developed to excess." Burlingame and Morris spoke in far different terms. "He was a champion of the people," declared the Maine congressman, and "his heart throbbed responsive to theirs. . . . he fell into conflict instantly with those tyrannic elements which, in every society, are seeking to destroy the rights of the people." He fought, regardless of danger. "No man knew better than he did the logic of events. . . . looking into the dark future, he saw, with the clear eye of his judgment, the very point where he must abdicate the leadership for the people's rights, or yield up his life." Burlingame stated that many of his listeners would remember "how the shadow of the event . . . was upon him ere he left this city."

Congressman Morris of Illinois echoed the sentiments of Burlingame. His tribute included the words: "Unless all truth is falsehood, and history speaks to the future of the past with a lying tongue, no brighter name will shine in its annals, among the true moral heroes of America." He closed with an injunction to his contemporaries and future generations of Americans: "Go, student of American statesmanship, and look over the bright galaxy of names which adorn the pages of your country's history; and when you come to that stone-mason's son, learn from him how to model your own character."

A few years later, in November 1863, Abraham Lincoln paused in the midst of the burdens of the Civil War presidency to pay his personal tribute to Broderick. The occasion was the presentation of a cane to Lincoln by a group of Californians—a cane that had once belonged to the departed senator. Lincoln accepted the gift and then made a short speech. At the outset he stated that while he had never known Broderick personally, he had learned from close personal friends that Broderick was devoted to "the cause of human rights." The impromptu tribute came to an awkward close as Lincoln declared it was a proud reflection that his acts were "of such a character as to merit the affiliation of the friends of a man like David C. Broderick."[10] However poorly the words were preserved by the reporter who heard them, there was no mistaking the sincerity of the tribute. Lincoln knew a great deal about Broderick, much of it learned from his friend Edward D. Baker, senator from Oregon, who shared the friendship of each. Lincoln named one of his sons for Baker, his dearest friend, and Broderick spent his last night on earth with Baker, whose life was to be sacrificed on one of the Civil War's early battlefields. A few days after he accepted Broderick's cane, Lincoln put the finishing touches to his classic tribute to the fallen of the battlefield at Gettysburg, who had given that last full measure that "government of the people, by the people and for the people shall not perish." It would not have been inappropriate for the President to have included Baker as well as Broderick, for they, too, had died in the battle to preserve democratic government.[11]

Broderick's career came to an abrupt conclusion on September 16, 1859, but his influence persisted long beyond his death. His political associates were demoralized by the tragic outcome of the duel, coupled with the defeat inflicted on them in the preceding election. For a time they cast about for expedients, seeking advice, searching for a program and policy without the sure hand of Broderick. A great many of those who were close to him shifted political affiliation and fell into that much belabored alliance with "Black Republicans." Others clung to Broderick's independent organization, still hoping to make it an effective antislavery political vehicle. Some looked to Douglas for leadership. The Little Giant, his political perceptions warped by ambition, advised them to rejoin the regular organization. They would then be able to influence the Democracy and marshal the California party behind the Douglas banner in the upcoming Charleston convention.[12]

As things turned out, Douglas not only failed to get the support of the California delegates to the Charleston convention, but he found

[10] Cincinnati *Gazette,* Nov. 13, 1863, quoted in Roy P. Basler, ed. *The Collected Works of Abraham Lincoln* (New Brunswick, 1953), VII, 13.

[11] Baker was elected to the Senate from Oregon following Broderick's death. He was killed in the battle of Ball's Bluff, October 1861. Hubert H. Bancroft, *History of California,* VII (San Francisco, 1890), 292–293; Allan Nevins, *The War for the Union* (New York, 1959), I, 298–299.

[12] Alfred Reddington to Douglas, Oct. 14, 1859; Charles E. DeLong to Douglas, Oct. 3, 1859; Richard P. Hammond to Douglas, Oct. 2, 1859; James Johnston to Douglas, Sept. 19, 1859; Colton to Douglas, Oct. 4, 1859; all in Douglas Coll.

them voting with the southern ultras against him. The California delegation, as fire-breathing as any delegation sent by the deep South, played a significant role in disrupting the convention of 1860, one of the final steps in the process of political dissolution which culminated in secession and the Civil War. During the election campaign of 1860, Douglas found the regular California Democratic organization divided—a substantial part in the camp of John C. Breckinridge. Even Douglas' professed advocate, friend, and supporter Milton S. Latham turned his back on the Little Giant for Breckinridge.[13]

California in 1860 went Republican by a narrow margin.[14] Lincoln's victory was due in part to the aid of former members of the anti-Lecompton Democratic party. In his own way, Broderick contributed to the victory. Perhaps his most important contribution was in championing and popularizing the antislavery cause through the long years of the decade of the fifties, when the Chivalry loomed large in the political arena. In season and out, in victory and defeat, Broderick had kept the faith, never overlooking a chance to strike at the peculiar institution and its supporters. He had seen the opponents of slavery emerge from the shadows of semirespectability and become a movement that included representatives drawn from all walks of society. In life he was an effective opponent of the Chivalry; in death he was a symbol of the cause of antislavery.

To the men and women of his own time, as well as those who came later, Broderick was a puzzling figure, difficult to appraise and understand. Their difficulty is apparent in the variety of descriptions and interpretations of the man and his career that have been produced. In part the difficulty grows out of the complex nature of the man himself. In the course of his thirty-nine years he played a bewildering variety of roles: stonemason's apprentice, stonemason, saloonkeeper, ward politician, city charter framer, volunteer fireman, customs clerk, congres-

[13] The California delegation at Charleston in April 1860 voted with the southern ultras of the resolutions committee, as responsible as any single incident for the disruption of the convention. See Allan Nevins, *The Emergence of Lincoln* (New York, 1950), II, 214; cf. Roy F. Nichols, *The Disruption of American Democracy* (New York, 1948), pp. 294–295, where the crucial nature of this development is described. Latham's role in the election of 1860 is described in Winfield J. Davis, *History of Political Conventions in California, 1849–1892* (Sacramento, 1893), pp. 113, 115–116, 123, 126, and William F. Thompson, "The Political Career of Milton Slocum Latham of California" (unpubl. M.A. thesis, Stanford Univ., 1952), pp. 86–90.

[14] Election Returns, 1860, Vol. 1759, Archives of the Secretary of State, Sacramento; Powell, "Southern Influences," pp. 145, 212–213.

sional candidate, minter and assayer, state senator, land speculator, politician, senator, and duelist.

Broderick was a complex man in whom were combined antithetical traits of character and personality. A man of powerful physique who was not averse to the physical in life, he avoided the soft pleasures of the flesh that were so much a part of San Francisco in his generation. He lived an ascetic life; he avoided alcohol, and his name was never associated with the women of easy virtue who abounded in the California of the 1850's. Uninterested in the diversions of other men of his time and circle, he found his greatest pleasures in reading and study. He had a consuming interest in political economy, history, and English literature. In time he came to a mastery of such fields that amazed the well-educated men with whom he came into contact. During the Lecompton crisis, when he was locked in battle for his political life, he plowed through the works of Daniel Defoe. In the midst of tumultuous political events he could isolate himself by concentrating on a prized piece of literature. Familiar with the great works in English, he had a special feeling for poetry, especially for such poets as the "mystic, incomprehensible, spiritual Shelley." For years he maintained two residences in San Francisco, one of which was known only to a small circle of close friends. Here he retired frequently with his books and stretched his mind with the ideas of the great writers of the past.[15]

Broderick's friends and enemies alike were struck with his ability to bind men to him with "hooks of steel." It was dismaying to his foes to see the manner in which his friends resisted the blandishments of

[15] The most recent appraisal of Broderick is that of L. E. Fredman, "Broderick: A Reassessment," *Pacific Historical Review,* XXX (1961), 39–46, which is essentially a summary of several hostile evaluations, notably that of John S. Hittell in the *Overland Monthly,* 2nd Ser., XIII, 103 ff.; no manuscript sources are cited, although a number of important collections are generally available to the serious researcher, and there are several rather obvious errors of fact and interpretation in the article. *McClure's Recollections,* pp. 30–33; Bancroft, *History of California,* VI (San Francisco, 1888), 733–737; A. P. Crittenden to John J. Crittenden, Sept. 18, 1859, Crittenden Papers, Library of Congress; and Frank Soulé, San Francisco *Times,* Sept. 20, 1859, are a few of the many appraisals of Broderick that refute Fredman's judgment that he was "the most successful, corrupt, and unprincipled" political gamester of the period. See also John B. Haskin in *Cong. Globe,* 36th Cong., 1st Sess., p. 752, Frank Soulé in San Francisco *Steamer Times,* Sept. 20, 1859, George Wilkes in *Wilkes' Spirit of the Times,* Oct. 22, 1859, and Lynch, p. 69, all of which shed light on Broderick's interest in literature. The records of the Library of Congress indicate his reading while a member of the Senate; a transcript of the record was supplied by David C. Mearns, Chief, Manuscript Division of the Lib. of Cong., to David A. Williams, Dec. 28, 1961.

power and the temptation of preferment to stay at his side. He was skilled far beyond the ordinary man in interpersonal relationships, and he was amply possessed of the matrix of skills that make for leadership. From his youth he exhibited a strong personal will and a willingness to use his strength and intelligence in behalf of himself and his friends. His rise from obscurity to the heights of political power was determined, in part, by that indomitable will. Men gathered around him because he was willing to undertake the burdens and responsibilities as well as the rewards of leadership. Such things, coupled with his strict adherence to his word in political matters, made it possible for him to build a political following and organization in California which was generally independent of faction.[16]

The manner in which Broderick affected and impressed his associates was displayed in the decades that followed his death. One of his associates, J. G. Carpenter, for the remainder of his life looked back upon the time when he had worked with Broderick as the finest of his years. His life, he declared, had been immeasurably enriched by association with Broderick, and he looked upon the duel at Laguna Merced as a great personal tragedy. Another of Broderick's friends frequently visited his grave to give vent to the deep and enduring grief which the death of Broderick brought him. A member of Congress stood among his sophisticated colleagues and confessed his love for Broderick. More than a decade after his death, a group of his friends organized an association to preserve his memory.[17]

Broderick was a man of considerable intelligence. He was also a man of great personal pride. Fierce pride brought him triumph as well as tragedy. It led to political success, but it also led to the field of honor as he responded to the provocations of his enemies in the 1859

[16] Broderick's friends and enemies commented on the fact that his following was largely a personal one, made up of men who were fiercely loyal to him. For typical comments of enemies, see Milton S. Latham to James W. Mandeville, Nov. 18, 1856, Mandeville Coll., Huntington Lib.; John C. Burch in *Cong. Globe,* 36th Cong., 1st Sess., p. 751; F. F. Low, "Political Notes," p. 52 ff., MS in Bancroft Lib.; Henry W. Halleck to Pablo de la Guerra, Jan. 29, 1852, De la Guerra Coll., Santa Barbara Mission Archives. His strict adherence to his "word" in political matters and his indomitable will were described by many contemporaries including Frank Soulé in San Francisco *Steamer Times,* Sept. 20, 1859; A. P. Crittenden to John J. Crittenden, Sept. 18, 1859, Crittenden Papers; *Alta California,* Dec. 30, 1853.

[17] Carpenter's granddaughter, Mrs. F. Fletcher Monson, Oakland, Calif., supplied the information in an interview. F. F. Low, "Political Notes," pp. 54 ff., MS in Bancroft Lib.; John Hickman, *Cong. Globe,* 36th Cong., 1st Sess., p. 753; *Alta California,* July 14, 1871.

campaign. That pride arose in part out of his humble birth as the son of a stonecutter. Born into the lowest echelons of society, blessed and burdened with a capacious intelligence which was amplified by reading and study, Broderick from youth was steeled by the spoken and covert insults and slurs that were the lot of an Irish immigrant's son. While some cower and fawn in the face of such an assault, others respond with defiance. Broderick was of the latter mold. Conceding nothing, he faced the world forthrightly, determined to establish through his accomplishments his equality with the proudest and best members of society.

His pride, his courage, and his intelligence spurred him on. His bold courage led him to defy a mob of thousands of inflamed men who were bent on lynching a prisoner and to plunge bodily into their midst in a hazardous but fruitless attempt to rescue the victim. It led him to defy an enraged armed antagonist whose anger made the revolver he waved more menacing. On two occasions pride and courage led him to the field of honor. He escaped with his life on the first occasion only because his opponent's bullet struck his pocket watch, a wild happenstance that would have taught prudence and caution to another man.[18] Broderick's success as a political leader was determined in large measure by these qualities of personality and character, which were also prominent in two towering political figures of the nineteenth century, Thomas Hart Benton and Andrew Jackson. Broderick emulated these men of other years. Like them, he was sharp and vehement in judgment and opinion, fiercely loyal to friends and equally strong in his antagonism to enemies. "No man ever doubted where to find him," for he freely and openly expressed his opinions. Like Jackson, he never forgot an enemy or a friend.[19]

Broderick's success in politics is not to be explained in terms of his character and personality alone. His ability to influence and move men

[18] "I never have known a man . . . who could so ill endure to be an object of pity or compassion," declared William F. Seward (*Cong. Globe,* 36th Cong., 1st Sess., p. 748). Gerritt W. Ryckman Statement, p. 2, MS in Bancroft Lib., and *Alta California,* June 12, 1851, describe Broderick's attempts to prevent a lynching. The clash with a fellow legislator is described in detail in the *Alta California,* Jan. 11, 1851. The duel which almost cost him his life is described in the New York *Times,* Apr. 17, 1852, and the San Francisco *Daily Evening Picayune,* Mar. 18, 1852; cf. Ben C. Truman, *The Field of Honor* (New York, 1884), pp. 486–489.

[19] *Alta California,* Dec. 30, 1853; John B. Haskin, *Cong. Globe,* 36th Cong., 1st Sess., p. 752. Broderick declared he was flattered to be compared with Benton in a political speech reported in the Sacramento *Union,* July 22, 1859.

grew in part from his identification with the antislavery cause. From the beginning of his political career in California until its end, he was the unrelenting and fierce foe of slavery. The question of motivation is difficult to answer, and there are a number of plausible explanations to account for his involvement, but the question of motivation is subsidiary to the fact itself. The record clearly shows that he was the most effective champion of the antislavery position in the Democracy of California in the 1850's from the time he arrived on the scene until he departed. In the first years of his stay, when he championed the right of Negroes to emigrate to the state, to his last political statement, the record shows that he was the archenemy of slavery in the West. In spite of the fact that his party was strongly influenced by friends of the peculiar institution, he remained a powerful force within it because he articulated the antislavery opinions of thousands of fellow Democrats. When he finally left the party, he took a substantial number of Democrats with him. His success then was based on the fact that he made himself the representative of a large part of the general citizenry, which looked with varying degrees of antagonism on the institution of slavery.[20]

But while Broderick, Sam Houston, and Thomas Hart Benton were battling to keep slavery out of the West, the party they represented was being captured by militant defenders of the institution and a number of pliable "doughfaces" who, once they became dominant on the national level, freely used "federal power" to strike at their enemies within the individual states. Benton was cut down in the early fifties, and Sam Houston was removed from the Senate a few years later. Broderick's political organization was badly mauled in the fall of 1859. The proslavery wing of the Democracy struck at antislavery sentiments and supporters by destroying the effective antislavery leaders of the party in the individual states. The process involved a substantial part of the membership, and periodic successes crowned these efforts.[21]

[20] His political enemies regarded him as a "Black Republican." See A. C. Blaine to James W. Mandeville, Nov. 11, 1856, Mandeville Coll.; Sacramento *Evening News*, Dec. 30, 1856, reprint of editorial "Is Broderick a Black Republican?" which appeared in the San Francisco *Globe*. In the elections of 1854, 1858, and 1859 Broderick mustered Free Soil and antislavery Democrats, who polled a substantial number of votes. See Election Returns, 1854, 1858, and 1859, Vol. 1759, Archives of the Secretary of State, Sacramento.

[21] Benton's career as a leader of the antislavery wing of the Democratic party and his defeat in the Senate race in Missouri in 1851 are described and analyzed in

In spite of everything that had been done to weaken and isolate Broderick and strengthen his enemies within the Democratic party, he remained a powerful and significant figure on the California political scene of 1859 until the meeting with David S. Terry on September 13.

To sum up a man's significance in words is always difficult. The man who lives and dies in obscurity may be as elusive to appraise and define as the flamboyant character who thunders through life noticed by all of his generation. The sensitivity and perceptiveness of the appraiser often determine as much as any other factor how accurate and complete the finished appraisal will be. But there are other circumstances that complicate the biographer's problems and shape his findings. In Broderick's case, two major problems are encompassed in the lack of introspective writings of the subject and the enormous amount of misinformation about him which circulates in the historical literature.

Broderick is an intriguing and puzzling subject who poses a number of problems to those who are sincerely interested in a realistic picture. Oftentimes facile pens have glided lightly over a lack of information, concealed ignorance, and limited understanding with pleasing and superficial generalizations. Some writers who should have been more wary have simply reproduced in modern dress the canards circulated by his enemies. Others have looked at the California past of which he was a part through spectacles ground by the mythmakers of his generation. The distortions divide Broderick and his political contemporaries into opposing camps of good men and bad. Broderick is the leader of the bad men; his enemies, who were also his political opponents, are the respectable, God-fearing men of property and distinction.

To separate fact from myth is one of the more responsible, albeit prosaic, tasks of the historian-biographer. In the course of producing this study, a number of myths involving Broderick have been revealed. One of the more persistent describes Broderick as an opportunistic

---

William N. Chambers, *Old Bullion Benton, Senator from the New West* (Boston, 1956), pp. 364–377; the significance of his defeat is described in Allan Nevins, *Ordeal of the Union* (New York, 1947), I, 6, 402. Sam Houston, equally unsympathetic to the militant defenders of slavery, described in a farewell speech how patronage had been used to defeat him in his bid for reelection to the Senate (*Cong. Globe,* 35th Cong., 2nd Sess., pp. 352–355). The election results of 1858 and 1859 indicate that Broderick's organization was a power locus in California politics; see Election Returns, 1858, 1859, Vol. 1759, Archives of the Secretary of State, Sacramento.

politician who mastered the subtleties of political chicanery in New York's Tammany Society. This allegation has become established through the years. It is found in the writings of most historians who have dealt with Broderick, and it has shaped their image of him, for Tammany and Tweed and political corruption are links in one chain. However, the facts clearly indicate that Broderick was never a member or even so much as a candidate for membership but on the contrary encountered the open hostility of the society when he was a rising figure in the ward politics of New York City. Far from the stereotyped Tammany-trained politician who worked his way with the electorate through devious schemes, Broderick was from the beginning of his political career until its end an egalitarian democrat who put his faith, and who would place ultimate political authority, in the hands of the general citizenry. He took his Jacksonian Democracy straight. In the urban setting of New York he blueprinted a system of municipal government which was permeated with democratic procedures. In organizing a structure for the California Democratic party he based party machinery on the general membership. In establishing a city government for San Francisco he proceeded along similar lines. In the thick of the great political battle of Lecompton he adamantly defended the right of the residents of Kansas to determine their destiny as citizens of a free or a slave state. When in the thick of the conflict he needed intellectual support, he turned to a seventeenth-century democratic philosopher and champion of popular sovereignty, Daniel Defoe.

Broderick was a champion of free labor as well. After his death Baker asked, "Who now can speak for masses of men with a passionate love for the classes from whence he sprang?" The son of a stonemason, himself a veteran of five years of arduous stonemasonry, he was ever dedicated to the laborer, the mechanic, the artisan, and the farmer of America. That devotion to their interests led him to champion popular democracy; it prompted him to push for mechanic lien laws and legislation preventing the forced sale of a citizen's home. It put him in the forefront of the battle against nativism and bigotry, and it pushed him into a frontal assault on the champions of a scheme to establish peonage in California. His role as a representative of "the classes from whence he sprang" ultimately led him to the center of the conflict between the slave and free societies which culminated in the Civil War. He was in those years of deep involvement committed to the cause of free labor, the archenemy of slavery in the Trans-Mississippi West—willing to hazard all, that freedom might prevail. His commitment cost him his life. When his friends turned to the writing of his epitaph, they produced: "David C. Broderick, Mechanic: Senator." It was entirely fitting. It was also entirely fitting that California's most significant figure of social reform, Henry George, should cut his political eyeteeth as a worker in the anti-Lecompton Democratic party organized by Broderick.[22]

Broderick was a highly publicized figure in his time who stepped toward oblivion when he agreed to face David S. Terry on the field of honor in 1859. In some respects his return to obscurity is understandable. A generation which collided at Sumter, Antietam, Shiloh, and Gettysburg, which experienced national tragedy in the deaths of thousands of its sons and the final wrenching folk trauma of Lincoln's assassination, was satiated with tragedy. The first-fallen are not always the first-forgotten, although in this case Broderick, the *homo politicus* who sought with political weapons what was subsequently secured with sabre and cannon, was apparently the first of the sacrificed to be forgotten.

In many respects, Broderick's career is symbolic of the generation which experienced the Civil War. His birth coincided with that of the Missouri Compromise; his death came on the eve of secession. In between those poles of life and death, as his life took shape and was given political thrust, events piled one upon another and reached toward Civil War. Molded by his times, he marched toward his personal rendezvous with destiny as his generation marched toward a similar confrontation.

[22] San Francisco *Times,* Sept. 14, 1859.

Index